Record

of the

Ninety-Fourth Regiment

Record

OF THE

Ninety-Fourth Regiment

Ohio Volunteer Infantry,

IN THE

War of the Rebellion.

CINCINNATI:
THE OHIO VALLEY PRESS,
143 RACE STREET.

Originally published circa 1890 by The Ohio Valley Press.
© Copyright 2020 by Commonwealth Book Company.
Printed in the United States of America.
All Rights Reserved.

INTRODUCTION.

The history of any one volunteer regiment in the War of the Rebellion is, doubtless, very much the same as that of other regiments of the same line of service. The President's proclamations calling for volunteers, at the dates and for the numbers hereinafter mentioned, gave opportunities for enlistment according to the judgment and inclinations of different persons. There were some men with fewer hindrances than others; and some men were more disposed to adventure than others; and doubtless some men were more ready to risk their lives than others; but all men who enlisted when they believed their services were required for the prosecution of the war and the preservation of the Union should be esteemed equally patriotic.

There was no regiment composed of men wholly of the same occupation. There was scarcely a company in which there were not men of nearly every profession and occupation. The volunteer army demonstrated a problem in a republican form of government which, in the minds of many people, especially in Europe, was of doubtful solution. It fully settled the question of the will and power of the people, in the absence of a large standing army, to fight their own battles, if necessary, in defense of the Republic. Everywhere, even among ourselves, there is a better understanding of the nature and stability of the Union. It is not at all probable that any sane man will ever again deem it possible to disrupt this Union by engaging in civil war. That question is settled by the arbitrament of arms.

The Ninety-fourth Regiment was one of the important factors in the war, and none the less important because of the hundreds of other regiments of equal valor engaged in the same struggle. The regiment was mustered at Camp Piqua, in Miami County, on the twenty-third and twenty-fourth days of August, 1862, and immediately went to the field, and from that time until the close of the war the regiment participated in every battle fought by the department of the army to which it was assigned; the principal engagements being the following, to-wit:

 PERRYVILLE, KY...............Oct. 8, 1862.
 STONE RIVER, TENN............Dec. 31, 1862; Jan. 1, 2, 3, 1863.
 CHICKAMAUGA, GA..............Sept. 19, 20, 1863.
 LOOKOUT MOUNTAIN, TENN .....Nov. 24, 1863.
 MISSIONARY RIDGE, TENN.......Nov. 25, 1863.
 RESACA, GA.....................May 14, 1864.
 KENESAW MOUNTAIN, GA........June 9 to 30, 1864.
 PEACH TREE CREEK, GA.........July 20, 1864.
 SIEGE OF ATLANTA, GA..........July 22 to Aug. 26, 1864.
 JONESBORO, GA..................Sept. 1, 1864.
 SAVANNAH, GA...................Dec. 10 to 21, 1864.
 BENTONVILLE, N. C.............March 19, 1865.
 JOHNSTON'S SURRENDER.........April 26, 1865.

That good soldiers and splendid men were to be found in every regiment is true; but we are inclined to regard with special favor those with whom we have more intimately borne the heat of the battle, suffered the fatigue of the march, and endured the privations of the camp. The members of the Ninety-fourth Regiment were as brave and true a body of soldiers as ever drew a saber or shouldered a musket.

The war had progressed considerably before the organization of the Ninety-fourth Regiment. The men of the regiment were generally active business men or laborers, and many of them were heads of families, which were dependent upon them for support. Such men did not go into the army of choice; they enlisted only when it became apparent to them that their services were actually needed to defend and preserve the Union.

The ties binding these men to their homes were the dearest on earth. Who, in all this world, will ever be able to give the sum of all the anguish and pain caused by the separations of families and friends in consequence of the war. Often both those going and those remaining at home were alike oppressed with a presentiment that they would not meet again. The volunteer knew not how his family would be provided for during his term of service. He would willingly risk his life for his country, but oh! how unwillingly he would leave his wife and children to suffer for the necessaries of life! Who, under such circumstances, can estimate the intense patriotism of the volunteer soldier? And more, who can comprehend the greater patriotism of the women, who, notwithstanding their great love for them, gave their husbands or sons to the armies of their country?

War is terrible; but to the boys in the service the realities of war were not so painful as they were to their families at home. The uncertainty and fear were more unendurable than the certain knowledge of the condition of things could be. But, during all this long period of the war, nothing but brave words, full of encouragement and hope, came from these patriotic women.

The men were not all in the war. But we owe a debt of gratitude to the brave men who stood by the President, the Congress, and the Army during the dark and perilous period of the war. But for them it would have been impossible for the Government and the armies to achieve victories. With a determined foe in front and secret enemies in the rear, the struggle would have been longer and uncertain had it not been for the loyal citizens.

This little book is a brief history of the Ninety-fourth Regiment of Ohio Volunteer Infantry. The committee charged with the preparation of the matter for publication have endeavored to make it as complete as possible with the material obtainable. Of course, the book is not wholly satisfactory, but it is the best that could be done under the circumstances. It would have been agreeable to the committee if special mention could be made of many officers and enlisted men who distinguished themselves by brave acts and heroic deeds; but the committee are of the opinion that they are unable to do equal and exact justice in all such cases, and rather than do injustice to any, even the most humble soldier of the regiment, it is deemed best to make no special mention of men, but trust to the memory and fairness of the members for a just recognition of deeds of special merit.

The book will be useful in many ways; and it will be especially valuable as a ready reference to facts which would otherwise be difficult to obtain. There will be constant changes, such as deaths, places of residence, etc.; but if the annual meetings of the survivors shall be kept up, as they ought to be, the material changes can be noted, and the book kept nearly accurate, until the last one of us is mustered out of this life. Then our children and relatives will esteem the book of inestimable value.

The magnitude of the great issue for which the war was prosecuted, on our side, will be better understood and appreciated with the increasing prosperity of the people, and the blessings vouchsafed under the Constitution as interpreted and construed by the arbitrament of arms.

There were enrolled in the armies a total of two million seven hundred and seventy-two thousand three hundred and sixty-six men, of whom three hundred and eighteen thousand and eighty-nine belonged to the State of Ohio. There were killed, and died of wounds and disease, during the war, three hundred and three thousand five hundred and four men. (See page 8.) There is no authenticated account of the number who have died since the close in consequence of wounds and disease caused by the war, but we know the number is very large. We may therefore conclude that the war settled the disputed question which furnished the pretext for a dissolution of the Union.

The years intervening since the war are increasing rapidly, and as they increase our numbers decrease. Many comrades are enfeebled, and are no longer able to perform labor. A majority of the soldiers were limited in their means of support, and, if unable to work, they are often without the means of a livelihood. It is true that a generous people do provide infirmaries for the unfortunate or destitute citizens of almost every community; but it seems as if the old broken-down soldier, who fought for the preservation of the Government, and who absented himself

TABLE OF DEATHS.

The total number of deaths, so far as known at the Adjutant General's office, at Washington, from the commencement to the close of the Rebellion, is as follows:

REGULAR ARMY	Commissioned officers	267
	Enlisted men	4,592
VOLUNTEER ARMY	Commissioned officers	8,553
	Enlisted men	256,427
COLORED TROOPS	Commissioned officers	285
	Enlisted men	33,380
	Total number of deaths	303,504

THE NINETY-FOURTH OHIO.

FROM PIQUA TO LOUISVILLE.

The Ninety-fourth Ohio Volunteer Infantry was recruited from the counties of Greene, Clarke, Miami and Darke. Companies A and G were from Clarke; E and H from Greene; B, C and D from Miami; and F, I and K from Darke.

It was enlisted in response to President Lincoln's proclamation calling for three hundred thousand more troops, under date of July 2d, 1862, which was prompted by the failure of McClellan's peninsular campaign and the defeat of our armies in the Shenandoah Valley. The recruiting at this time was remarkable by there being an absence of the drum-beating, speech-making and display of flags which had characterized the enlistments of the year previous.

The regiments of 1861 have been inclined to regard themselves as being entitled to a greater share of honor than those of 1862, because they were the first to respond to the call for troops; but great as is their honor, it does not excel that of those who sprang to arms when the tide of battle was rolling almost on the shores of our own State. We had then learned that the war was destined to be long and terrible; we had seen the wounded from the fields of Fort Donelson and Shiloh, and the sick from the hospitals, who had obtained a brief furlough to receive the kind attentions of home. All these had taught us to look on the dark side of the picture of war, and when we enlisted knew full well that wounds and suffering, hunger and thirst, weary limbs and sleepless nights, were in store for us, but not so soon as actually came, for we were told that we would be thoroughly drilled and equipped before we took the field. This, like many another promise, was not fulfilled, and one week from the time of muster-in found us in Kentucky facing a victorous enemy, while the men who had but two days before constituted an organized division of the Union Army were going to our rear as paroled prisoners of war.

The first recruiting commissions were issued July 15th, and the entire regiment, consisting of one thousand and ten men, was recruited and mustered in within a few weeks. The companies began to assemble at the appointed rendezvous, "Camp Piqua," early in August. The location was upon a part of the farm known as "the Colonel John Johnston farm," at Upper Piqua, the site of the Shawnee Indian Agency.

Here we began drilling in squad and company drill without arms; but few of the officers knowing any more of tactics than the men in the ranks, made our progress slow. On Saturday and Sunday, August 23d and 24th, we were mustered into the service by companies by Captain Drake of the United States Army; each company being drawn up in two ranks, the men, with their right hands raised above their heads, repeated the oath which made them soldiers in the service of the United States. On Wednesday, the 27th, we drew arms and accoutrements, but neither uniforms nor canteens. The following morning, the 28th, we broke camp and took up the line of march for Piqua, where we were placed on board a train on the Dayton & Michigan Railroad and started for Cincinnati, where we arrived about dark of the same evening. We were again formed in line and marched to the ferry, where we crossed over the Ohio River into Covington, Ky., where the citizens were apprised of our arrival by the ringing of the bell on the City Hall. In a short time they served us a substantial supper, and we were assigned quarters in halls and public buildings. On Friday, the 29th, we drew our uniforms, which made the regiment have more of a military appearance, and gave the men the feeling that at last they were full-fledged soldiers. On Saturday, the 30th, the regiment was loaded on the cars of the Kentucky Central Railroad for Lexington, where it arrived the same evening and learned of the disastrous battle which had been fought that day at Richmond, about thirty-five miles distant, where our new troops, under General Nelson, had been badly defeated and a large number captured by a greatly superior force of Confederate troops under General E. Kirby Smith.

This was not encouraging to a regiment which had just been mustered into the service and totally unacquainted with battalion maneuvers, and knowing but little of company drill or the manual of arms. That night we rested on the ground near the cemetary, supperless. On the following morning, Sunday, the 31st of

August, we left our camping ground and marched into the town and formed on the square at the court-house, where we were told we would be fed, but after waiting for some time and getting nothing we received an imperative order to march at once and formed our column, moving out in the direction of Tate's Creek Ford, on the Kentucky River, sixteen miles south-east. The band marched at the head of the regiment, playing that once popular air "We're coming, Father Abraham, three hundred thousand more." The weather being very hot, the roads dry and dusty, and with nothing to eat and very little water to drink, having no means of carrying it with us (canteens not having as yet been issued), would have made it a hard march for veterans, but more especially for soldiers whose uniforms were taking the first dust and who were totally unused to hardships. During the march several were overcome by the heat and had to be left by the roadside. In the evening, a short time before reaching the bluffs overlooking the river, a heavy shower came up and drenched the men thoroughly; shortly afterwards it became dark. The regiment was halted where the road commenced to descend towards the river; the Colonel ordered one company to be placed on picket. While this was being done and the men were finding their places in the darkness, the remainder of the regiment laid down upon the ground, wet, hungry and exhausted, and many soon fell asleep; but their sleep was of short duration, for a party of rebels concealed in the thick cedars skirting the road fired at short range and threw us into temporary confusion. Six or eight cavalrymen, whom we had rallied during the day from the stragglers met on the road, were seated on their horses near the right of the regiment when the firing began; suddenly wheeling, they dashed back through the mass of men in the road, injuring some seriously and adding no little to the confusion. A random fire was kept up for some minutes by our men, but after the Colonel had peremptorily ordered it to cease and it still continued, he declared he would shoot the first man who fired another shot; this had the effect to stop it.

That was a long and weary night, full of alarms, sleeping with guns in our hands, ready to spring to our feet at a moment's notice. One man missed his brother from the ranks, and fearing that something had happened to him, crept down to the road where the firing had begun and there found a dead man. To assure himself whether it was his brother or not, he pulled off his boot, knowing that he had a toe missing on one foot. His worst fears were realized, for it was indeed his brother, cold in death. When morning dawned we found ourselves occupying a bluff overlooking the river, with bluffs of a like character on the opposite side. The march and fast of the previous day had made us extremely hungry, and we began to look for something to eat, but all we could find was some green coffee which had just arrived in a wagon from Lexington, and green corn growing in an adjacent field. While roasting the corn some of the boys scattered in search of drinking water, and while they were gone the stillness of the morning was broken by the boom of a cannon from the opposite bluff. Then came the screeching of a shell over our heads; this was followed by others in rapid succession. The companies were formed in line separately and posted in such positions that it seemed that we had a much larger force than we actually had. The firing lasted about half an hour, during which time we got a lesson in dodging shells which lasted us during the remainder of the service. The Colonel learned that a large force of rebels, consisting of infantry, artillery and cavalry, were in our immediate vicinity, so he ordered in the pickets and made preparations to retreat. He gave his horse to his orderly and sent him in haste to Lexington for reinforcements of cavalry. Dividing the regiment into battalions he placed one on each side of the road, which was protected by stone fences, and began to quietly withdraw. The movement was executed so deliberately, and in such perfect order, that the rebels were not at first aware of what was taking place. When they discovered that we were gone they started their cavalry in pursuit; they overtook us after we had fallen back six or seven miles, and attacked the rear while marching in the road.

Up to this time we had kept in the edges of the fields, on either side of the road; but, deeming it safe, and as the marching was so much better, had returned to the road, and were marching in column when the firing began. Here the enemy had us at a disadvantage for a short time, but a line of battle was quickly formed across a field on the south side and at right angles to the road, and their advance was temporarily checked. We had at this time seventy-five or a hundred of our men taken prisoners, most of whom were getting water at a spring on the north side of the road when the attack began. After remaining in line a short time, the firing not being renewed, the march toward Lexington was resumed. We had proceeded a short distance when we saw a cloud of dust and heard the clatter of approaching cavalry in our front. The head of our column was just entering a deep cut in a hill, and the first impression was that the enemy had us surrounded. Colonel Frizell halted the regiment and ordered those in advance to open ranks, which they did by clambering up the steep banks on either side of the road, so as to be better prepared for an emergency; but when they approached we discovered to our joy that they were Union cavalry, consisting of four companies of the 9th Pennsylvania Cavalry, under the command of Major Jordan. They dashed rapidly through the cut, cheering as they went, and in a few minutes we heard the crack of their carbines as they engaged the enemy in our rear. After marching about a mile farther, we were again halted and formed in line in a corn-field to receive the enemy, but the cavalry was able to hold them in check, and the march to Lexington was not again interrupted.

The loss of the regiment at the ford on the night of August 31st was as follows:

Killed: PERRY F. WIKLE, Co. F.
ISAAC HOLLEPETER, Co. I.
Wounded: First Sergeant H. C. CUSHMAN, Co. A.
Corporal MARTIN KESSLER, Private JESSE BYRKETT, Co. D.
WILLIAM H. BIERLY, Co. F.
WILLIAM H. TENNENT, Co. I.

The total loss reported was two killed and nine wounded for that day. Early next morning two outposts held by men from Company H were attacked by cavalry directly after the regiment had started to Lexington. Privates James Doole and Nathaniel Studevant were mortally wounded; the remainder were captured unharmed. Soon after this Private Levi Falknor, of Company B, was disabled by the cavalry advance while he and others were engaged in destroying a bridge.

We arrived at the Fair Grounds near Lexington about six o'clock in the evening, weary and discouraged, to find the military authorities making preparations to evacuate the place. Colonel Frizell rode into the city to endeavor to procure something for the regiment to eat, and Major King was left temporarily in command (Lieutenant-Colonel Bassford at this time being on leave of absence in Ohio). The Major ordered us from our temporary encampment and marched into the edge of the city; it was then beginning to grow dark. An officer on horseback approached the head of the column and inquired what regiment it was. Lieutenant Winger, of Company A, being nearest to him, answered, "The Ninety-fourth Ohio." "Who is in command?" said the officer. "Major King at present," said the Lieutenant. Just then the Major approached and inquired what was wanted. The strange officer then replied in a somewhat haughty manner, "Follow in the rear of that regiment," pointing to the 73d Indiana, which was marching down a cross street. Major King remarked, "These men have had nothing to eat for two days, and the Colonel has gone to make arrangements for supper for them." The officer replied in a loud and angry tone, "My name is Jackson; I command these troops; march in the rear of that regiment." So away we marched west toward Versailles, twelve miles distant.

Colonel Frizell did not learn at first what had been done; but when he did, started to overtake us, which he did after we had marched about four miles. During the night we overtook the wagon train, and obtained a supply of "hard tack," which relieved our pinching hunger. We marched and munched, and slept *on foot*, during that dark weary night, halting frequently to let the cavalry pass to front or rear, as the occasion demanded, arriving at Versailles at daylight, where we rested about two hours and again took up the line of march toward Frankfort, just as the enemy's cavalry was approaching town. Our column now consisted of about five thousand men, mostly infantry. We had with us two regiments of cavalry and a battery of heavy artillery, but not supplied with ammunition. The battery was placed in position on a knoll on the east side of the town, with the 52d O. V. I. in support, where they remained until the whole column was again in motion, when they also withdrew.

The force at this time consisted of the following named troops: The 52d, 93d, 94th, 98th and 105th Ohio, 73d Indiana, and such fragments of the 12th and 16th Indiana and 18th Kentucky as had escaped capture at Richmond, Kentucky, in the disastrous battle of the 30th of August; also, the 9th Pennsylvania and 9th Kentucky cavalry. The battery before alluded to need not be considered as augmenting the force numerically, since it was manned by details from the infantry. Our brigade at this time consisted of the 93d, 94th and 98th Ohio and the 73d Indiana, commanded by Colonel Gilbert Hathaway, of the latter regiment.

We were not attacked during this day (September 2d), but during the afternoon, on the near approach of the enemy's cavalry, we left the road and formed in line of battle. We were, however, soon withdrawn, and the march was resumed, arriving at Frankfort about ten o'clock at night, where we rested until three o'clock the next morning (September 3d), when we again essayed to force our blistered feet into our shoes and try the realities of another day's march through the stifling dust, beneath a burning sun. We marched about eighteen miles, and encamped near a stream where the water was standing in stagnant pools covered with green scum, but this was so much better than no water at all that it was accepted gratefully.

On September 4th we marched about the same distance that we did the previous day, passing through Shelbyville in the afternoon, and encamping a few miles beyond. September 5th we marched from here to a point about seven miles from Louisville and halted in a beech grove, where we went into camp, or rather fell down exhausted without making any attempt at arranging the camp in order, hardly caring what became of us so long as we were not required to move our blistered feet and aching limbs. It is proper to mention here that at the last camp before this Joseph Walker, of Company A, from Springfield, detailed as teamster, received a kick in the forehead from a mule, which resulted in his death in the hospital at Louisville a few days later. We remained here a few days, performing no service but picket duty and holding regimental dress parade every evening.

One day an order came to pack up and fall in, without any explanation as to what was intended, and with all the mystery which attends army movements. After marching about a mile, we halted and went into camp in a beautiful grove, where we remained about ten days, drilling and doing picket duty. Here knapsacks and canteens were issued to us for the first time. Another mysterious order came, and the camp was again moved three or four miles nearer Louisville. Here our little division was encamped on a series of hills, hardly any two regiments being encamped together. In the meantime we had received the accession of some Illinois and Indiana troops, and a sort of temporary reorganization took place, General W. T. Ward being placed in command of our brigade. Our first regimental inspection took place at this camp. Colonel Frizell now began a vigorous course of drill, but was careful not to select the smoothest location for the evolutions, thinking it best, probably, to acquaint us with the fact that battle-fields are not always located on level ground.

It was during our stay in this camp that we participated in the grand review in Louisville. It was a terrible hot day, and the regiment suffered severely from heat and thirst on the long, tiresome march through streets where scarcely a breath of air was circulating, under the fierce rays of a midday sun. A great many men were overcome by the heat, and the general result to the command was equal to an ordinary battle, minus the glory. About the middle of September, all the troops under General Nelson were withdrawn to the immediate vicinity of Louisville. Our regiment went into camp in an old orchard west of and adjoining the Catholic cemetery. Here we began throwing up earth-works, the main line passing through our camp and extending to our left through the Catholic and "Cave Hill" cemeteries. This work occupied more than a week. After the completion of the fortifications, we were subjected to a vigorous course of drill and discipline, as it was not known at what time the enemy would attack us; it was known that the rebel army under General Bragg had invaded Kentucky and was marching in the direction of Louisville, and might reach that city before we received sufficient reinforcements to hold him in check. Every morning at two o'clock we were called up and marched out to the intrenchments in Cave Hill Cemetery, where we would remain in line until daylight, at which time we would return to camp.

This continued until the arrival of the advance of General Buell's army, on September 25th. Our exposed position at this time can be better understood by quoting a dispatch from General Buell (while on the march north) to General Nelson, in command at Louisville:

HEADQUARTERS ARMY OF THE OHIO,
September 22d, 1862.

MAJOR-GENERAL NELSON:

I dispatched to you last evening from Horse Cave, but the courier did not leave until after I arrived here last night. I learned since, with tolerable certainty, that the enemy marched in force to Elizabethtown. He may go rapidly through to attack Louisville; or, if he thinks you too strong to be easily beaten, he may go to Bardstown to effect a junction with Smith; or he may halt at Elizabethtown to complete the junction and fight me there. The latter I consider more probable, considering I am close at hand. If he marches on Louisville he will probably go by way of Shepherdsville, and it might be possible for him to reach there Thursday. In any event you should be reinforced to the last man without a moment's delay. My own movements depend so much on the movements of the enemy that I can hardly tell you what to do. If you have only the force you speak of, it would not, I should say, be advisable for you to attempt the defense of Louisville, unless you are strongly intrenched.

Under no circumstances should you make a fight with his whole or main force. The alternative would be to cross the river or march on this side to the mouth of Salt River and bridge it, so as to form a junction with me. But, as I tell you, so much depends upon circumstances that I must leave the question to your discretion. I only offer you my suggestions in regard to it. This much do at any rate: Send a million of rations down the river, say opposite Brandenburg, to make them safe, to be subject to my order, and have a boat bridge made to be thrown rapidly across the mouth of Salt River for my use, if I require it. Lose no time. Steamers should be opposite Salt River subject to my orders.

Bear in mind in these arrangements that the enemy will probably have a small cavalry force at the mouth of Salt River. All steamers used for the service referred to should be kept constantly under steam and ready to escape if threatened. Communicate with me daily. I shall probably continue on the Louisville pike, at least as far as Elizabethtown. I shall be at Bacon Creek to-night, or beyond there if the enemy should be determined to stand at Elizabethtown. Your advance on the Louisville pike, with the means of crossing Salt River, would undoubtedly have an important effect, and perhaps give you an opportunity of acting an important part.

I received your dispatch in answer to mine from Dripping Spring.
[Signed] D. C. BUELL,
Major-General Commanding.

THE PERRYVILLE CAMPAIGN.

On the arrival of General Buell's army our regiment was transferred to the 9th Brigade, 3d Division, 1st Army Corps. This corps was commanded by Major-General A. McD. McCook, and was composed of three divisions. Only two divisions of the corps participated in the campaign which terminated in the battle of Perryville; these were the 3d Division, commanded by Brigadier-General Lovell H. Rousseau, and the 10th Division, commanded by Brigadier-General James S. Jackson; the 2d Division, under General Sill, having been detached to march upon Frankfort to intercept General Kirby Smith, and prevent him forming a junction with Bragg.

Rousseau's division was composed of the 9th, 17th, and 28th Brigades, commanded respectively by Colonel Len. A. Harris, Colonel William H. Lytle, and Colonel J. C. Starkweather. Harris' brigade, to which we belonged, was composed of the following: 2d Ohio, 33d Ohio, 94th Ohio, 10th Wisconsin, 38th Indiana Infantry, and Captain Simonson's 5th Indiana Battery.

On October 1st, 1862, our army marched out of Louisville, McCook's corps passing through Shepherdsville about noon, encamping the first evening some miles beyond that place. On

October 2d, after a hard march, we encamped near Taylorsville in a drenching rain. We remained here all the following day, having crossed Salt River and encamped adjoining the town. We had bivouacked in an open field, and were preparing to go to sleep, when we heard artillery firing in the direction of Bloomfield. The bugle sounded and we fell into line and marched rapidly until we came within a few miles of the place, when, as the firing had ceased, we halted and formed in line across a field and laid down in line the remainder of the night. On the morning of the 4th we marched to Bloomfield, where we saw some of the effects of the fight of the previous night. We staid here the remainder of that day. That night the regiment went on picket about a mile beyond the town and in close proximity to the enemy. On the morning of the 5th (Sunday), we were relieved and returned to camp. On the morning of the 6th we resumed the march in the direction of Danville, and, after marching about fifteen miles without any incident worthy of mention, encamped on some low hills adjoining a large body of timber. On the morning of the 7th the march was resumed. A greater portion of the day we passed along a timbered ridge where the population seemed to be loyal, judging by the number who lined the road, greeting us with cheers and words of encouragement as we passed along. Late in the afternoon we descended into an open, well cultivated country, and encamped for the night on a stream about a mile west of Mackville. On Wednesday morning, October 8th, we were aroused about four o'clock, and, after a hasty and scanty breakfast, were on the march by five o'clock in the direction of Perryville, from whence proceeded the sound of distant artillery, which indicated that a fight was in progress. Harris' and Lytle's brigades of Rousseau's division took the advance, and we marched rapidly a distance of nine or ten miles until we came within the vicinity of Perryville about noon, where we halted and formed in line to the left of the road near the Russell house, where our regiment was held as a reserve of Harris' brigade. During this time artillery firing was going on from two batteries posted in our front.

We will here digress sufficiently to give a brief description of the ground upon which the battle of Perryville was fought. The country is somewhat broken, and lies in a series of irregular ridges on each side and nearly parallel with the course of Chaplin River. The course of the Chaplin is northward past the town of Perryville, and for about two miles beyond, where it bends to the west. A smaller stream, called Doctor's Creek, flowing from the south-west, joins the Chaplin north of the town. On the fields and woodlands, enclosed between these two streams, the battle was mainly fought. Bragg's force was posted on the eastern range of hills beyond these streams, and on the same side upon which the town is located. Our force occupied the western range of hills facing the enemy, with the streams about midway between the lines. McCook's line of battle was formed as follows: The right of Rousseau's division rested near a barn on the right of the Perryville and Mackville road, near the Russell house, extending to the left, on a commanding ridge, through a corn-field, to a skirt of woods; Lytle's brigade on the right; Harris' brigade on the left; the right of Terrill's brigade of Jackson's division resting near the left of Harris' brigade in some woods extending to the left, on a hill overlooking Chaplin River to the north, the left of his line being bent to the rear, in order to occupy the high ground. Starkweather's brigade and Stone's and Bush's batteries, of Rousseau's division, were posted to the left and rear of Terrill's brigade on commanding ground. Webster's brigade of Jackson's division was posted to the left of Russell's house, and in the rear of the center of Rousseau's line on the right.

At the time when the line was formed it was distant from the water about six hundred yards. The whole command was suffering for water, having marched rapidly at least ten miles over a country where all streams were dried up by the protracted drought. The water procured at the stream near our camp, which we left in the morning, was all exhausted before reaching the battle-field.

Realizing the necessity for a supply of water, General Rousseau attempted to advance his line to the stream, which here stood only in stagnant pools; but the enemy, who had up this time been partially concealed, advanced in force and opened on our line with three batteries of artillery, with the evident determination of cutting us off from our supply of water and placing us at a disadvantage at the very opening of the engagement. This was about two o'clock P. M., and was practically the beginning of the *real* battle of Perryville, which raged with unabated fury from right to left until night put an end to the bloody but unsatisfactory conflict— the fighting which had been going on during the morning and forenoon having been mainly between detached bodies of troops. The enemy had choice of position; he marched from Harrodsburg to give us battle in the vicinity of Perryville. The battle was fought upon ground broken by many hills and ravines, which afforded admirable opportunity for concealment and the massing of troops. At least three divisions of the enemy assaulted Rousseau's and Jackson's divisions, and the partially dry beds of the streams afforded no obstacle to the enemy's advance. The strength of the corps at this time was about 12,500, against which the enemy hurled at least 20,000 of his veteran troops—the flower of the rebel army.

General Buell's army, as stated by himself, numbered at this time 58,000 effective men, the most of whom were within supporting distance, and yet the brunt of the fight was permitted to fall upon McCook's, the smallest of all the corps, with the assistance of a small portion of Gilbert's corps, which lay within easy supporting distance on the right. We can not give all the details of the battle, but will endeavor to show from the reports of regimental and brigade commanders the part taken by our regiment on that eventful day.

At the beginning of the engagement, the Ninety-fourth was the reserve of Harris' brigade, but was not allowed to retain this position but a short time, as we were ordered by an aid of General McCook to take a position nearly a half mile to the left, where a regiment in Jackson's division had broken and eight companies had been driven from the field. We moved promptly, at double-quick, by the left flank, and reached the spot, filled the broken gap in the line and commenced firing. This was done none too soon, as the enemy was making a dash for the breach, with the evident intention of passing through and cutting off the left wing. This was frustrated by the prompt action of our regiment. The condition at this part of the line was extremely desperate at this time, as Jackson, commanding the division, and Terrell, commanding the 33d Brigade, had both been killed, and Webster, commanding the 34th Brigade, fell mortally wounded shortly after. The left of our regiment touched the right of Starkweather's brigade, which formed the extreme left of the line, and gallantly held its own against fearful odds until nightfall. After firing rapidly for some time the enemy gave way in our immediate front. We advanced the line more than a hundred yards and held this position about half an hour. About this time the enemy made a vigorous onslaught on the troops on our immediate right and captured four guns of a battery; the two remaining guns of which, with their caissons, dashed rapidly past us through the woods and took up position on the next range of hills to the rear. We were ordered to the support of this section, and took position at the foot of the hill on which the artillery was posted, which place we held till the close of the engagement. During the night we were transferred from our position on the left to the right, where the remainder of our brigade was in position. We bivouacked, expecting fully a renewal of the engagement in the morning; but daylight revealed the fact that the enemy had retreated during the night, and the fact was subsequently revealed that he had moved in the direction of Harrodsburg to form a junction with Kirby Smith's column.

Herewith is appended the report of Colonel Joseph W. Frizell, commanding the Ninety-fourth Ohio Infantry:

ARMY OF THE OHIO.
IN THE FIELD, October 10, 1862.

SIR: I have the honor to make the following report as to the part my command (Ninety-fourth Ohio Regiment) took in the action of the 8th instant at Chaplin Hills. I formed my regiment by order of General Rousseau, as a reserve, on the left and in the rear of Simonson's battery; but before it became necessary for me to go directly to the support of the battery, I was ordered, by an aid of General McCook, to the support of Terrill's battery. I moved up by my left flank, in double-quick, about eight hundred yards, some two hundred yards to the left of the battery, where I found the enemy in great force and where our forces had given way. I had scarcely halted my command and fronted when a most murderous and incessant fire from infantry was opened upon me. My men stood their ground for about three-quarters of an hour, when the enemy began gradually to fall back. Fresh troops at this moment came up and took our position, but was informed that I must again take the front. Knowing that I was almost out of ammunition, my only alternative was to resort to the bayonet. I moved forward with the expectation of using cold steel, but was satisfied to find that the enemy had promptly left when they saw us making towards them. They gave way entirely in front of us, and after advancing some one hundred and twenty-five yards, and not being supported, I did not feel authorized to proceed forward. My regiment remained in this position some half an hour; nothing occurring of note except that a rebel colonel came a little too close to us to make observations, when one of Company F's men shot him off his horse. He was brought inside of our lines and expired a few moments afterwards. My attention was diverted to my rear, when I saw a portion of Terrill's battery was going past me in hot haste, and heavy volleys of infantry to the right and rear of me. I immediately formed my men so as to meet the enemy's right, who appeared to be driving our men down the ridge we first occupied. The enemy, however, was checked before they reached our last line. I remained until I received your order to take another position, about dark. The numerous dead bodies found upon the ground in front of the position I occupied showed that the enemy were severely punished. In the early part of the engagement, Captain John C. Drury, of Company B, fell, shot through the heart. A finer officer or a braver man fell not that day. In the death of Captain Drury the company lost a gallant leader; the regiment, an officer whose place I am fearful will never be filled. The officers and men of the regiment behaved most gallantly, going into action under a fire almost unprecedented in the annals of war for severity. It was astonishing to see the line stand as steadily as if it were practice. Lieutenant-Colonel Bassford and Major King displayed great coolness and bravery, and these gentlemen were entitled to great credit for the successful action of my command on this occasion. James E. Edmonds, Acting Adjutant, rendered great aid. I commend him for his activity and gallantry. Sergeant-Major William D. Putnam, during the hottest of the fire, attracted the attentive admiration of the officers of the regiment and incited the men by his great courage and daring. Our Chaplain, Reverend William Allington, gave ample proof of a Christian and kind-hearted gentleman by his incessant care to our wounded men. I went into action with five hundred men. My loss in killed, 8; wounded, 25; prisoners, 2; missing, 5--total 40.*

Respectfully, your obedient servant,

J. W. FRIZELL,
Colonel Ninety fourth Ohio Volunteer Infantry.

LIEUTENANT G. A. VANDEGRIFT.

Honorable mention of our regiment in this engagement is made by the brigade, division and corps commanders. Colonel Len. A. Harris, commanding the 9th Brigade, says: . . . "At this time the firing was very heavy. I now sent back for the Ninety-fourth Ohio, Colonel Frizell commanding, but was informed that they had been directed by Major-General McCook to support a section of artillery which General Terrill was working." He says later, in his report: "Captain Drury, Ninety-fourth Ohio, fell gallantly fighting at his post." Brigadier-General Lovell H. Rousseau, commanding the 3d Division, in speaking of the fighting of the 9th Brigade, says: "The 2d Ohio, moving up to the support of the 33d Ohio, was engaged before it arrived on the ground where the 33d was fighting. The 38th Indiana, Colonel B. F. Scribner commanding, then went gallantly into action on the right of the 2d Ohio. Then followed in support the Ninety-fourth Ohio (Colonel Frizell). I wish here to say of this regiment that, although new and but a few weeks in the service, it behaved most gallantly under the steady lead of its brave Colonel Frizell." Major-General Alex. McD. McCook, in his report of the battle, says: "When the 2d and 33d Ohio, 38th Indiana and 10th Wisconsin fought so well I was proud to see the 94th and 98th Ohio vie with their brethren in deeds of heroism." In

---

*The revised statement of the losses in the battle of Perryville makes that of the Ninety-fourth forty-nine.

proportion to the numbers engaged and the duration of the battle, the losses were scarcely equaled by any general engagement during the war. That the result was not more decisive was not due to the men engaged, nor to the officers in direct command on the field. The total loss, killed, wounded and missing in the Army of the Ohio aggregated 4,241, of which McCook's corps lost a total in killed, wounded and missing of 3,299.

A list of killed and wounded, found upon the muster rolls, Columbus, Ohio, is as follows:

Killed: Captain JOHN C. DRURY, JOSEPH E. HARRISON, Co. B.
TILLMAN WILSON, Co. D.
ABRAHAM COY, JOSEPH MILLER, Co. E.
JOHN R. JACOBY, Co. H.

Died from Wounds: ELMER BRECOUNT, Co. C.
SYLVESTER JONES, Co. G.
JACOB ETTER, Co. I.

Wounded: Sergeant A. B. HUSTON, GRIFFITH M. D. GIRARD, JAMES WALES, Co. B.
JOHN A. EDMONDS, SAMUEL C. BOWMAN, Co. C.
ADAM G. CORNWELL, Co. E.
FELIX WINGFIELD, Co. G.
ANDREW JACKSON, GILBERT DEHART, Co. H.

October 9th, 1862. Our brigade moved farther to the right of the line and encamped in a piece of woods bordering on an open field. When it was known that the enemy had withdrawn, a detail was made from our regiment to go to the field to search for the dead and wounded. This detail went to the part of the field where we had been engaged the day before and there met a body of rebel cavalry roaming through the woods, with whom they talked, but who showed no disposition to molest them when they learned what was their mission, saying they also were looking for their wounded. The dead were collected and taken to our camp, where they were buried the same day.

October 10th. We moved from our camp, passing across the battle-field and crossing the Chaplin River; encamped on the hills on the eastern side. After going into camp it began raining heavily. Having no tents, we made the best shelters we could with corn-fodder and straw, but which was poor protection against the storm.

October 11th. Moved camp a short distance to the Harrodsburg and Perryville turnpike, where we were joined by Sill's division from Frankfort.

October 12th. Marched from this camp to Harrodsburg and went into camp south of the town, near the Soldiers' Home grounds.

October 13th. Learned that the enemy had moved in the direction of Danville; we marched to within a few miles of that place and went into camp.

October 14th. Marched to Danville and passed in review through the town — reached the vicinity of Stanford and encamped.

October 15th. Marched through Stanford in morning and Crab Orchard in evening and encamped about two miles beyond the latter place.

October 16th, 17th, 18th and 19th were spent at this camp. On Sunday, the 19th, we had inspection. Our camp was situated at the base of a cliff on a bank sloping toward a creek. It was so steep in places that we had to drive stakes in the ground to keep the camp-fires from rolling down the hill.

October 20th. Broke camp and marched toward Lebanon, and encamped at night on a high wooded hill.

October 21st. Marched through a hilly country all day and halted at night at Rolling Fork—a clear, pure stream, which afforded the first good drinking water we had had for three weeks, as nearly all the streams on our line of march were dry and stood in stagnant pools.

October 22d. Left the camp at Rolling Fork and resumed the march, crossing the stream seven or eight times during the forenoon. We reached the Lebanon turnpike toward evening, but had to wait a long time to let Schoepf's division pass. We then took the road and marched by the side of a wagon train, in a stifling dust, for a long distance, reaching Lebanon after dark; but instead of going into camp, passed on to New Market, which was seven miles beyond. This place we reached about ten o'clock at night, after marching about twenty-eight miles since leaving camp in the morning. After leaving Lebanon, the men began dropping out of ranks and going to sleep by the roadside, so that when the regiment reached camp there were not more than one hundred and fifty in ranks; we went into camp in a thick woods.

October 23d. The stragglers of the night before came into camp during the forenoon, when we were moved into an open field, where we put up shelters of rails.

October 24th. It grew cold and snowed, and we suffered severely on account of poor shelter and lack of clothing.

October 25th. Remained in camp, suffering from the inclement weather.

October 26th. Still in camp; the weather began to grow milder and the snow melted away.

"At about this time General Buell left the army with General Thomas and retired to Louisville. On the 26th of October he directed General Thomas to put the army in motion towards Bowling Green and Glasgow."

FROM BOWLING GREEN TO MURFREESBORO.

"While General Buell's army was concentrating at Bowling Green and Glasgow, he was relieved by General W. S. Rosecrans. This change occurred October 30th, in compliance with General Order No. 168, War Department, dated October 24th, 1862. By the same order the troops of the department were called the 'Fourteenth Army Corps.' This designation soon gave place to the more appropriate and popular one, 'Army of the Cumberland,' the name which the original portions bore under Generals Anderson and Sherman."

The reorganization of the army by General Order No. 8, on the 7th of November, assigned General Thomas the command of the "center," comprising the divisions of Generals Rousseau, Negley, Dumont and Fry. (All of the division of General Dumont, and part of that commanded by General Fry, were left back in Kentucky and along the railroad.) General McCook commanded the right wing—the wing embracing the divisions of Generals Johnson, Davis and Sheridan. General Crittenden commanded the left wing, embracing the divisions of Generals Wood, Palmer and VanCleve.

Rousseau's division reached camp on the Barren River on the evening of November 3d, 1862. During the day the column marched along a ridge road called the "Hogback." Toward the close of the day the troops turned to the left into the low ground, and, after wading the stream, encamped not far from Bowling Green.

Soon after reaching the camp the army was turned out to be reviewed by the new commander, General Rosecrans. In the review on the 7th, General Rousseau's division made a splendid appearance, because of the full ranks, steady and solid appearance of all the regiments and batteries. The troops marched out in bright sunshine, leaving overcoats in camp, but the afternoon brought rain and freezing weather, with a drenching and all the discomforts of exposure under such circumstances.

The march toward the South began on the 9th. Our portion of the army reached Lost River that day, and on twenty miles to Franklin, Kentucky, on the 10th. On the 11th we reached Mitchellville, just thirty-seven miles north of Nashville. After leaving Mitchellville, the division passed by way of Tyree Springs; encamped for a time at Edgefield Junction, and again for a week at Edgefield, commencing December 4th.

The next move placed the entire center in camp (Camp Andy Johnson) three miles south of Nashville. During the march through Kentucky and up to this camp, the regiment lost large numbers left in hospitals by the way on account of sickness. Company K reported five deaths from the time of leaving Bowling Green until the regiment reached Nashville. Company I started with ninety-four enlisted men when leaving Ohio, and now reported thirty-five for duty. This camp was a pleasant place—not much drill—good water and rations plenty, and an occasional trip to the picket posts.

While in camp here the Regular Brigade was made by bringing together the battalions in this army and uniting in brigade organization, with Lieutenant-Colonel Carpenter in command of the six battalions. Christmas night orders were issued for the advance of the army toward Murfreesboro, and next morning, Friday, December 26th, our brigades moved out of the camps and on through mist and rain on the Franklin pike to Brentwood. From here Rousseau's division turned to the left, following Negley over to the Wilson pike and on south, and after a march of ten miles encamped at Owens' store.

Saturday, December 27th. The division found the cross-roads on the way over to the Nolensville pike almost impassable, in consequence of the heavy rain the night before. The troops and trains of the center changed positions slowly. The head of the division did not reach Nolensville until night.

Our brigades were scattered along with the trains; the Ninety-fourth was kept in the rear, and encamped that night near the road upon which the trains were moving, a part of the regiment being placed on picket.

Sunday, December 28th. Marching was quite difficult, with all of the circuits to avoid bad places in the roads, and the delays on account of wagons sticking in the mud. It was 3:00 P. M. before our regiment reached the Nolensville pike. After a march of three or four miles, we halted beyond the town. By this time the sick in the regiment had reached such numbers, and the cases were of such character, that orders came to leave them here. Wheeler reached the rear of our army, and captured and paroled all of these, Tuesday, the 30th. Some of these returned to duty the following March; many others were permanently disabled, and were discharged.

After leaving Nolensville the division labored on through the rude defiles on the way to the Murfreesboro pike. The rear of the division did not get over the eight miles until Monday, the 29th. After reaching the pike the rear closed up, and the division was again united, at a little town called Stewartsboro.

Tuesday, December 30th. Rousseau's division moved down the Murfreesboro pike through mud and rain, halting at times on the way, until 4:00 P. M. The column filed to the left of the pike and was massed in the rear of the position occupied by Negley's division, in a cedar grove near the railroad. The lines of battle were completed in front of the center, in double line of battle, with Rousseau's division in reserve.

Our division was aroused for breakfast at 4:00 A. M. of the last day of the year 1862. At about 9:00 A. M. our three brigades—Scribner's, Shepherd's and Beatty's—were hurried to the front and to the right of the pike; while halted here for a few minutes, the men of our regiment heard read the address of General Rosecrans. The disaster to the right wing of the army required the presence of the reserves. Rousseau's division went into the cedars at double-quick, at the order from General Thomas, and formed on General Sheridan's right, to support him should he maintain his position, and to resist the enemy should he fall back. At this stage three divisions—Negley's, Sheridan's and Rousseau's—from left to right, were in line at right angles to the position first occupied by Sheridan. After these dispositions had been made, the enemy repeatedly assailed the three divisions. For some time his attacks were repulsed, but Sheridan's division, having exhausted its ammunition, went to the rear. Then came the supreme crisis of the battle. After Sheridan's division left the line, both of Negley's flanks were in air, and Rousseau was in the same condition; both divisions being completely isolated, and soon after were each nearly surrounded by the overlapping lines of the enemy. Both divisions were subjected to a cross-fire of musketry and artillery at short range. While it was utterly impossible for them to maintain their positions, it verged closely upon an impossibility for them to secure new ones with safety to themselves and the army. In the emergency General Thomas ordered both Negley and Rousseau to withdraw to a new line. Each was at first covered by cedars. But the enemy was in their rear as well as in front, and it was impracticable to give mutual support, as their insulation was too positive and the necessity of rapid movement too imperative. It was necessary to form a temporary line to save the artillery before a permanent one could be established. General Thomas therefore first directed that a new line should be taken, running along a depression in the open ground in the rear of the cedar woods, to be held until the artillery could be retired to high ground near the Nashville pike, where the permanent line was to be established. Rousseau's division, leaving its position under heavy fire, drew back to this depression, having first posted its batteries on the high ground farther to the rear. The exultant enemy soon emerged from the cedar woods, but fell under the musketry of Rousseau's division at short range. The troops that formed here and resisted this attack were Scribner's, Shepherd's and Beatty's brigades, Loomis' and Guenther's batteries, with the Pioneer brigade and Stokes' battery. This short and decisive conflict saved the center and the army. The enemy was here repulsed and driven back to the woods. After hard fighting, Rousseau's, Negley's and Palmer's divisions were firmly connected, and other dispositions made which placed the whole army in a continuous line.

General Rousseau says of the conflict: "As the enemy emerged from the woods in great force, shouting and cheering, the batteries of Guenther and Loomis—double-shotted with canister—opened upon them; they moved straight ahead for a while, but were finally driven back with immense loss. Four deliberate and fiercely-sustained assaults were made upon our position and repulsed." (Official report.)

Our regiment went into the cedars on the double-quick, as described by the reports of Generals Thomas and Rousseau, and held its place in line during the day, except when led out by Colonel Frizell in two charges made that day. One of these, made under the eye of General Thomas, brought out the words, which led to our use of the term, "The Gallant Ninety-fourth." He said in the last review at Washington, in the last days of May, 1865, as he rode alone with Major Snider to the center of the regiment: "I remember this regiment at Stone River, when, from my position, I saw you led out in a charge against the enemy, when you cleared your front. It was a gallant thing to do. You earned a reputation that day which has been sustained by you on every field from that day forward! I have known much of this gallant regiment, and have followed your history after you left my department and the army I had the honor to command."

After the enemy had been fully checked at all points, the lines were readjusted. The regiment was under severe fire from sharp-shooters; several of the men were picked off, and went to the woods in the rear. After a time General Rousseau came up and led the regiment to a position on the right of the 38th Indiana, and while at this point Colonel Frizell was wounded and carried from the field, leaving the command to Major King. (Lieutenant-Colonel Bassford was absent at the time, after ammunition.) No change occurred in the situation of the regiment during the rest of the day. Lieutenant-Colonel Bassford returned and assumed command after dark. The line was felt by the enemy late that evening, after which both armies rested on their arms in close proximity. Our men lay upon the ground, surrounded with dead and wounded, without rations, without fires, and endured the cold and mud as best they could.

January 1, 1863. Our regiment was placed in position behind a battery for support, and was not changed during the remaining days of the battle. Our division was not actively engaged during the 1st and 2d of January. The weather on the 3d was unfavorable to active operations. That evening at 6:00 P. M. one brigade of our division (Beatty's) and Spear's brigade of Negley's division now advanced, driving the enemy through the woods, beyond his line of trenches, and breaking his center. During that night Bragg retreated. The 4th was occupied in burying the dead, and on the 5th we moved through Murfreesboro and went into camp in the old rebel quarters west of the town.

The loss of the regiment, according to best reports, was forty-nine killed and wounded. This can not be made to include all the slightly wounded. Colonel Frizell was lost to the service from a severe shoulder-wound received here. Captain David Steele, commanding Company E, received a mortal wound the first day of the battle. The list of wounded embraced those following, with others whose names are not on the rolls.

Killed and died of wounds:
        Captain DAVID STEELE, Co. E.
        JAMES LOCKHART, STEVEN D. TAYLOR, Co. G.
        JACOB ARN, Co. I.

Wounded: Colonel JOSEPH W. FRIZELL.
Corporal ANDREW J. CLACE, WILLIAM H. HAIN, DANIEL JENKINS, Co. A.
Corporal GEORGE DOLLINGER, Co. B.
Lieutenant BURTON C. MITCHELL, EMORY CHAMBERS, JOHN E. ROBERTS, Co. C.
ELI H. FENTERS, HARVEY HUGHES, Co. D.
LEWIS C. COTTRELL, Co. E.
HIRAM MCCLURE, JOHN H. REIS, Co. F.
JOSIAH REED, Co. I.
Sergeant JEFF. R. MARTIN, THOMAS B. WHITE, Co. K.

From the organization at Piqua until disabled by a wound at Stone River, Colonel Frizell was constantly with the regiment. He was taken to the "Brick House Hospital" late in the afternoon, December 31st. At the hospital he was cared for, in company with a large number of officers from the Regular Brigade, by our regimental band, and shared with them a portion of the wild turkey caught while on the double-quick into the cedars that morning. Colonel Frizell was found permanently disabled, and was discharged from Nashville in February, 1863.

ADDRESS OF COLONEL JOSEPH W. FRIZELL

AFTER BEING WOUNDED.

The following address, by Colonel Frizell, was delivered to his command immediately after he was wounded at the battle of Murfreesboro:

"HOSPITAL ROOM NO. 9, SPRUCE STREET,
"NASHVILLE, TENN., January 6, 1863.

"*Officers and Soldiers of the Ninety-fourth Regiment O. V. I.:*

"Allow me — though laboring under severe pain from my wound, received on the 31st ultimo — to say to you that your gallant conduct on Wednesday last is to me, in my severe affliction, a source of great consolation and comfort. I know not how well other troops behaved during Wednesday's hard and desperate conflict; that they behaved well is saying little in their behalf. But when I say that your conduct during the day's terrific fighting has never been excelled by any regiment that ever trod the battle-ground, I only say what I firmly believe.

"It was your coolness, when at different times lying under the enemy's terrible fire of infantry and artillery, that saved you. It was your ready and willing compliance to my orders that has still strengthened and increased my confidence in you. For these, soldiers, accept my hearty thanks.

"The history of the Ninety-fourth Ohio since its organization, up to the present time, is indeed a singular and almost a mysterious one — unlike that, perhaps, of any regiment that has yet entered the field. It is worthy of your many reflections that you may be benefited in future thereby.

"It doubtless strikes the minds of many of you that you were saved at the Kentucky River from Kirby Smith's sixteen thousand veterans, when they had you well-nigh surrounded, as a miracle. You yet think that your lives were saved in the same manner at Perryville, when five times your number opposed you, and when many of your gallant comrades fell at your feet to rise no more. And still, perhaps, you think that your lives were miraculously spared on Wednesday last. Let me tell you, brave soldiers, what wrought this miracle that has saved so many of you so far through all these terrible scenes. It was your coolness, your cheerful and implicit obedience to orders, when under fire.

"Recollect that men, panic stricken, voluntarily commit suicide. Let me ask you if you were not at least a dozen times, on Wednesday last, in such a position, had you attempted to run, that probably not twenty of us would have been saved. Upon reflection you must admit that such would have been the case.

"Now, soldiers of the Ninety-fourth, let me hope that you will be as cool and obedient in the future as heretofore, and that you will as readily and as cheerfully respond to the orders of your gallant Bassford and King as you have to mine. They are worthy of your confidence, and able still to add new laurels to those you have so nobly won.

"From the condition of my wound, comrades, it is extremely doubtful whether I will ever again be able to lead you into another engagement. My prayer is for your happiness and safety.

"I again return you my hearty thanks for your uniform kindness and soldierly bearing.

"J. W. FRIZELL,
"*Colonel Ninety-Fourth Regiment O. V. I.*"

SIX MONTHS AT MURFREESBORO.

On the 5th of January, 1863, the Army of the Cumberland went into position in the vicinity of Murfreesboro. General Thomas placed his divisions on the Woodbury, Bradyville, Manchester, and Shelbyville turnpikes; General McCook posted his command from the Shelbyville road across the Salem turnpike to Stone River, where his right rested; and General Crittenden disposed his command from General Thomas' left so as to cover the Liberty and Lebanon turnpikes, resting his left on Stone River.

The camps of Rousseau's division were arranged in line, the 1st Brigade on the north end of the line and connected with the Regulars on the south; and next in the line came the brigades of Beatty and Starkweather. Soon after reaching this camp Companies I and K were detached for duty at the Convalescent Camp on Stone River, returning some time before the opening of the campaign.

By authority of General Order No. 9, War Department, January 9th, 1863, the troops of the Army of the Cumberland were organized into three corps d'armée, designated the Fourteenth, Twentieth, and Twenty-first, corresponding in the main to the former grand divisions of "center," right, and left wings, without change of commanders.

While here our regiment suffered much from sickness, in common with other regiments of our age. The fatigues of the campaign and the exposure while lying in mud and water during the battle, and afterward in the rebel camps, made a large amount of typhoid fever. Measles spread as an epidemic, and many of our "good soldiers," strong and equal to every exposure and danger to this time, went down to death. One evening the enlisted strength at dress parade was but ninety-six; the remainder of the four hundred left after Stone River were dead, or sick in quarters in the hospitals or the Convalescent Camp near by. March 15th, five men died in the camp of the regiment, three of them in quarters in Company B.

On the 16th of March the divisions of the 14th Corps were placed in new camps in level country upon the south-east side of town, and on the 19th the entire corps paraded for the first review since the battle of Stone River.

On the 21st the Ninety-fourth was made a part of a strong column for a reconnoissance out on the Manchester pike. The brigade was under command of Colonel Scribner, and was accompanied by Loomis' battery. Skirmish lines were engaged with the enemy near Hoover's Gap that day. The third day all returned to their camps. The regiment marched sixty-four miles during this trip.

On the 1st of May the large Sibley tents were turned in and exchanged for shelter tents.

During the latter part of May the regiment made a trip to Nashville and return to guard a wagon train.

During May and June, 1863, all of the regiments present were much engaged in drill upon the level plain near our camps. The exercises embraced movements for the battalion, frequently by brigade and division, and occasionally the entire corps was in the field.

Generals Thomas and Rousseau made frequent visits to see the maneuvers of the 1st Brigade and enjoy the music made by the band of the regiment, now detached and acting as brigade band.

The captured men from the retreat through Kentucky and Nolensville rejoined here all along through the months of March, April, and May.

May 27th. The brigade maneuvers were attended by Generals Rosecrans, Thomas, and Rousseau.

June 1st. The 14th Corps turned out for review. Scribner's brigade was placed on the right, as in the review of March 19th.

THE TULLAHOMA CAMPAIGN.

Marching orders were received on the 23d of June, and the next day the whole army was in motion. The 14th Corps led out on the Manchester pike, Reynold's (4th) division leading, followed by Rousseau's and Negley's divisions.

Wilder's brigade of mounted infantry encountered cavalry posted seven miles from Murfreesboro, and pressing them back on their reserves drove the whole force through Hoover's Gap, a defile three miles long, and took position at its southern entrance.

He was soon attacked by a large body of infantry, but held his ground until General Reynolds joined him with his other two brigades, when the enemy withdrew, and the 14th Corps rested for the night in another of the passes through the hills in front of the enemy.

Skirmish lines from our regiments were engaged with the enemy, and all of the brigade brought within range while supporting Wilder's brigade in the gap on the 25th and 26th.

The enemy fell back on the 26th, and the divisions of the 14th Corps advanced toward Fairfield and met a strong force posted in the heights north of Garrison Creek. General Thomas drove the enemy steadily at all points during the day. After pursuing some distance, the divisions were dispersed so as to offer a battle front, extending from the Fairfield road to within five miles of Manchester.

Early on the 27th the 14th Corps was in motion far in advance of Hoover's Gap—Rousseau's and Brannan's divisions to Fairfield, and Negley's on their left in support, and Reynolds' directly on Manchester.

The enemy retreated from Fairfield, and the column passing that way turned toward Manchester, where, about midnight, the whole corps was concentrated.

Early on the morning of the 28th, Wilder led the advance toward Tullahoma, followed by Rousseau's and Brannan's divisions. When about five miles out the division halted and posted a line of pickets. During all of this advance rain fell every day for two weeks from the day of starting. At this time the roads were almost impassable for artillery and trains.

"On the 29th there was an advance toward Tullahoma until the front of the army was within two miles of the place. Early on the morning of the 30th, after learning that Bragg had evacuated the position, General Rosecrans ordered the army in pursuit. Rousseau and Negley overtook the enemy at Bethpage bridge and engaged sharply with lines of skirmishers.

"The swollen streams—especially Elk River—formed behind Bragg a barrier to rapid pursuit. In some instances the cavalry forced the passage of the river at the moment of engaging the enemy, but in the main the pursuit either by cavalry or infantry was entirely fruitless. It developed the fact, however, that General Bragg had crossed the Cumberland Mountains, and that Middle Tennessee was again the possession of the Army of the Cumberland."

After the close of the campaign the 1st Division was encamped for several days near Dechard Station, and from this place continued the advance over the first range of mountains, arriving at Cowan Station on the 14th of July. The division remained in camp here until August 6th, when we were again advanced into Anderson Valley and placed in camp on Crow Creek.

Scribner's brigade remained in the vicinity of the station, while the other brigades were encamped a few miles down the valley. While here the troops lived upon the best of everything; peaches, green corn, chickens, pigs, and potatoes were found in abundance. Much of the foraging was carried on after night on account of the watchfulness of the provost guard, and toward the close of our stay an order was issued requiring a roll-call every two hours. In spite of these precautions the men cleared up the valley, and at the same time escaped the guard-house.

The regiment was commanded by Major King for several weeks following the battle of Stone River. Colonel Bassford was sick in quarters and at Nashville during this time; he rejoined and was in command the most of the time that summer until detached with a recruiting party. Major (now Lieutenant-Colonel) King went home on sick leave soon after. These changes gave the command to Major Hutchins, recently promoted from Company D. Lieutenant-Colonel King rejoined in the mountains below Bridgeport, but was found unfit for field service, and was sent to the hospital at Chattanooga.

CHICKAMAUGA AND CHATTANOOGA.

On September 2d, 1863, the 1st Division, under command of General Baird, began the movement toward Chickamauga from their camps in Anderson Valley. Scribner's brigade was led up a trail in the mountain side toward the east. The weather was hot; the march was rapid and tiresome. It was up hill for a long ways, and a march on for eight miles before reaching water. At last the troops were halted in the vicinity of a large spring of clear, cold water. After a short rest we were marched four miles beyond the spring and placed in camp.

Baird's division was united on the 3d at Bridgeport; on the 4th crossed the Tennessee and was encamped near by. After a rapid march from here on the 5th, the head of the division reached the foot of Sand Mountain. The column was halted to allow the trains to pass up the mountain, and during the halt in the valley everybody went foraging, gathering in chickens, pigs, potatoes, etc. Early the next morning the brigade was aroused and set to work at helping the wagons up the hill. At 3:30 P. M. the artillery and trains were on top and our column began climbing up the road. The distance to the top was one and one-half miles; the road was steep in many places. The troops were worn upon reaching the top, but continued the march across the plateau until late that night.

September 7th, at 5:00 A. M., our column began the march down the mountain into a narrow valley. The brigade closed up by noon. After a two hours' rest, the division made a short march and encamped together.

During the 8th and 9th there was no movement by our part of the army. The army trains kept passing all of the 8th. General Negley's division had the advance and was beyond Lookout Mountain.

September 10th the 1st Brigade moved out rapidly for four miles and halted at the foot of the mountain. Here the regiment relieved the 10th Wisconsin at helping up the train. After reaching the mountain top we marched all of that day and began the march down at night. Many men fell over rocks and into crevices, filled with dust, as they marched in the dark. At nine o'clock the brigade encamped in McLemore's Cove.

The movement of the 14th Corps into McLemore's Cove, through Stevens' and Cooper's Gaps, deserves some notice here.

"On the 9th, the 2nd Division, General Negley, moved over Lookout Mountain and threw forward skirmishers to Bailey's Cross-roads. During that evening and next day, the 1st Division, General Baird, crossed the mountain to the eastern base. Reports reached General Thomas that the enemy's cavalry was drawn up in line in front of General Negley, and that a heavy force, consisting of infantry, cavalry, and artillery, was concentrated at Dug Gap, beyond Negley's position. On the night of the 9th, Bragg formed a combination of three divisions and a cavalry force to move against Negley the next day. During the 10th, Bragg made effort to move against Negley, but subordinates failed to carry out his orders. He did not, however, abandon the project, and at night gave orders for a far heavier combination for the 11th. During the night of the 10th, Baird's division closed up toward Negley's position, and Reynold's and Brannan's divisions were ordered forward early in the morning."

From the careful movement, and the precaution taken, it was shown that our corps was in a dangerous position; the enemy was close at hand, and rumor said the movement to intercept Bragg's retreat to the south had been successful. In fact, Bragg turned from his retreat, and ordered an attack upon General Thomas, expecting to defeat our corps before the corps of McCook and Crittenden could be brought to his aid.

"The fact of concentration was revealed with greater emphasis before the 14th Corps on the 11th. It is now known that Bragg clearly understood the exposed position of the three corps, and turned to take advantage of the situation. While instructions were being prepared to General Thomas to hasten his movement on Lafayette, Bragg had just moved his headquarters from Lee & Gordon's mill to Lafayette, and was planning to move seven or eight divisions against the divisions of Negley and Baird in McLemore's Cove. At 3:00 A. M. the men of the 1st Division were in line behind their stacks, and remained in position until daybreak, and then began a rapid movement forward. At 8:00 A. M. the division reached General Negley's position, and was formed on the left. Soon after it was learned that the enemy was advancing through Cutlett's and Dug Gap in heavy force, while another column was approaching from the north. It was then apparent that the trains, and even the command, would be endangered should battle be accepted without change of position, and General Negley decided to withdraw as speedily as possible.

He sent the trains toward the mountain, and followed with his own division, leaving General Baird's 1st Division to check the enemy until he could assume a new position north of the Chickamauga, and in turn cover the withdrawal of Baird's line, and prevent a flank movement on the left."

When Negley's division had gained a position and formed in line of battle, Baird's division withdrew, step by step—first the skirmishers, then the main line—until they, too, had crossed the stream. The enemy pressed the line as the division retired, and the troops were compelled to fight, suffering and inflicting loss. The division had hardly crossed the stream before the enemy appeared with heavy lines on the opposite side, and opened with artillery, while a heavy force formed in line of battle on the left of the line. The artillery of the 2d Division responded from a hill to the rear, and Starkweather's and Stanley's brigades became warmly engaged, and so far checked the enemy that our 1st Division was able to form a new line behind General Negley. (This part of the movement began about 4:00 P. M., and will be remembered by the men on account of the rapid marching, the heat, and clouds of dust made by the wagons hurrying to the rear). This was made by order of General Negley, by which the brigades of General Beatty and our own Colonel Scribner, went to the rear to protect the trains from the enemy's cavalry. These timely, cautious, and dextrous movements saved these divisions, and their safe retirement from the presence of an army may be regarded as one of the pivotal events of the campaign, having completely foiled the enemy by their skillful withdrawal.

"Generals Negley and Baird took a strong position before Stevens' Gap, and were soon joined by the remaining divisions of the corps. The four divisions were disposed for defense in the following order from right to left: Negley, Baird, Brannan, and Reynolds—the whole covering Stevens' and Cooper's Gaps. But these preparations for defense were not necessary, as Bragg turned from Thomas to direct Polk's corps and other forces against General Crittenden's corps; first, to crush him, and then turn again against the Fourteenth."

Bragg's order for the movement against Crittenden is attached:

HEADQUARTERS ARMY OF THE TENNESSEE.
LAFAYETTE, GA., 6:00 P. M., Sept. 12.

LIEUTENANT-GENERAL POLK:

General: I enclose you a dispatch from General Pegram. This presents a fine opportunity of striking Crittenden in detail, and I hope you will avail yourself of it at daylight to-morrow. This division crushed, and the others are yours. We can turn on the force in the Cove. Wheeler's cavalry will move on Wilder, so as to cover your right. I shall be delighted to hear of your success. Very truly yours,

BRAXTON BRAGG.

Afterward Buckner's corps was moved in support.

General Bragg thus refers to the movement and its failure:

"Early on the 13th I proceeded to the front, ahead of Buckner's command, to find that no advance had been made on the enemy, and that his forces had formed a junction and recrossed the Chickamauga. Again disappointed, immediate measures were taken to place our trains and limited supplies in safe positions, when all our forces were concentrated along the Chickamauga, threatening the enemy in front.

"Lafayette was five miles distant from Dug Gap, ten miles from Lee & Gordon's mill, eighteen from Alpine, and fifteen from Ringgold. Bragg's army was mainly between Lafayette and Dug Gap, on his left, and Lee & Gordon's mill on his front, and hence he held interior lines of extreme shortness for operations against an army divided into three parts.

"It is, therefore, demonstrable that, had General Thomas moved rapidly on the direct road to Lafayette, through Dug Gap, as ordered, the defeat of the corps, or its capture, would have been inevitable, and the fate of the corps would have been the fate of the army. It is, accordingly, not surprising that, when General Rosecrans had full knowledge of the facts, he frankly stated in his official report that, 'It was, therefore, a matter of life and death to effect the concentration of the army.'"

When it was evident that General Bragg's army was concentrated north of Lafayette, McCook's corps was forty miles distant from Crittenden's by the nearest road, and the distance from Lee & Gordon's mill and from McLemore's Cove (14th Corps) to Bragg's army was less than between the positions of Thomas and Crittenden, while McCook's (20th) corps was much farther from Thomas or the position of the 14th Corps than from the enemy before Lafayette. But, notwithstanding the wide separation of the corps, the intervening mountains, and the concentrated forces of the enemy in proximity to Crittenden (21st Corps), the Army of the Cumberland was united in time for battle.

In abandoning the offensive from the 13th to the 18th, Bragg lost his best opportunity to overwhelm a single corps. During this time Crittenden's corps stood before his army on the opposite bank of the Chickamauga. Had he moved forward he would have forced this single unsupported corps back upon Chattanooga, or westward upon Lookout Mountain, and while doing this he would have covered his communications through Ringgold to Dalton.

There was no change in the position of the 14th Corps during the 12th. From the 13th to the 17th there was some advance of a portion of the corps from day to day.

Within the regiment or division the notes show that on the 13th the 1st Division was encamped about the large spring that came from the mouth of a cave in McLemore's Cove.

September 14th and 15th. The troops put up shelter tents and took the "top rails" from the fences, according to custom.

September 16th. Orders for the march next day at 5:00 A. M. All sorts of rumors afloat as to the purpose and the place to be reached.

Thursday, September 17th. The troops were in line at 5:00 A. M. At six o'clock the movement began. Our division moved toward the east and halted, after passing over six miles, near General Crittenden's corps. During this day artillery was heard in front. At 4:00 P. M. the Ninety-fourth was placed on picket along the edge of a creek in a corn-field. No disturbance on the line that night.

"The night of the 17th Bragg announced his plan, and prescribed the movements of his army for execution on the following morning. Three corps in their order, from right to left—Hood, Walker, Buckner—were directed to cross the Chickamauga. At Reed's and Alexander's bridges and Ledford's Ford Buckner was to press upon Wood's division of the 21st Corps, in front of Polk's corps, while this corps next in line to the left was to demonstrate on the line of direct approach, and, if not met by too much resistance, to cross and attack any force he might meet. Hill's corps was to cover the left flank. The cavalry covered the gaps in Pigeon Mountain. Had these movements been executed promptly, as ordered, the larger portion of Bragg's army would have been on the left flank of Rosecrans' army and in rear of the left, with a fair prospect of grasping all the roads east of the Chattanooga Valley, as at the time fixed for the execution of the movement General Rosecrans was not prepared to defeat it. It was a repetition of the initiative of the same commander at Perryville and Murfreesboro, only on a grander scale. The conditions here were different, and though he was nearer the rear of the Union Army, and had designated heavier columns for his favorite movement, there were obstacles that gave more embarrassments than in his other battles. In preparing for battle on the 18th he had overlooked causes of detention, and this mistake gave General Rosecrans time to throw his army to the left, between him and Chattanooga, upon the shortest roads thither. The roads designated for his columns were narrow and unsuited for the movement of artillery. A stream with few bridges and few fords was in his way, and the movement of a large army by the flank on transverse roads involves embarrassments which almost always cause detentions not anticipated; so that at nightfall on the 18th Bragg was by no means ready for battle on the 19th, having failed to deliver it on the 18th as he had planned. But his preparations were in advance of those of General Rosecrans, as he had the initiative and moved on shorter lines. Night marches alone could give partial finish to Rosecrans' provisions for the engagement now plainly imminent."

September 18th. Early in the day the clouds of dust trending to the north-east had made evident the character and purpose of the movement of the Confederate Army by the right flank. At an early hour there was a demonstration in front of Palmer's division of the 21st Corps (Crittenden's) to the right of Crawfish Springs, and at noon Wood's division of that corps was threatened. These were intended to conceal the heavy movements down stream. Within the regiment the soldiers discussed the reports that the rebel army had turned from the retreat to Atlanta, and in turn were hugging close to the Union Army, with the intention of retaking Chattanooga. Another was that Bragg had been reinforced by Longstreet's and Hill's corps from Lee's army.

"The mounted brigades of Colonels Minty and Wilder were on the watch at Reed's and Alexander's bridges over the Chickamauga, and it was not until late in the afternoon that the heads of column appeared before them.

"These two brigades resisted so persistently that Bragg mentioned their action as one cause of delay. But they were finally forced back and the enemy secured the crossings; the lower one, at Reed's bridge, was wrested from the enemy late that evening and burned by Colonel Dan McCook's brigade of the reserve corps. Bragg held the river from General Wood's position to Reed's bridge, and, under cover of the night and the forests, his movements were perfectly concealed—none of the commanders there were able to learn what forces crossed the Chickamauga late at night. As two corps of the enemy remained in position across the Chickamauga, and his cavalry was on the right bank, far up the stream, it was very critical to move the Army of the Cumberland by the left flank. The movement of the 14th Corps, with the 20th following from the right, toward General Crittenden's position, was accomplished with great caution and consequent slowness during the day, so that at 4:00 P. M. of the 18th no troops had reached the rear of Crittenden, though it was well known that the enemy had forces far beyond Wood's position at Lee & Gordon's mill. At this hour General Thomas was directed to relieve a part of Crittenden's corps—the divisions of Palmer and VanCleve—with Negley's, that they might be placed upon Wood's left, and, with Baird's, Brannan's, and Reynolds' divisions, to take position at Kelly's, on the Lafayette road."

The Ninety-fourth was recalled from picket at 5:00 P. M. and joined the brigade, then marching with all of Baird's division on the way to the left. After a short march the troops were halted, rations issued, and supper prepared. At seven o'clock the division moved north on the main road to Chattanooga from Lafayette. The march was continued until midnight, when the troops halted for a short rest.

Saturday, September 19th, at 2:00 A. M. our troops were still on the march in the main road to the north-east, as many believed, to Chattanooga. The fences were burned along the road during the night. The troops marched in silence—occasional shots from out-posts of the enemy upon our right, and the hum of voices in the column as the men talked of the approaching battle, were all that could be heard during that weary all-night march. The changes in the positions of the divisions were effected for the most part during the night, and at early dawn there were five divisions in front of the enemy.

"At daylight Baird's (1st) division reached Kelly's house, and was formed in line on the right of Brannan's (3d) division. These divisions formed the left of the Union Army, and were placed in such position as to cover the roads leading from Reed's and Alexander's bridges over the Chickamauga.

"Soon after these divisions had taken position before Kelly's house, General Thomas was informed by General McCook, of the reserve corps, who had bivouacked on the road to Reed's bridge, that he had succeeded in burning the bridge after a brigade had crossed. Believing this brigade to be isolated, Colonel McCook suggested that an effort should be made to capture it.

"Deeming the suggestion worthy of experiment, and wishing to explore his front, General Thomas directed General Brannan to leave one brigade within supporting distance of General Baird, and with the other two reconnoiter the road to the burnt bridge, and, if practicable, capture the isolated brigade. General Thomas, sharing in the prevailing ignorance of the exact movements of the enemy, had been forming his lines in nearness to a heavy force.

"Although the armies had been maneüvering in closest proximity for twelve days, each army commander was ignorant of the special dispositions of the other, and a mere tentative advance became the initiative of one of the bloodiest battles of the war.

"General Bragg had hoped to conceal his effort to throw his army between General Rosecrans and Chattanooga. The latter had discerned the movement of troops to his left, but neither he nor any of his officers were aware that seven-tenths of General Bragg's army were on the west bank of the Chickamauga early on the morning of the 19th.

"After forming line in the woods before Kelly's house Baird's division stacked arms and prepared breakfast. After this the men rested and slept about their stacks until the advance of Brannan's division. At this time the brigades moved forward in support of the movement directed for General Brannan. The whole division advanced rapidly, driving the enemy. The rebels gave way, leaving many dead in their track, and two hundred prisoners. After other dispositions in General Brannan's line, both divisions pressed the enemy back some distance. This done, the line was halted for readjustment, when it was learned that a large force was moving upon the right and rear of these isolated divisions.

"Bragg had reinforced his right with Walker's corps in support of Forrest. General Baird prepared for resistance by ordering the Regulars to change front to the south, but before this change could be made, Liddill's large division was upon them, and both this brigade and our own (Scribner's) were driven from position with the loss of ten guns. Starkweather's brigade was thrown before the enemy, but it, too, gave way. Fortunately reinforcements were at hand to press back the enemy from the right and rear of Baird. Portions of Brannan's division charged the pursuing enemy, driving them in turn, and while doing so gave time for a better resistance. The brigades recovered from their temporary confusion, and in a short time the entire division line was restored on the right of Brannan."

In the charge spoken of the 9th Ohio recovered Battery H, 5th U. S. Artillery, posted with the Regulars.

Lieutenant Van Pelt, in command of Lomis' battery (A, 1st Michigan Artillery), posted with Scribner's brigade, fought with saber and pistol until killed there. The four guns lost were finally recovered at Mission Ridge.

"The capture of the guns in the 1st Division, and other guns on the field, was mainly due to the fact that the conflict occurred on ground thickly covered with forest trees and undergrowth, and consequently unfavorable for the rapid movement of artillery, as also for its effective use. This opening passage of arms was the type of the fighting in its first stages from left to right. Excepting a few small fields, the whole region between the Lafayette road and the Chickamauga was thickly wooded, and divisions and brigades from each army were often hotly engaged while in complete isolation in the densest woods, for when armies meet unexpectedly on such a field methodical movements are impracticable, as also continuous lines, until there has been an immense waste of strength.

"When General Thomas was assured by the advance of Baird's and Brannan's divisions that he had the Confederate Army in his front, he requested General Crittenden, whose corps was nearest him and not engaged, to send him support. Palmer's division reached him, and almost at the same time Johnson's division of McCook's corps. Reynolds' (our own 4th) division arrived soon after. As yet Bragg had not advanced his troops to the gap between the right of our division (Baird's) and the left of Crittenden's corps. His object had been to envelop Crittenden, supposing that the extreme left of the Union Army rested at Lee & Gordon's mill. When his cavalry met Brannan's infantry, overlapping his right flank, Bragg threw Walker's corps against Brannan and Baird, and was compelled soon after to direct his reserves, and one division from his extreme left, to his right, where Walker's corps had been broken and routed. The time spent in the execution of these movements, and surprise from the unexpected conditions of the engagement, permitted three divisions to secure alignment on the right of Baird. The first movement of Brannan and Baird had been regarded by Bragg as intended to turn his right flank, and until its security had been attained other dispositions were suspended. This prevented the advance of his central columns upon the unoccupied ground between Thomas and Crittenden, and robbed him of his greatest advantage."

The opening battle of the 1st and 3d Divisions Saturday morning was full of experiences for the Ninety-fourth. The regiment joined in the charge upon the enemy at the first advance, rushing down through the woods in obedience to orders. A battery was overtaken in the charge, but there was no thought that it could be dragged back to our lines, for just then the enemy opened fire in rear of the regiment, and, looking about, it was found that in the charge the regiment had advanced beyond the brigade and was alone, without support upon either side— none of the other regiments to be seen. The regiment then faced to the rear and marched against the lines now closing in behind us. Upon reaching the enemy our regiment opened fire and held firm until the troops on our right gave way. The regiment fell back a short distance and again restored the line. The position of the regiment at this time was upon the left of the Regular Brigade, joining one of the battalions of the 18th Infantry. After joining here our line was moved to the right, and upon forming repulsed a fierce charge upon our position. Meantime the gap to the right of Baird had been closed by the divisions of Johnson and Palmer, and the roar of battle now extended along this front. During the afternoon, while formed on the left of the Regulars, Colonel Moore, of the 33d Ohio, found the regiment and led the way to the brigade, a short distance to the rear. From the first advance in the forenoon until near nightfall the regiment kept a place on the front line. Separated from brigade commander and regiments, there was no thought except that it was their business to stay, " orders or no orders," fighting as best they could at every chance.

In spite of frequent changes of front, and once when compelled to fight through a line to the rear, the loss by capture was quite small. So far as can be learned, the gallant fellows who went down to Andersonville from this field were captured in the change in the position of our lines that night.

"After the repulse of the enemy's right wing a complete lull ensued here, and during this quietness the whole of both our and Brannan's divisions were retired to a commanding position on the road to Reed's bridge. The divisions still retained their original positions—Brannan's the extreme left of the army, ours (Baird's) next on his right. This change was made by General Thomas to make the left stronger in anticipation of another assault upon it. During the assault upon the right, Brannan's division was sent from the left, while Reynolds and Palmer were retiring before a destructive fire. This timely reinforcement, the quick re-formation of portions of these divisions, and the most effective use of several batteries of artillery, arrested a disaster. After this repulse the enemy moved through a gap to the left of Woods' position, but were met here and driven back by Negley's division, which had advanced from the Widow Glenn's, and by Brannan's, which came upon him from the vicinity of Kelby's house. The whole right of Bragg's army had been broken up and repulsed, and his central forces, though more successful in maintaining lines, had suffered equal losses. At the time Brannan's division had been moved to the right in the afternoon, Scribner's and Starkweather's brigades were advanced to Johnson's division in support, leaving the Regulars alone on the road to Reed's bridge to hold the ground previously occupied by two divisions.

"These changes were merely provisional, and General Thomas, as night approached, selected ground for a new and more compact line, and designated the respective positions of the five divisions which he had handled during the day; but before Johnson's division and Baird's two brigades (Scribner's and Starkweather's) could be withdrawn, they were attacked by Cleburne's fresh division, supported by Cheathem's, and a severe night conflict ensued, lasting for an hour, with heavy losses on both sides and final repulse of the enemy."

The Ninety-fourth shared the dangers and aided in this final repulse of the day. The strong lines of the enemy forced our men slowly backward at the same time the enemy appeared upon the left of the regiment. After retiring some distance, the brigade re-formed the line. The fighting continued until after dark, and after its close the brigade was marched to a large open field to the rear (the new position spoken of above); here the men stacked arms, built fires, and laid down to rest. The night was cold and everybody was quite uncomfortable. At the opening of the battle, the regiment threw off knapsacks for the charge, and not returning the same route, were now compelled to sleep without blankets. After such rough handling, being on the front line from the opening of the battle, the regiment was well-nigh worn out with fatigue and excitement and could sleep anywhere.

"Both armies lost heavily during the day. The loss of officers in the Confederate Army was quite large. But, heavy as were the losses, each army knew that the battle had not been decided, and would be renewed on the morrow. Neither army was willing to yield without further fighting, and yet to neither was there the assurance of ultimate victory. As they lay on their arms in close proximity, there was to each the oppression of doubt with regard to the issue. Bragg, however, had more troops in reserve available for the next day than Rosecrans. Longstreet reached Ringgold with several brigades that evening. Breckinridge's division had not been engaged at all, and two others only slightly, while nearly all of the brigades of the Union Army on the field had been fully engaged. General Rosecrans, being on the defensive, was compelled moreover to diffuse his army more widely, not only to cover the two main roads to Chattanooga from the field, but those also in proximity to his flanks.

"But notwithstanding General Bragg's reserves, he had cause to feel uneasiness with regard to the work before him. He had been completely foiled in his strategy and tactics. He had expected to find Crittenden's corps on the left of the Union Army, but his own enveloping lines had been taken in flank, and the right half had been fearfully shattered. At the opening of the battle, his army had been well in hand for offense or defense, while General Rosecrans had been compelled often to throw forward divisions and brigades without support on right and left, and the National Army was now before him with continuous lines, and having the choice of strong positions in the rear. Besides, this army was yet upon the roads to Chattanooga, which he had expected to grasp after he had doubled its left upon its center and pressed it back upon the mountain passes. In all his special expectations and dominant aims, Bragg had been disappointed and defeated.

"Our army attained a continuous battle front only at the close of the engagement. The three corps of the army were in such position at the opening of the battle, and such the necessary haste of movement to the most threatened, that their organizations could not be maintained. Thus General Thomas had three divisions from his own corps and one from each of the other two; and on the right center and right of the army the remaining divisions of McCook's and Crittenden's corps were in regular alternation. This mixing of divisions gave an expression of improvision to the battle front strongly significant of the emergencies of its formation. In forming the new line in the evening, General Thomas did not change the orders of the divisions for the left of the army, but modified their relations so as to give greater compactness and strength to the front that should be offered to the enemy. The order from left to right was: Baird,

Johnson, Palmer, Reynolds, and Brannan. Baird's division was well re-fused, facing the east. The battle front coursed around the north-east corner of Kelly's farm, crossed the Lafayette road a little south of his house, and extended thence to the south-west. Baird's, Johnson's, and Palmer's divisions were east of the road, and Reynolds' and Brannan's were west of it.

"The division line was moved out to a new position before day on Sunday, and was formed as the extreme left of the army. According to the arrangement for the order of battle for this day, agreed upon at the conference of corps commanders and other general officers the night before, Negley's division should be relieved from the right and take position on the left, in anticipation of another attack upon the left flank.

"After the troops had reached the new position, the men built barricades of logs, stones, and rails found in the woods, and kept under cover. Our brigade made the left of the line at that time, and was in extreme peril, because of the fact that all of the ground occupied by a division of troops the day before was open to the enemy, and the Lafayette road to the left and rear was uncovered. Soon after this, one of Negley's brigades (Beatty's) reached our line and formed on the left of our brigrade, and this formed the only support for the left in the storm of battle, which all expected would soon come upon them."

The Ninety-fourth was in line upon the left of a battery, an excellent position for defense, the battery being placed in such a position as to enfilade lines of the enemy approaching the left and front of the line of battle.

"At half-past eight o'clock Sunday morning, the skirmishers opened in our front, and soon after the enemy made a furious assault upon the left of the line, which rapidly extended to the right. Against the left the assault was made by Breckinridge and Cleburne. The left brigade of the former struck the left of Baird's division, and the other two brigades soon overpowered Beatty's brigade next on our left. With this brigade displaced, the left flank was greatly overlapped. Upon the firmness of the flank depended the possession of the road to Rossville. In this attack Breckinridge's left brigade and Cleburne's division were so shattered that it was not deemed safe to swing the overlapping brigades into the rear of Baird's division. This for a time saved the left of our line, especially as the other divisions on the left of Cleburne were repulsed with equal emphasis, as Bragg's attack swept from left to right. For an hour he maintained the conflict with great vigor, in part with fresh troops, but his whole right was broken as on the previous day. General Cleburne reported the loss of five hundred men in a few minutes, and Breckinridge's left brigade was almost annihilated, having lost its commander, General Helm, and two colonels killed and two colonels wounded. Generals Stewart and Cleburne mentioned in their reports the effect of the National artillery as the most destructive in their experience. The left, in the initial conflict, was again triumphantly successful, but disasters on the right, and a second attempt to overwhelm the left, for several hours threatened the complete overthrow of the whole army. In the maintenance of the left, Stanley's brigade of Negley's division rendered timely assistance.

"The conflict continued with occasional quiet spells upon the left. The demand for troops here, and the quietness of the enemy on the right, led General Rosecrans to believe that Bragg was moving his army to the right, and so strong was this belief that he finally decided to withdraw the right of the army. Soon after, the right center and the divisions of the right were ordered to move to the left, and it was while this movement was taking place that Hood's assault was delivered, and the right center broken. When this assault reached Brannan's division, the right flank went back under fire in some confusion; but the left being secure, order was soon restored, and the lines maintained their positions until a lull in the conflict gave opportunity to take a new position.

"During this time everything was concentrated in the effort upon the right center of our army, and matters were quiet in front of our division, in its place at the other end of the line. For a time after the disaster on the right there were but five divisions in line against the whole rebel army. These divisions were all firm, but the enemy was concentrating on both flanks of the line which lay across the Lafayette road; and soon, under the inspiration of partial victory and the hope of complete triumph, most vigorous and persistent assaults were made, whose successful resistance, under the circumstances, makes the closing struggle of this great battle one of the most remarkable which has occurred in modern times—one of the grandest that has ever been made for the existence of army or country. From morn till night the five divisions which had previously constituted Thomas' line, with such other troops as reached him from the right under orders, or drifted to him after the disaster, and two brigades from the reserve corps, successfully resisted the whole Confederate Army. The issue of the first attack upon the left did not deter Bragg from a renewal of effort to turn the left flank and gain the Rossville road in our rear. The next assault was made with stronger lines and greater force, and this time with partial success. The left of Thomas' line had not yet been reinforced, except by a brigade from Wood's division placed in support of our 1st Division (Baird's).

"The rebel corps were extended to the right beyond the scene of the first attack, and intended to wheel to the left and envelop our exposed left. Breckinridge swung around and was soon able to move southward on the Lafayette road and take in reverse the main line near Kelly's. This movement was met and overwhelmed by the reserve brigades of Johnson's, Palmer's, and Brannan's divisions, which were in fortunate freedom for this most threatening emergency. This rebel division was routed and driven back around Baird's division to join the broken ranks of Walker's corps and Cleburne's division, which had been routed in every attack upon Baird, Palmer, and Johnson. These attacks were furious and persistent, but without impression upon the firm, defensive line."

Within the regiment the time of the second attack was fixed at 3:00 P. M. The fighting on this line surpassed anything ever known by our men up to that date. There was a continuous roar of artillery and musketry along the entire front. The battery posted on the right of the regiment was served with deadly effect. Their guns were loaded with grape and canister, and at each discharge carried down numbers from masses engaged in the assault. As in the morning, a complete cessation of the deadly strife followed this repulse, and none of the troops on the left were engaged until late in the evening, when the order came to withdraw the line.

"At 3:35 P. M. General Garfield and Colonel Thruston, Chief of Staff to General McCook, joined General Thomas. The former bore instructions from General Rosecrans, giving Thomas discretion as to the immediate withdrawal of the army. The reply was brief but emphatic: 'It will ruin the army to withdraw it now. This position must be held till night.'

"Seldom in war has such a burden of responsibility fallen upon a subordinate as upon General Thomas at Chickamauga. The battle was left to him before noon on the 20th. He received no instructions from the commanding general. He was ignorant of the disaster on the right until the oncoming left wing of Bragg's army revealed it.

"Uninformed as to the general situation, he could not anticipate emergencies, but he was strong and versatile to master them as they were developed. It was not a light matter to command the Army of the Cumberland as a whole against a vast army that had been gathered from the east and the west to crush it; an army superior in numbers and inspired by the hope that in winning a decisive victory the general contest would be decided also. But to take command of half the Army of the Cumberland, with no supporting cavalry, with exposed flanks and unconnected lines, to be supreme on the field by the demands of the situation rather than by the orders of a superior, and under such circumstances to contend successfully against Bragg's whole army, was an achievement that transcends the higher successes of generals.

"General Thomas did all that was possible with his forces on both days of battle. He suggested for the whole army a position whose strength he demonstrated with a part. He discerned the importance of turning all the troops gathered on the Dry Valley road against the enemy's left flank. His generalship in this battle can not be measured alone by his success in repulsing all the forces that moved against his lines on both days. What he suggested, as well as what he achieved, must be taken to give full breadth to his military skill. Had his advice been taken the battle of Chickamauga would never have been fought, but Chattanooga would have been fortified from choice, as it afterwards was from necessity.

"He saved his corps, and with it the army, by his cautious advance toward Lafayette; and in the battle which he would have avoided, he used every resource with the greatest skill to defeat the enemy. A general less calm and self-reliant in undefined emergencies, less stubborn in defense, less quick in disposing troops in the crises of battle, or less masterful of resources and advantages, would never have saved the Army of the Cumberland at Chickamauga. No commanding general fought such a battle during the war, and no other subordinate commander wrought such a deliverance for an imperiled army and an imperiled cause.

"There was but one Chickamauga and but one Thomas.

"It should not, therefore, be a matter of surprise that when General D. H. Hill, after the war, mentioned three distinct causes for the failure of the Southern arms, one of these was the stubborn resistance of Thomas in this battle. Neither is it strange that he was ever afterwards known as the ROCK OF CHICKAMAUGA."

General Garfield sent the subjoined note after joining Thomas. This is copied here because it shows the situation on the Thomas line Sunday afternoon:

HEADQUARTERS GENERAL THOMAS.
BATTLE-FIELD, FIVE MILES SOUTH OF ROSSVILLE,
September 20, 1863, 3:45 P. M. (<i>By Courier</i>).

GENERAL ROSECRANS:

I arrived here ten minutes ago *via* Rossville. General Thomas has Brannan's, Baird's, Reynolds', Wood's, Palmer's, and Johnson's divisions here still intact after terrible fighting. Granger is here closed up with Thomas, and both are fighting terribly on the right. Sheridan is in with the bulk of his division in ragged shape, though plucky for fight.

General Thomas holds his old ground of this morning. Negley was coming down on Rossville from the road passing where we saw the trains on our route. I sent word to him to cover the retreat of trains through Rossville. I also met the 4th Independent Battery at that place and posted it in reserve in case of need. As I turned in from the Rossville road to General Thomas I was opened on by a battery; one orderly killed; Captain Graves' horse killed; my own wounded.

The hardest fighting I have seen to-day is now going on. I hope General Thomas will be able to hold on here till night, and will not have to fall back farther than Rossville; perhaps not any. All fighting men should be stopped there, and the Dry Valley road held by them. I think we may retrieve the disaster of this morning. I never saw better fighting than our men are now doing. The rebel ammunition must be nearly exhausted. Ours fast failing. If we can hold out an hour more it will be all right. Granger thinks we can defeat them badly to-morrow if all our forces come in. I think you had better come to Rossville to-night and bring ammunition.

Very truly yours,
JAMES A. GARFIELD, <i>Brigadier-General.</i>

In the evening Thomas received orders from General Rosecrans to withdraw the army, as shown by General Thomas' official report and by General Garfield's letter from Rossville.

At 5:30 P. M. General Reynolds was directed to withdraw from position and form a line near the road leading through the gap to the Dry Valley road at McFarland's to cover the retirement of the other divisions. In moving as directed General Reynolds encountered a brigade of the enemy's troops that had moved around his right flank to his rear. This brigade was routed by Turchin's brigade, and was finally driven around Baird's left flank by Willich's brigade of Johnson's division. When Reynolds' division had formed near the road, the divisions, as rapidly as practicable, left the line and moved toward Rossville.

Baird, Johnson, and Palmer were attacked as they withdrew, and this fact gave the Confederate generals opportunity to report that their last attack dislodged our forces. The Ninety-fourth, along with the other regiments on the extreme left, fell back parallel with the Lafayette road, reaching the main road in the vicinity of Cloud Springs, and from here on to Rossville. As soon as his troops were in motion General Thomas rode to Rossville, and upon their arrival commenced the formation of the army to resist the advance of the enemy.

The following extract from a telegram sent that evening from Rossville will give the situation there:

HEADQUARTERS DEPARTMENT OF THE CUMBERLAND,
ROSSVILLE, GA., 8:40 P. M., September 20, 1863.

MAJOR-GENERAL ROSECRANS:

I have this moment returned from the front. I wrote you a long dispatch as I arrived on the field and while the battle was in progress, but it was so difficult to get communication to the rear that I fear you have not yet received it. Thomas has kept Baird's, Brannan's, Reynolds', Woods', and Palmer's divisions in good order, and has maintained almost the exact position he occupied this morning, except that his right has swung back nearly at right angles with the Gordon mills and Rossville road. General Thomas has fought a most terrific battle and damaged the enemy badly. General Granger's troops moved up just in time, and fought magnificently. From the time I reached the battle-field, 3:45 P. M., till sunset, the fight was by far the fiercest I have ever seen; our men not only held their ground, but at many points drove the enemy splendidly. Longstreet's Virginians have got their bellies full. Nearly every division on the field exhausted its ammunition, got supplies and exhausted them again. On the whole, General Thomas and General Granger have done the enemy fully as much injury to-day as they have suffered from him, and they have successfully repelled the repeated combined attacks of the whole rebel army, frequently pressing the front and both flanks at the same time. The disaster on the right can not, of course, be estimated now; it must be very considerable in men and material, especially the latter. The rebels have done their best to-day, and I believe we can whip them to-morrow. I believe we can crown the whole battle with victory. Granger regards them as thoroughly whipped to-night, and thinks they would not renew the fight were we to remain on the field. Your order to retire on this place was received a little after sunset and communicated to Generals Thomas and Granger. The troops are now moving, and will be here in good shape and strong position before morning. I hope you will not budge an inch from this place, but come up early in the morning, and if the rebels try it on accommodate them. * * * *

J. A. GARFIELD,
Brigadier-General, Chief of Staff.

The loss in the 1st Division was 2,213. The loss in killed and wounded in the regiment can not be made out from the rolls now, but it is believed the number did not equal that of the other regiments in the brigade. Our loss in captured was light compared with those. For the first time our captured went down to prisons from the field. The rolls tell the end of many a gallant soldier who "died at Andersonville."

Killed: GEORGE LOHNES, Co. A.
JOHN MATTHEWS, Co. B.
Wounded: Lieutenant H. C. CUSHMAN, SAMUEL S. COWAN, LEMUEL ALBIN, EDWIN N. KITCHEN, GEORGE W. TWIST, Co. A.
MATTHIAS DYE, Co. B.
BENJAMIN F. MATTOX, AARON TOMIRE, Co. C.
SAMUEL FOLKER, Co. D.
ADAM KERSHNER, Co. E.
Corporal WILLIAM E. SMITH, Co. F.

On this field, as at other times, the loss of the regiment was not in proportion to the exposure endured or the fighting performed by the brigade. During both days the regiment kept its strength in the line held by Baird's division, and assisted in repelling every assault made upon it.

During Sunday the regiment kept under cover of a breastwork made of logs and stones, and while here, from early dawn all day long, made every shot count upon the masses that swarmed in the woods before that line. A great deal of the firing by the enemy was without effect, because delivered while advancing and in the face of volleys from that low breastwork.

On the morning of the 21st there were indications that the enemy was advancing against the position at Rossville. The brigade and division lines were completed, stretching across the hills in the gap commanding the roads. The regiment was placed in position for the support of an Illinois battery, close to the guns, and, as the rebel advance involved the use of artillery, the men found the position quite uncomfortable. There was slight loss among our troops by shell and grape-shot. At 9:00 o'clock that night the regiment was sent forward to picket, with instructions to present a bold front, while the troops retired to Chattanooga.

Tuesday, September 22d. At 1:00 o'clock A. M. the regiment returned to the works to find the lines vacated. The battery stole quietly down the hill, and at this time the army was on the way to Chattanooga. At 3:00 A. M. the regiment left the works at Rossville Gap, and by 8:00 A. M. was in position, with the entire division, before Chattanooga. General Rousseau met our brigades in the formation at Rossville on the morning of the 21st and assumed command of the division. Rousseau's division was established upon the left of the corps and next to Palmer's division of the 21st Corps. The troops began the work of entrenching at once upon being placed in line. Late the same evening the bands along the lines played delightful music. Thousands of soldiers cheered, all of which served to prove that the Army of the Cumberland was not discouraged.

September 23d. The regiment was in line behind the Chattanooga and Knoxville Railroad, with the greater portion sent to work on a line of trenches in front of this position. The work was commenced the day before, and on account of expecting an attack the men toiled all night. Great clouds of dust could be seen in the direction of Rossville, made by the enemy closing up to our lines. Our batteries were used upon the enemy the entire day. The music of the bands and the cheering were heard all along the front of the army. At 6:00 o'clock that evening the regiment went into the breastwork in front of the railroad, the left of the brigade line and the first line.

September 24th. The enemy tried our front, opening upon the camps with artillery, and, engaging the pickets, work was continued upon the trenches during the entire day. A reconnoissance in front brought on a brisk fight, with some loss in killed and wounded among the troops sent out. After tattoo that night the regiment was aroused from sleep by an attack upon our lines. The men took their places in the trenches, but the enemy did not venture near enough to engage the main line. General Rousseau took his position with the Ninety-fourth and encouraged everybody near by with his cheering words.

September 25th and 26th. The work on the trenches was continued at the front amid the music of the bands, the play of batteries on both sides, and the rattle and alarms on the picket lines.

On the 27th the picket lines agreed to cease firing, except in case of an advance. The request was sent from our lines under a flag of truce, and was accepted by the other side.

September 28th and 29th. The regiment marched to the front early on the 28th for picket duty near the Rossville road. The lines here were so close that the men could talk to the "Johnnies." Papers were exchanged and coffee traded for tobacco. A large train of ambulances sent to the battle-field returned, passing the regiment on the 29th. These brought a portion of the wounded from our army, left upon the field for five or six days without attention.

October 4th. After several days of rain the trenches in the low ground filled with water, and everything about camp was afloat. For several days and nights past the men did little else than stand about the fires and try to keep warm. About this time the reports came in about the burning of our supply trains coming from Stevenson. This was known to be a serious matter, because the army was forced from this time on to depend upon a single line of railroad for supplies. The regiment moved to a hill in the rear of the second line of works to get on dry ground.

(Extracts taken from notes made at the siege of Chattanooga, by Sergeant Lane, Company H; Sergeant Beck, Company F; and Corporal Rohr, Company I:)

"October 5th. At 11:00 A. M. the enemy opened fire with heavy pieces from Missionary Ridge. The range was well estimated. Many shells were dropped in our camps along the front lines, but as the men kept under cover of strong works we lost but few in wounded. Our supplies are short. The ration is estimated at one-fourth, and the men urged to be sparing on account of the small quantity in store. The enemy continued firing upon our camps until 2:00 A. M. of the 6th. At times shells came entirely too close for comfort and helped to disturb sleep.

"October 8th. 'Grape vine' reports say the rebels are placing heavy guns in front of the brigade. We know from the size of the shell found in camp that at least one 32-pounder is in position in our front. Details from the regiments continue to work on the intrenchments. A portion of the Ninety-fourth have put in some labor on Fort Rousseau. At this time the papers and prominent officers have much to say that may be called praise for the part performed by the 14th Corps in the battle of Chickamauga. Scribner's brigade performed its part with much credit during both days of the battle.

"October 9th. A large detail of the regiment was sent to work on the forts. The men suffered from hunger. They were easily fatigued, and could do but little work.

"October 10th. Very little food. Parched corn is a luxury and in great demand. The men take rations of corn issued to mules and horses, leaving them to starve. At 8:00 o'clock P. M. the regiment received enough bacon and crackers for supper.

"Sunday, October 11th. At 2:00 P. M. the brigade assembled

to hear a reading by James E. Murdoch, of Cincinnati. He read 'The Sleeping Sentinel,' 'The Story of Joseph,' and Psalm xxxix. There is not an ounce of rations in the camp. The men offer good prices for an ear of corn, with little prospect of finding it.

"October 12th. The regiment was sent to picket the front to-day, and while out exchanged papers with the 'Johnnies.' In one paper we read that one Confederate corps stripped nearly all of the prisoners taken by them at Chickamauga. They took their shoes and started them to prison barefooted. The papers sent from our side seem to effect desertions. Seventeen came in at a post near the regiment a few days ago.

"October 13th. The Ohio troops vote for Governor to-day. Brough tickets are in demand in the regiment, while Vallandigham finds few supporters. How earnest is the soldiers' wish that people at home may be as firmly united in their support of the Union party as are the men here in the field fighting for their country.

"October 14th. In the count of votes yesterday it was shown that the Ninety-fourth gave 287 for Brough, and six for Vallandigham.

"October 20th. At 1:00 P. M. to-day the entire division packed up and moved to the extreme right of our lines, directly in front of Lookout Mountain. The regiment was posted on a hillside, and from the camp could see the movements of the enemy on the mountain. For several days the men were engaged in fixing up quarters.

"October 20th the changes of commanders and consolidations of corps became known to the army. The President's order of October 18th, which created the Military Division of the Mississippi, with General Grant in command, placed General Thomas at the head of the Army of the Cumberland.

"At the time of this change of commanders the Army of the Cumberland comprised the 4th, 11th, 12th, and 14th Corps, and three divisions of cavalry. In compliance with the President's order of September 28th, the 4th was formed on the 9th of October by the consolidation of the 20th and 21st, and at the same time the reserve corps was attached to the 14th.

"Under the new organization there were three brigades in each division, designated as the 1st, 2d, and 3d, and three divisions in each corps similarly distinguished. Major-General Gordon Granger was assigned to the command of the 4th Corps, and his division commanders, in the numerical order of divisions, were Majors-General John M. Palmer and Phillip H. Sheridan, and Brigadier-General Thomas J. Wood. The commanders of the 1st, 2d, and 3d Divisions of the 14th Corps were, respectively, Major-General Lovell H. Rousseau and Brigadiers-General Jeff. C. Davis and Absalom Baird. The 1st Division was increased by the addition of Negley's division. A new 2d Division was made from the reserve corps, and the 3d Division received Reynolds' division. Our 1st Brigade received Beatty's brigade, and, as a commander, General W. P. Carlin, from the old 20th Corps.

"The dominant problem was that of supplies. Upon its solution rested the fate of the army. General Grant telegraphed to General Thomas: 'Hold Chattanooga at all hazards. I will be there as soon as possible. Please inform me how long your present supplies will last, and the prospect for keeping them up.'

"The response was: 'Two hundred and four thousand and sixty-two rations in store-house. Ninety-six thousand will arrive to-morrow, and all trains were loaded which had arrived at Bridgeport up to the 16th—probably three hundred wagons. *We will hold the town till we starve.*'

"General Thomas assumed command of the army the same day, and directed General Hooker to hasten the concentration of his command, and his preparations to move, according to previous instructions."

The record of Lane, Beck, and Rohr says "that on October 23d the regiment was aroused at 4:00 A. M., and at 6:30 A. M. marched two miles toward Lookout Mountain to picket along Chattanooga Creek, the reserve stationed at a tan-yard near by.

"October 25th. Orders received at night to keep arms and accouterments within reach, that line can be formed quickly in the morning.

"October 26th. The regiment formed promptly at the call, and stood in the trenches from 4:00 o'clock until daylight, expecting an advance upon our lines. Arms stacked for breakfast, then the troops were returned to quarters at 9:00 A. M. Some of the men have not had a bite to eat since yesterday at noon. At 10:00 A. M. the regiment was formed and sent to division headquarters, and from there to a high position to the left of the camp to finish a fort.

"October 30th. Shells from Lookout Mountain drop very close at times. The men are at work splitting boards for houses, and are building fire-places.

"October 31st. The shells went wide of the mark to-day. They exploded high in the air. The distance, estimated by sound, was about three miles, counting from the puff of smoke from the battery on the mountain until the report was heard.

"Sunday, November 1st. Inspection at 9:30 A. M. The men have half rations of crackers and a little meat (beef). All are hungry and weak, but know the rations must be made to hold out the required time, and can do nothing to avoid suffering. During the past two weeks there has been much distress among the troops on this account.

"November 4th. The regiment was on picket again at Chattanooga Creek. The reserve post was shelled by the battery on the mountain, but all escaped without injury.

"November 5th. Slight artillery fire along our front, and plenty of starvation within the camps—horses and mules dying every day. During the past week the men have received barely enough to keep them alive and on their feet. Last Sunday the Ninety-fourth drew a cracker and a half, went to picket duty on Monday, and drew again Tuesday evening.

"November 8th. On picket again to-day. Last night three-fourths rations of crackers, and a little sugar, coffee, and meat was issued. This made all hands feel good.

"November 13th. Pay-rolls made out to October 31st, and the Paymaster is in the camp.

"November 19th. Again on picket for a two days' trip, two-thirds rations and one hundred rounds of cartridges carried by each man."

LOOKOUT MOUNTAIN AND MISSIONARY RIDGE.

November 23d was the opening of the battles about Chattanooga. A part of General Granger's (4th) corps carried Orchard Knob, and by this means the lines of the army were enabled to advance and secure high ground near Missionary Ridge. During the assault Johnson's division (14th Corps) took position in the trenches near camp, and remained here until ten o'clock that night. At this time Carlin's brigade was moved to the front on the north side of Fort McCook, and remained in the trenches until morning.

On Tuesday, November 24th, the brigade moved to the front and halted in front of Fort Negley. During the forenoon the forts in the rear of the line kept up a brisk fire upon the lines of the enemy in the direction of Rossville and the mountain. At about 12:00 M. General Hooker's troops began the battle upon the mountain side. The divisions of Geary, Osterhaus, and Cruft engaged in the assault upon the enemy's lines on the Craven farm. These troops drove the enemy before them in disorder around the nose of the mountain, within sight of the army below.

At 4:30 P. M. Carlin's brigade moved to the mouth of Chattanooga Creek. Leaving the remainder of the army in position, they crossed the creek and filed up the mountain, found the left of General Hooker's line, and with strong skirmish lines pushed the enemy into the rocks far beyond the White house. Severe skirmishing was kept up until nearly midnight. The White house was occupied as headquarters by Generals Hooker and Carlin. The loss in the regiment was a few slightly wounded. Among the killed in the 40th O. V. I., during the day, was Private Alexander White, of Company K, Ninety-fourth.

The sun came out clear and bright next morning. Not a sign of the enemy was left. The men built fires upon the mountain sides, on account of the cold, and to celebrate the victory. All rejoiced over the success of our arms, and felt rewarded for all the dangers and exposure suffered by them, as they saw the flag planted on the top of the mountain. Then the hills and valleys resounded with shouts of joy from the whole army.

The men of the Ninety-fourth will ever remember that day as they stood in line of battle, in the midst of rocks and trees, far above the army, and gave cheer after cheer while looking at the old flag on that rock far above their heads.

After burying the dead, the brigade returned to the valley at 11:00 A. M. started for a position with the division across the valley and facing Missionary Ridge. The division was formed as the extreme right of General Thomas' army and Carlin's brigade on the right of the division. The Ninety-fourth took its place on the front line before the ridge, and awaited the signal for assault. At 4:00 P. M. the lines moved forward with double lines of battle and skirmishers, leading through woods, creeks, brush, and the resistance made by artillery on the top of the ridge and the skirmishers directly in front. Before starting upon the last rapid advance, the lines were halted in the timber and closed up. Then on, with cheers, for the works at the foot of the ridge. The rebels fled from rifle pits, then from first and second lines of intrenchments, with our troops following closely. The lines closed up and kept on, after halting a moment at the foot of the Ridge. The enemy tried to defend the last line at the crest, but soon gave way, as our men climbed up the hillsides and swarmed over their lines. All along the front of the division the "Johnnies" were routed, and driven in confusion from their last line. Our brigade and division lines were halted in the works, and took possession of prisoners, killed and wounded, cannon, and small arms. Johnson's division rested within the rebel works, the scene of the last fighting. Other parts of the army were sent in pursuit, and made many captures that night. The loss in the charge in the regiment was one officer (Captain McLaughlin, Company B) and ten or twelve enlisted men wounded.

At 10:00 A. M. our division joined in the pursuit, going in the direction of Graysville. At nine o'clock that night the rear guard was overtaken, and dispositions made to intercept them, if possible. The 2d Brigade coming up delivered a volley, and this was the signal for a scamper of the enemy in all directions. In their flight they left behind three guns, colors, small arms, and wagons. The pursuit was continued on to Graysville. Here the brigade halted for the night, and the Ninety-fourth went to the front for picket duty. While out that night the men gathered in a few more of the stragglers hiding in the woods. Next morning the march was continued toward Ringgold. The enemy dropped muskets, clothing, and all sorts of plunder. Other captures were made and another gun captured.

About 11:00 A. M. of the 27th the brigade was again placed in line, and skirmishers sent out to engage the rebel line near Ringgold. The enemy was routed and driven from position. The troops remained here and engaged in the destruction of the railroad until Sunday, when the 1st and 3d Divisions returned to Chattanooga. The rest of the army was sent to the relief of Knoxville. The advance reached Parker's Gap, beyond Graysville; from here to Chattanooga the distance was about twenty-four miles At nine o'clock that night the regiment reached the old quarters near Battery Rousseau.

Chattanooga notes by Rohr:

"Since the battle the regiment has performed a full share of the work required to complete the forts and earthworks. The ration is light, and we have about the usual detail for picket. (December 5th to 20th.)

"December 28th. About this time the old regiments began reënlisting as veteran volunteers. Near the camp of the Ninety-fourth three regiments enlisted a second time for three years, and were started North on furlough. These were the 38th Indiana in the 1st Brigade, 69th Ohio in the 2d Brigade, and 79th Pennsylvania in the 3d Brigade.

"January 21st, 1864. Carlin's brigade struck tents and moved out in front of Fort Wood. On the 23d the regiment formed a part of a scouting expedition; the distance marched was forty miles, the troops returning on the 25th.

"From January 15th full rations were issued, and the soldiers were cheerful and contented, or, to say it another way, 'the boys of the Ninety-fourth are as lively and full of sport as lambs in early spring.'

"On the 17th of February General Grant ordered the Army of the Cumberland forward on a 'formidable reconnoissance' toward Dalton, with instructions to occupy the place, if possible, and repair the railroads. At the time there was some probability that it might be successful, as it was supposed that Johnston had weakened his center especially to strengthen Polk against Sherman in Alabama. Two days later, however, General Thomas received information that Johnston had in hand six divisions, comprising from thirty to forty thousand men, and that no troops had been sent away except one brigade of infantry. This intelligence did not, however, induce General Grant to recall the movement, though it rendered General Thomas hopeless of success."

On the 22d of February all the forces that could be safely withdrawn from Chattanooga and the line of communication were put in motion towards Dalton.

Our 1st Division (General R. W. Johnson), with Baird's (3d) division, advanced on direct roads to Ringgold for operations on the right flank. General Davis' (2d) division advanced to Ringgold on the 23d. On the 24th our lines engaged in skirmishing during an advance of three or four miles, driving the enemy beyond Tunnel Hill. The enemy formed a new line, and opened with his batteries from a hill one mile from town. General Palmer (14th Corps) then withdrew and encamped three miles to the northwest.

Davis' and Johnson's divisions were in the advance toward Tunnel Hill on the 25th, with Colonel Harrison's mounted infantry in front, and Colonel Boone's on the left flank; and Colonel Long's brigade, supported by Grose's brigade of Cruft's division, was at Farnell Station, on the Dalton and Cleveland Railroad. These pairs of divisions advanced on different lines, flanking and driving the enemy beyond Tunnel Hill. Davis' division, with Johnson's in support, pursued and found the enemy in Buzzard's Roost. Baird and Cruft also encountered the enemy in Rocky Face Valley.

At this juncture General Thomas joined his troops, and at once became convinced that the enemy's forces outnumbered his own, and besides were posted so as to more than double their strength in defense. Deeming further menace impracticable, he advised the immediate withdrawal of the troops to their former positions.

The following extracts from dispatches bear upon the situation:

Thomas to Grant from Tunnel Hill, Ga., February 26th, 1864, 7:30 A. M.: "I arrived here last night. Davis and Johnson occupy the pass at Buzzard's Roost. They have a force equal to theirs in their front who outnumber them in artillery. It is not possible to carry this place by assault. General Palmer made the attempt to turn yesterday with Baird and Cruft's divisions, but was met by an equal force, exclusive of their cavalry, in an equally strong position as at Buzzard Roost. Our transportation is poor and limited; we are not able to carry more than sixty pounds per man. The country is stripped entirely of subsistence and forage. Prisoners taken yesterday report that a portion of Cleburne's division has returned. I will await the development of this day and advise you further."

Thomas to Grant, February 27th, 1864, 10 P. M.: "I have just returned from the front. My troops, after ceaseless labor under the greatest embarrassments for want of transportation, reached within three miles of Dalton, where they were received by the enemy strongly posted, and in force fully equal to my own in infantry."

The following letter describes well the experiences of the regiment during these days of active work:

[From the Springfield (Ohio) News of March 12, 1864.]

A PORTION OF A LETTER FROM THE NINETY-FOURTH OHIO, BY CHAPLAIN ALLINGTON.

CHATTANOOGA, TENN., March 1, 1864.

MR. EDITOR: The newspapers East, West and North have scattered broadcast over the land intelligence concerning the reconnoissance toward Dalton, Ga., from this city, but are almost as oblivious of the Ninety-fourth Ohio as the papers published in Springfield. To what purpose are we the first in the fight and the last to leave it? Such are the opinions expressed and proposed by many a member of our regiment on reading the accounts of the recent expedition. On Monday, 22d ult., rumors were obtained respecting a probable advance on the birthday of Washington. Before dawn the various camps around the city were astir, and soon following daylight we led to the front, arriving at Rossville. We were preceded by General Baird's division. That night we camped at Ringgold. What desolation is here! Railroad torn up, depot destroyed, hotel and warehouses burned, and the town deserted. Here, also, are the tombs of Hooker's braves, who confronted death and Cleburne in the rebel retreat from Mission Ridge. During this day's march, which was rapid, the men were hilarious, as if progressing to a banquet, passing jokes and jibes in profusion from file to file, occasioning at times the most boisterous laughter. This morning the rebel cavalry visited this vicinity, but retired on the approach of our forces.

Tuesday, 23d. Last night we were ordered to be ready to march this morning at four o'clock. It was a lovely morning, the air cool and invigorating; a splendid day for a battle. Nor had we long marched before anticipating an opportunity of testing our strength and prowess. Our mounted infantry were in the advance, skirmishing. We were halted and formed in line of battle, and, throwing out as skirmishers Company B, the extreme left of the regiment, thus marched for miles through thickets of briars, over and through numerous ditches and fences, unvaryingly driving the enemy, whether on horse or foot, behind barricades or in the open field. Approaching an ugly though hastily constructed barricade formed of fence-rails, and commanding an open field over which we were to march, Company A, under Lieutenant Cushman, halted behind a cluster of houses, and then appearing as fearless and undaunted as the braves of Valley Forge or Waterloo, never hesitating, marched direct toward the point of danger, closely followed by the regiment. A moment's suspense, a volley, and a skedaddle. The field over which the foe retreated appeared suddenly to swarm with graybacks hard pressed by the "Boys in Blue." But little rest was allowed the rebels. The mounted infantry, omnipresent throughout, soon charged on the fleeing foe, and before night chased them through Tunnel Town.

Upon their return the divisions of the 14th Corps were posted as follows: Baird, at Ringgold; Davis returned to his former position at Rossville; the 1st and 2d Brigades of Johnson's division were posted at Tyner's Station, and the 3d at Graysville.

The regiment remained in camp at Tyner's until March 19th, when both bridgades marched over to Graysville. This was five miles from the other post, and on the Atlanta Railroad, nineteen miles from Chattanooga. At Graysville the camps were regularly laid out, and when completed presented a beautiful appearance. The Ninety-fourth was located in a little cedar grove. While here, on the night of the 21st, our camp was covered by a deep snow. The weather was pleasant, and this taste of winter lasted but a day or two. The regiment was about free from sickness from this time on until mustered out. Exposure and hardships were successfully resisted, and from this time forward the losses were caused by bullets. At the close of the Atlanta campaign there were some cases of severe illness, and some died. With this exception it was counted always in the companies that the entire strength was for duty. The strength was a little above three hundred officers and men. The duty at Graysville consisted in serving as pickets at Parker's Gap occasionally.

April 11th. Company F was detached from the regiment and sent to guard a bridge over the Chickamauga.

April 14th found the regiment at Parker's Gap, in Oak Ridge. The 2d Ohio was relieved by our regiment, and we in turn by the 37th Indiana on the 19th.

April 29th. Five days' rations issued; one hundred rounds of ammunition given to each soldier; baggage ordered to the rear, and active preparations being made for a campaign.

THE ATLANTA CAMPAIGN.

On the 1st of May, 1864, the Army of the Cumberland was well in hand awaiting orders to advance. The 4th Corps was at Cleveland, the 20th was mainly in Lookout Valley, and the 14th (General Palmer) was before Chattanooga.

Soon after the return from Chickamauga General Rousseau was called to an important command at Nashville, and General R. W. Johnson placed in command of our 1st Division. General Carlin was placed in command of the brigade, which, at that time, consisted of the 2d, 33d, and 94th Ohio Regiments of Infantry, 38th, 42d, and 88th Regiments Indiana Volunteers, 10th Wisconsin Volunteers, 15th Kentucky Volunteers, and 104th Illinois Volunteers.

The movement of the 14th Corps began with the advance of Davis' and Baird's divisions on the 2d. Our 1st Division closed to Ringgold on the 3d. On the 7th the corps moved upon Tunnel Hill. The enemy made a show of resistance for a time, but soon fell back to Buzzard Roost. Strong skirmish lines pressed the enemy into his intrenchments at the gap on the 7th.

On the afternoon of the 8th Johnson's division was advanced in support of the other two divisions. On the 9th the Army of the Cumberland was engaged on the east, north and west of Buzzard Roost. Carlin's brigade, supported by the remainder of the division, felt the lines of the enemy on the west.

May 10th, 1864. Killed in action at Buzzard Roost: Milton Hardacre, Company A; Sergeant John W. Steele, Company E.

The loss in killed was slight, but in all of these operations before this gap a great many were wounded. The action, though less severe, was continued the next day. The army then began the movement through Snake Creek Gap. The 14th Corps passed through on the 12th, and on the 13th advanced toward Resaca. Johnson's division marched in double lines of battle the greater part of the afternoon of the 13th. General Kilpatrick was wounded, and was being cared for in a fence corner awaiting the arrival of an ambulance. Our regiment passed him this afternoon. Just before dark the line of skirmishers covering Carlin's brigade came to a halt, and, as they found the enemy's line too strong, they intrenched. The brigade line did the same. The 1st Division Hospital was established by our regimental band that evening, as ordered by Surgeon Marks, Division Medical Director, and forty-nine of the Regulars (our 2d Brigade) cared for. None of Carlin's brigade injured that evening.

The plan of the battle for the 14th was a movement with the right of the 14th Corps on a pivot. Johnson's division was close to the enemy, and each division to the left became engaged in succession as they wheeled upon the pivot in their advance.

"Carlin's brigade of Johnson's division was the first to encounter the fire. The regiments crossed Camp Creek and advanced some distance over the open ground under a severe fire of artillery and musketry. The passage of the creek disordered the lines of the regiments somewhat, and, as it was seen they could not hold the enemy's works should the assault succeed, the front line withdrew and found shelter and a parapet at the bank of the stream." (*History of Army of the Cumberland*). This quotation tells the story of this charge.

Our regiment was in the first line of the brigade and pushed far to the front toward the rebel works on the open ground beyond the creek. At the failure of the charge the right half found shelter in a ravine, to which they penetrated. The companies of the left wing returned to the creek. Here, with dead and wounded, they kept up their fire and held their ground rather than return to shelter in the woods to the rear. After night the regiment was withdrawn to the left and rear, behind works. This assault failed partly on account of the strong works and destructive fire of the enemy and partly on account of our brigade lines reaching the enemy's position one after the other, instead of a simultaneous advance. This was caused by the distance the lines were halted from the enemy the night before. It was a succession of charges, and in some cases a failure of supports.

VanHorne says of the brigade aligned with Carlin's brigade: "General King, perceiving Carlin's repulse, halted his brigade to the left and rear. The men of the 33d Ohio complained of the fire of the Regulars to their left and rear. The Ninety-fourth lost some of the best men in ranks during the charge and while lying in that exposed position between the lines the rest of the day. The total loss was fixed at fifty-seven killed and wounded; the slightly wounded in some cases not included in these figures."

The loss by companies was as follows, as far as can be learned from the rolls and members of the regiment:

Killed and died of wounds:
  LEMUEL ALBIN, PETER BABB, THOMAS J. FILBERT, OLLY GORDON, JOHN H. SIDENSTICK, Sergeant JOHN SYMMONDS, Co. A.
  DAVID M. HARRISON, Co. B.
  WILLIAM C. HARRIS, PETER M. PRUGH, Co. C.
  JOSIAH FETTERS, Co. D.
  OSCAR CHRISTIE, GEORGE W. HUSTON, Co. E.
  WILLIAM H. CROWELL, Co. F.
  JAMES B. CROSS (First Sergeant; awaiting muster as First Lieutenant), WALES A. BELL, THOMAS HARDIN, Co. G.
  First Sergeant JOHN F. SHEARER, JOHN H. BULL, GILBERT DEHART, JASPER N. GREEN, ALFRED JONES, CORNELIUS STOUP, Company H.
  JOHN POTTER, THOMAS D. REED, Co. K.

Wounded: ISAAC M. COLLISON, Sergeant JOHN V. PURSELL, Co. A.
  BENJAMIN M. KEPNER, JOSEPH LEWIS, JACOB RANKIN, Co. B.
  ROYAL W. GROSVENOR, CHARLES ROBERTS, Co. C.
  Lieutenant JAMES E. MITCHELL, WILLIAM FINDLAY, HARRISON FUGATE, Co. E.
  First Sergeant DAVID B. HALE, GEORGE W. BYMASTER, WILLIAM H. NEAR, ISAIAH WOOD, Co. G.
  Sergeant JOHN C. GATES, GEORGE W. WISSINGER, Co. I.
  CHARLES H. BAYMAN, JOHN J. MARSHALL, VALENTINE WOLF, Company K.

During the 15th our brigade skirmish line kept up a heavy fire; artillery was used also along the entire front of the Army of the Cumberland, but the assault or general advance was not repeated.

During the night the enemy abandoned Resaca, and on the morning of the 16th the place was occupied by General Thomas' army. Orders were issued for rapid pursuit, and our corps moved by way of Calhoun. The advance was continued, pressing the enemy closely, on the 18th, and that day our camps were located near Kingston. On the 19th the enemy was in force about Cassville, strongly intrenched, with orders to attack the 14th Corps as it came up, but Hood delayed until the opportunity was lost. The whole of Johnston's army held a commanding position on the night of the 19th on a ridge before Cassville, but concluding it was untenable, he crossed the Etowah the next morning.

General Thomas' army rested about Cassville for a few days, in order to bring up supplies for the next stage of the campaign. On the 23d the army was again in motion, with wagons loaded with forage and subsistence, for a flank movement or circuit to the right in the direction of Dallas. Our corps crossed the

Etowah south of Kingston, marching by Euharlee and Burnt Hickory, at night on the 24th. The 14th Corps encamped some distance in the rear of the latter places. The next morning the march was resumed. Johnson's and Baird's divisions were delayed by the trains, and did not reach the front during the engagement of the 20th Corps at New Hope Church. The next day, the 26th, was spent in closing up the armies on the position of the enemy, now intrenched in dense forests, in a country almost unknown to both armies.

On the afternoon of the 26th one division deployed from the left and rear of the 4th Corps. The lines of the opposing armies were now in closest proximity. For days a continual battle was in progress by strong skirmish lines, taking advantage of every species of cover, and fortifying by making strong trenches.

The movement toward the right flank of Johnston's army on the 27th by Wood's division was supported by our 1st Division. In this the loss in killed and wounded was slight, as compared with the principal column of assault, and was found mostly in General Scribner's brigade and the Regulars. General Johnson was severely wounded, and turned over the command of the 1st Division to Brigadier-General John H. King.

The divisions intrenched their respective positions during the 28th. Our troops were engaged in brisk skirmishing along the entire front.

On June 1st began the movement to the left from the position held by the division on the extreme left since the 27th of May. On the 4th and 5th the line was gradually extended toward the railroad, fortifying as it advanced. This was followed by the retreat of the enemy to the mountains north of Marietta.

On the 6th our camps were placed in the vicinity of Ackworth, and a rest ordered until the 10th of June. On the 10th of June our corps advanced six miles from Ackworth, passing Big Shanty on our way to Kenesaw Mountain. A skirmish line covered our front or advancing columns until they were up within artillery range.

On the 11th our movement was to gain some distance to the left and front; then followed two days of constant rain, preventing all motion. On the 14th our corps advanced a mile to the front. It was on this day that General Polk was killed by a shell from Captain Simonson's 5th Indiana Battery, while he and Johnston were overlooking our movements from Pine Hill.

The members of our regiment will remember the battery at

Perryville, as a detail from the regiment helped serve it during that battle.

The line held by the enemy in front of the center, and the place of the death of General Polk, was called Pine Hill. The movements on the left of our line caused the abandonment of this line on the night of the 15th. On the 16th our lines were advanced slightly. Early on the 17th our corps moved over the works at Pine Hill in the direction of Kenesaw, and encountered a line of skirmishers before a series of hills extending south-west from Kenesaw Mountain. The 18th was occupied in deploying for position. On the 19th the 14th Corps advanced toward the base of Kenesaw. By this time the position of the enemy was well defined- "The lines were in view, running along the base of the large mountain over the small one, thence on the hills to the south-west. The position was one of great strength, and was covered by defenses of every type."

The operations up to this time during the month of June were carried on through three weeks of rain, making army movements almost impossible; but the time was employed in strengthening our lines by trenches and skirmish pits and extending the line toward the right without exposing the depot of supplies at Big Shanty. The 20th was occupied in the movement by the right flank.

On the 22d, during the heavy cannonading throughout the front of our army, several of the regiment were hurt by pieces of shell. Lieutenant Hardy and Private Harner, of Company C; First Sergeant VanTilburgh, Company F; Sergeant Abel Haughey, John VanCleaf and D. W. Carpenter, Company E, made up the list. The loss in the division up to this time from June 1st was slight—probably it did not exceed one hundred killed and wounded.

From the 22d of June on until the enemy fell back, our troops were under fire in trenches in close contact with those of the enemy. The fight with small arms was almost incessant, with a liberal use of artillery.

During the last two weeks of our stay before Kenesaw, our regiment lay behind a line of works that were defended by a portion of the 4th Corps in the investment. The killed on both sides had been hastily covered by the dirt thrown up for a breastwork, or were left unburied just over the works. The rains and hot weather in that low position in the thick woods had the effect of producing smells worse than ever before known. There was no such thing as leaving it, as part of the bodies were in the works that sheltered our position. While here "Jud" Wesler, Company D, was killed by a sharp-shooter. This was July 1st.

Before the flank movement to the right, ordered July 1st, was fairly started, Johnston withdrew his army on the night of the 2d below Marietta. Our Army of the Cumberland followed upon the main road on the morning of the 3d, through Marietta, on the direct road to Atlanta. The rear guard of the enemy was reached four miles below Marietta and our lines formed again, and by midnight pressed again close up to the enemy's line. July 4th was celebrated at this place by heavy skirmishing along our front and considerable artillery firing. An entire line of pits was captured. Our 2d Brigade cleared their front by a charge of skirmishers. This position was called Smyrna Camp-ground. The fight was noisy but not desperate, and was intended to aid the advance of our troops toward the crossings on the right.

ACROSS THE CHATTAHOOCHIE.

During the night of July 4th, Johnston's army was withdrawn to the works covering the crossings of the Chattahoochie. Our lines were closed up against the enemy, and again were met by a severe resistance at all points. Our lines were held here until the 9th, when the enemy fell back to his next line south of Peachtree Creek.

On the 17th our corps crossed the Chattahoochie, and on the 18th continued on a general right wheel toward Atlanta. Our line of battle was formed facing Peachtree Creek. The 19th was occupied in crossing parts of the Army of the Cumberland over Peachtree Creek. Early the next morning (the 20th) the remainder crossed. These, including our division, were deployed in front of the works of the enemy on the south side of the creek. During the afternoon of the 20th, the enemy made a furious sally upon the line occupied by the 20th Corps, General Newton's division of the 4th Corps, and our 1st Brigade (Johnson's division) of the 14th Corps.

Our brigade was commanded by General Anson G. McCook, and was in double line of battle, the Ninety-fourth in the second line. Both lines were protected by a half finished parapet. The attack swept from left to right, and soon again after the first repulse, the enemy came on against our lines from Newton's division on the left to Johnson's division on the right. All were repulsed. Charge after charge failed. In this action artillery was used with fearful effect; and, though much exposed, the enemy did not reach a single gun.

The regiment lost Private Robert Ricket, Company A, killed, and seven or eight others wounded. The loss in the brigade was estimated at two hundred.

July 21st was occupied by our lines closing up, skirmishing along the whole front, and intrenching each position. The enemy retired to the immediate defenses of the city. The line of the 14th Corps was extended west of the railroad. Constant skirmishing and cannonading were maintained.

On the 22d, while the Army of the Tennessee was changing position to close in upon Atlanta, General Hood sallied out from his works and struck the exposed flank. This time he gained a temporary advantage, but in the final issue was defeated with heavy loss. General McPherson was killed early in the engagement. In our front the "Peachtree line" was abandoned, and our troops pressed forward to establish our lines close up to Atlanta, or to occupy it if the place was evacuated, as we then thought it was. While in this position the regiment covering the front of our brigade was driven back, and a call made for volunteer skirmishers from the regiments on the road. Our regiment sent its quota, and as they went to the right and front on a charge, they carried rails with them, and when the position was reached they made breastworks of them, and were soon under cover. The regiments filed in and held the line all day. On this day our regiment built three lines of works, besides marching several miles from the "Peachtree line," and fighting at different times. In the "front into line" of skirmishers just spoken of, several of the Ninety-fourth were wounded. Harrison Nicodemus, of Company B, and Fred. B. Ledbetter, Company E, were among these. General Carlin returned from his leave about this time, and assumed command of our brigade, and soon after the division.

After the 22d our lines were strengthened, and the two armies kept within fortified lines, each inviting the other to attack. Our regiment occupied various positions, none of them far from the first taken on the 22d. The Army of the Tennessee was moved behind our lines to the right on the 27th, and on July 28th fought again to repel a final attack on the extreme right.

The attack fell, for the most part, upon General Logan's 15th Corps. During the progress of this action there was heavy skirmishing along the whole front of the Army of the Cumberland. August 3d Johnson's division was moved to the right, and kept up a show of active operations to mask movements on the right.

THE SIEGE OF ATLANTA.

The flanking movements toward the right continued. On the 7th our 14th Corps carried a line of rifle-pits and established a line close up to the works of the enemy. The loss to the entire corps was about five hundred. From this time our troops kept on in their daily round of shooting and entrenching. The long 30-pound Parrott guns reached our works on the 10th, and added to the music. Just before the movement on Jonesboro the situation in our regiment was about as follows. A letter dated August 25th, 1864, says:

"All quiet before Atlanta at this time. The men lie in their pits and watch each other, talk and laugh at the jokes that are practiced upon them. The skirmish line is the 'circus' of the army. But few men are hurt unless there is an advance; then, of course, all talk ceases and they are enemies again. The 'Ninety-fourth' is on the front line, and the rebs are about eighty yards in front of the regiment. The regiment has occupied this position for three weeks, with no relief. Yesterday relief was offered, but as they were well fixed and had good works the commanding officer returned an answer saying they did not want to be relieved. Since the regiment occupied these works two men have been killed; John Miller, of Company F, and Henry J. Hobbs, of Company I.

"The regimental band came out from their quarters with the second line the other evening for a serenade in the trenches. The rebs in front said their favorite was 'Dixie,' and would like to hear it. The band played 'Dixie;' then they yelled for the 'Federal Doodle.' The next night a rebel band came out on the line and entertained Yanks and rebs. I could hear their notes plainly from here. The first visit of the band was not so well received. At the opening, 'Long Live America,' a volley came over. The men of A and F replied, without stopping or interrupting the music; after this they seemed as anxious to listen as our men.

"This is about time for the return of the O. N. G.'s; the draft comes off, too, about this time. You will have some exciting times this fall. I hope the people of the North will send us about fifty thousand volunteers; if not volunteers, then drafted men. This, in my opinion, is the only way to end the war honorable to us."

Others of the regiment killed and wounded from the time of taking position before Atlanta until our leaving the last position beyond Utoy Creek were as follows:

Killed: JACOB L. WOLF, Co. I.
Wounded: SAMUEL R. COLLISON, Co. A.
JOHN O. KESSLER, Co. D.
WESLEY HUDSON, Co. H.
JESSE T. BRUSH, Co. I.

On the night of the 26th of August our corps, now commanded by General Jeff. C. Davis, was withdrawn from the trenches below Utoy Creek to take part in the flank movement against the communications of the enemy far to our right. Our movement was effected with but little disturbance. A detail of about forty men, under command of Captain Winger, with other similar details, was left to cover the front of our brigade. These withdrew to our main lines in the morning, and when hard pressed fell back without loss, all reaching the regiment in our position along Utoy Creek on the right of the 4th Corps.

Our corps remained in position during the 27th, covering the movement of the 4th Corps to our right. On the 28th our corps passed the 4th at Mount Gilead, our 2d Division in the advance, and by late in the afternoon encamped in line east of the Atlanta and West Point Railroad, facing east.

That night and the next day were spent in thoroughly breaking up the railroad. The arms were stacked near by. The track was heaved up in sections the length of a regiment, then separated rail by rail. Bonfires were made of the ties and of fence rails, on which the rails were heated, carried to trees or telegraph poles, wrapped around and left to cool. The work of destruction was continued until twelve and one-half miles of the road were thoroughly dismantled.

On the 30th our corps, with the 4th, moved to Couch's house and camped in line of battle. Next day, August 31st, a strong detachment of our corps was ordered forward to feel for the Macon Railroad. General Baird's division, with Mitchell's brigade of General Morgan's division, made this column. The leading detachment reached the railroad four miles above Jonesboro. Our 1st

Division moved to Renfrew's, covering the trains, and late in the afternoon was ordered to support General Howard's Army of the Tennessee, which had been attacked by Hardee's and Lee's corps. Carlin moved the division as ordered, but did not reach the field until after the complete repulse of the enemy. The stragglers captured this day by the advance of the 14th Corps said that Hardee's and Lee's corps had passed down to Jonesboro—the attack coming from there proved the situation. Two corps of Hood's army were at Jonesboro.

September 1st. All parts of the army turned on Jonesboro. Our division reached the railroad, and two brigades, with the three of General Morgan's division, were formed in double lines for an assault on the works occupied by Hardee's corps. Baird's (3d) division was formed on the left for support, our 1st Brigade of Carlin's division in reserve.

The lines advanced at four o'clock through thick swampy woods toward the works of the enemy, extended along a wooded ridge. The obstructions in the form of swamps, ditches, and thickets delayed them and gave trouble in keeping direction and alignments. The lines were halted under partial cover, and again, at 5:00 P. M., the rectified lines moved forward along the whole battle front. The entire line carried the works, and held as captives one general officer, the remnants of a brigade of infantry, eight guns, and some battle flags. During the night about one thousand more were brought in, captured or surrendered. This action was the most brilliant and successful of its type during the campaign—a battle of the 14th Corps against Hardee's corps posted behind strong defenses.

September 2d. Our corps remained about Jonesboro to collect the material left by the enemy and bury the dead.

Atlanta was evacuated on the same day. As the advance approached from the 20th Corps on a special reconnoissance, they were met by the mayor, who made a formal surrender of the place. The advance of our army was intrenched at Lovejoy's Station when the movement began toward Atlanta.

There was slight skirmishing at Jonesboro. On the 7th our corps reached Rough and Ready, and on the 8th reached our camp near Atlanta, to the right of the Campbelltown road. Our brigade was in the rear covering the movement, and was engaged as skirmishers on the return march.

Atlanta was ours, and fairly won. After a campaign of four months our troops rested in quiet camps, and rejoiced over the fruits of victory. "The aggregate casualties of the Army of the Cumberland during the campaign, from the 1st of May to the 6th of September, were as follows: 196 officers and 2,855 enlisted men were killed; 810 officers and 14,973 enlisted men were wounded; 104 officers and 2,603 enlisted men were captured; in all 21,534 men. During the campaign 43,153 were reported sick to Major George E. Cooper, Surgeon United States Army, Medical Director of the department. Of these, 26,184 were sent to the rear, 207 died from disease, and 1,067 died from wounds. Almost all others, sick or wounded, were returned to duty.

"General J. M. Brannan, Chief of Artillery, reported the capture of four guns by the 20th Corps at Resaca, in battle, and four left by the enemy in his fortifications; ten guns captured by General Jeff. C. Davis at Rome; twenty left by the enemy in Atlanta, and eight captured by the 14th Corps at Jonesboro. He also reported the expenditure of 86,611 rounds of artillery ammunition, 11,815,299 rounds of infantry ammunition, and the loss of 1,439 artillery horses. These statistics reveal the cost of war." (*History Army of the Cumberland.*)

THE PURSUIT OF HOOD.

On the 3d of October, 1864, the bulk of our army started to our rear after Hood, who had gone to destroy our communications, and invade Tennessee and Kentucky. General Thomas, with the force thought necessary for the protection of the important stations—Alatoona, Rome, and Chattanooga—went by rail some days in advance. After our assembly and stacking arms in our camp below Atlanta, about noon of this day, a count of the stacks in the Ninety-fourth showed just one hundred and fifty rifles. At the opening of the campaign, on the 8th of May, in the woods near Tunnel Hill, a count of stacks showed two hundred and eighty-seven. The difference represented the losses from the 1st of May to October 1st—killed, wounded, sick, a few furloughed, and a small squad sent to Nashville after supplies.

Before leaving Atlanta, on the March to the Sea, many men absent on account of wounds, furloughs, and details returned to duty with the regiment, so that it numbered above two hundred— probably two hundred and twenty-five—muskets on the "Great Raid." From the time the regiment reported to the army at Louisville until muster-out, more than the usual demand was made for officers to serve on the brigade and division staffs. At the opening of this campaign, on account of losses and the cause just named, there was present one officer to command each company, by transfer or exchange of companies.

Carlin's division encamped on the north side of the Chattahoochie the first night out, near the old battle-field of "Smyrna Camp-ground." From here, by different routes leading from Marietta and Kenesaw Mountain, the army followed after Hood. On the 6th the position of the 1st Division at Kenesaw was passed. Line was formed near Lost Mountain and light works built. Ackworth was reached on the 9th, and Alatoona Pass on the 10th at night, Carlin in the rear.

October 11th, at about 3:00 A. M., the regiment crossed the Etowah. The troops were halted near by until 8:00 A. M., when the march was resumed towards Kingston.

Our regiment, with the other Ohio regiments, voted for State officers and members of Congress while on the march north toward Kingston. The voting began at noon. The ballot-box was a drum. Companies A and F finished at noon. The regiment started on a rapid march. The judges and clerks marched outside the column. The men passed their tickets out and these were slipped in a hole in the drum-head. This moving ballot-box was carried by the owner, Jesse Tarbutton, of Company G. The remaining eight companies voted during the afternoon. The ballots were counted and a return made to the headquarters of the division before six o'clock that evening.

The division camped about two miles from the town that night; on the 12th turned toward Rome, and camped within three miles of town. Here again, it seemed to us, the trail was lost; or, it was not known in what direction Hood was leading. Toward evening, on the 13th, our column turned again toward the north, marching until late at night; on the 14th passed through Calhoun and on toward Resaca, camping near there that night; on the 15th moved on in the direction of Dalton, and crossed a portion of the battle-field of May 14th. From here our head of column turned to the left through Snake Creek Gap and marched on the road extending from Dalton to Lafayette. That night the armies went into camp at Taylor's Ridge, where Ship's Gap divides it. Our portion of the army remained here until the 18th, then followed down the Chattooga Valley on the Summerville road, reaching a point near that place on the 19th, and on the 20th reached the vicinity of Gaylesville, Alabama, where we remained in camp until the 28th, drawing our supplies of corn, potatoes, and meat from the farms of that rich valley about the mouth of the Chattooga.

When it became known among the soldiers that Hood had reached our "cracker line," the "living upon the country" began in earnest; and after our columns reached the country west of the lines tramped over during the early summer, there was a system about this business. Upon reaching Gaylesville all hands made themselves comfortable at once, and, in addition to the regular details, sent out for corn, the men helped themselves, as they could find opportunity, to anything that would add to their comfort. Three days' rations of coffee, sugar, salt, and hard bread were issued; the meat and other material, such as flour, corn-meal, molasses, potatoes, etc., to complete the issue for five days, was found in the country. The citizens (bushwhackers one-half the time) learned for the first time that war was a serious business.

A party of soldiers from the 4th Corps, near us, at a farm-house one evening were unable to find a single pig on the whole farm, but plenty of signs. In the center of the barnyard was a large pond, and in the center of the pond stood a wagon, the bed just above the water. One said: "What do you reckon that old 'goose-nest,' or 'dry-land schooner,' according to 'Couchy,' is doing out in that pond? I'll go see." He stripped and waded out to find all of the pigs in the wagon, quartered and salted. The entire party stripped and pulled the "schooner" out. They found a yoke of oxen in their travels. They found some "apple-jack" also. At about 11:00 P. M. they passed our camp on their way to the 4th Corps, the whole party—guns, pork, applejack, and all, in that wagon—and it is safe to say, at the rate they traveled and the amount of noise made, there was not much sleep in the camps on that road while they were passing.

The return march of the army began on the 28th of October. General Thomas had been directed to look after Hood in his march across the Tennessee.

The division closed up to Rome on the 29th by a rapid march of twenty-two miles, or twenty-six for both days. Our portion of the corps adopted a plan for rapid marching this day that enabled the troops of the 14th Corps to out-march everybody pitted against them from that time forward. The plan was regular rests at the end of each hour—rapid marching for the hour, then a rest of ten minutes.

At Gaylesville orders were received directing the issue of clothing, and to make up the last mail for the North for forty days. The corps moved on to Kingston November 1st, and rested here until the 12th. The preparation of the army for the march to Atlanta began in earnest. The regimental band was detached from here and assigned to duty at post headquarters in Chattanooga. Sick and wounded men, surplus artillery and baggage, were shipped to the rear. On the 8th the regiment voted for the re-election of President Lincoln.

THE MARCH TO THE SEA.

"On the 12th of November, 1864, the railroad and telegraph communications with the rear were broken, and the army stood detached from all friends dependent on its own resources and supplies. No time was to be lost; all the detachments were ordered to march rapidly for Atlanta, breaking up the railroad *en route*, and generally to so damage the country as to make it untenable to the enemy. By the 14th all the troops had arrived at or near Atlanta, and were, according to orders, grouped into wings, the right and left, commanded respectively by Majors-General O. O. Howard and H. W. Slocum.

"The right wing was composed of the 15th Corps, Major-General P. J. Osterhaus commanding, and the 17th Corps, Major-General Frank P. Blair commanding. The left wing was composed of the 14th Corps, Major-General Jefferson C. Davis commanding, and the 20th Corps, Brigadier-General A. S. Williams commanding.

"The 15th Corps had four divisions, commanded by Brigadiers-General Charles R. Woods, William B. Hazen, John E. Smith, and John N. Corse.

"The 17th Corps had three divisions, commanded by Major-General Joseph A. Mower and Brigadiers-General M. D. Leggett and Giles A. Smith.

"The 20th Corps had three divisions, commanded by Brigadiers-General N. J. Jackson, John W. Geary, and W. T. Ward.

"The 14th Corps had also three divisions, commanded by Brigadiers-General William P. Carlin, James D. Morgan, and Absalom Baird.

"The cavalry division was commanded by Brigadier-General Judson Kilpatrick, and was composed of two brigades, commanded by Colonels Eli H. Murray, of Kentucky, and Smith D. Atkins, of Illinois." (*Sherman's Memoirs.*)

There had been some changes in the 1st Brigade of Carlin's division. Before the opening of the Atlanta campaign an exchange of regiments gave the 21st Wisconsin to the 1st Brigade and the 38th Indiana to the 3d. After the lines were beyond the Chattahoochie the regiments that enlisted in "'61" left for home. The first to leave was the 10th Wisconsin; next the 2d Ohio. Colonel Anson G. McCook, as senior, in the absence of General Carlin, was in command of the brigade at the time his regiment started home. Next to command the brigade was Colonel Taylor, 15th Kentucky, until this regiment went away, not many days after. Colonel H. C. Hobart was next assigned to the command of the brigade, and was in command at the muster-out.

After the loss of the regiments named by expiration of term of service—from the last days of July, 1864—no other changes occurred until the organizations were separated at Washington in 1865. The regiments were as follows: 33d and 94th Ohio Volunteers, 88th Indiana Volunteers, 42d Indiana Volunteers, 21st Wisconsin Volunteers, and 104th Illinois.

For administration and for fighting the brigade was divided into wings. The lines were always encamped or intrenched in a double line of battle. The wing commander was the senior field officer present with the wing. At the opening of the Atlanta campaign this form of division was not closely followed, but later on in the campaign the wings alternated each day, and the leading wing that day became the first line of battle in case of fighting. In closing to Resaca, on the 13th of May, the Ninety-fourth was in the second line. On the 14th the regiment was on the first line.

At Peachtree Creek the regiment was in the second line. From Atlanta, and after, the first three regiments named were called the right wing, and the senior officer present and assisting in the administration of the brigade was Lieutenant-Colonel Bryant, of the 88th Indiana Volunteers. The left wing was the remaining three, and the senior officer present was Lieutenant-Colonel Hapeman, of the 104th Illinois Volunteers.

The strength of the army, as officially reported December 1st, was as follows: 55,329 infantry, 5,063 cavalry, and 1,812 artillery;

in all, 62,204 officers and men. The strength of our 14th Corps was given at the same date at 14,416 officers and men.

"With all of the efforts made to purge this army of non-combatants and sick men, it may be assumed that all present were able-bodied, experienced soldiers, well-armed, well-equipped and provided, as far as human foresight could, with all the essentials of life, strength, and vigorous action.

"The greatest possible attention had been given to the artillery and wagon-trains. The number of guns had been reduced to sixty-five, or about one gun to each thousand men, and these were generally in batteries of four guns each. We had in all about twenty-five hundred wagons, with teams of six mules to each, and six hundred ambulances, with two horses to each. The loads were made comparatively light, about twenty-five hundred pounds net; each wagon carrying in addition the forage needed by its own team. Each soldier carried on his person forty rounds of ammunition, and in the wagons were enough cartridges to make up about two hundred rounds per man, and in like manner two hundred rounds of assorted ammunition were carried for each gun. The wagon-trains were divided equally between the four corps, so that each had about eight hundred wagons, and these usually on the march occupied five miles or more of road. Each corps commander managed his own train; and habitually the artillery and wagons had the road, while the men, with the exception of the advance and rear guards, pursued paths improvised by the side of the wagons, unless they were forced to use a bridge or causeway in common.

"The chief commissary of the army reported 1,200,000 rations in possession of the troops, which was about twenty days' supply, and a good supply of beef cattle to be driven along on the hoof. Of forage the supply was limited, being of oats and corn enough for five days, but it was known that within that time we would reach a country well stocked with corn.

"All the material at Atlanta not needed for the expedition was sent to the rear or devoted to destruction with a large portion of the city. The garrisons north of Kingston moved to Chattanooga." (*Sherman's Memoirs.*)

The 14th Corps left Kingston on the 12th and reached Cartersville that night, Chattahoochie River on the 14th, and Atlanta on the 15th. Here there was a delay of one day in the movement of the 14th Corps. This corps remained in Atlanta with the rear guard of the right wing to complete the loading of the trains and the destruction of the buildings of Atlanta which could be converted into hostile uses. Company C of our regiment was detached upon the return to Atlanta to headquarters of the 1st Division as provost guard. From this time forward the regiment had nine companies together until reunited for muster-out.

The march from Atlanta began on the morning of November 15th, the right wing and cavalry following the railroad southeast toward Jonesboro; General Slocum, with the 20th Corps, leading off to the east by Decatur and Stone Mountain toward Madison.

Early on the morning of the 16th the 14th Corps moved out of Atlanta by the Decatur road. General Sherman rode with our column, and describes this morning in the following words: "As we reached the hill just outside of the old rebel works we naturally paused to look back upon the scene of our past battles. We stood upon the very ground whereon was fought the bloody battle of July 22d, and could see the copse of wood where McPherson fell. Behind us lay Atlanta, smouldering and in ruins; the black smoke rising high in air and hanging like a pall over the ruined city. Away off in the distance, on the McDonough road, was the rear of Howard's column, the gun-barrels glistening in the sun, the white-topped wagons stretching away to the south; and right before us the 14th Corps, marching steadily and rapidly, with a cheery look and swinging pace that made light of the thousand miles that lay between us and Richmond. Some band by accident struck up the anthem of 'John Brown's soul goes marching on.' The men caught up the strain, and never before or since have I heard the chorus of 'Glory, glory, hallelujah!' done with more spirit or in better harmony of time and place. Then we turned our horses' heads to the east; Atlanta was soon lost behind the screen of trees, and became a thing of the past."

The first night out we camped near Lithonia. That night and next day the left wing was engaged in destroying the railroad on toward Social Circle and Madison. Next day, the 18th, our part of the corps passed through Covington and camped near the place, and from here turned to the right for Milledgeville *via* Shady Dale.

Sherman says: "We found abundance of corn, molasses, meal, bacon, and sweet potatoes. We also took a good many cows and oxen and a large number of mules. In all these the country was quite rich, never before having been visited by a hostile army; the recent crop had been excellent, had just been gathered and laid by for the winter. As a rule we destroyed none, but kept our wagons full and fed our teams bountifully."

On the 23d our corps reached Milledgeville. On the 24th we resumed the march on the direct road to Sandersville, which was reached on the 26th, and then swept eastward toward the Georgia Central Railroad; on the 28th crossed the Ogeechee River, and on the 29th passed through Louisville. From Louisville our corps moved to Buckhead Church, north of Millen and near it; on the 3d of December reached Lumkin's Station, on the Augusta road, and burned the buildings—this was ten miles north of Millen; on the 5th marched to the Savannah road and went into camp about seventy miles from that city.

The army now turned south on the four main roads leading to Savannah. "All the columns then pursued leisurely their march; the trains were in good order, and the men seemed to march their fifteen miles a day as though it was nothing. The corn and forage becoming more and more scarce, but rice fields beginning to occur along the Savannah and Ogeechee rivers proved a good substitute both as food and forage. The weather was fine, the roads good, and every thing seemed to favor us."

No enemy opposed us, and we could only occasionally hear the faint reverberation of a gun to our left rear, where we knew General Kilpatrick was skirmishing with Wheeler's cavalry, which persistently followed him. But the infantry columns had met with no opposition whatsoever.

McLaw's division was falling back before us, and we occasionally picked up a few of his men as prisoners, who insisted that we would meet with strong opposition at Savannah.

Our corps marched on the left, touching the river. Crossing a swamp on the 8th, reached Ogeechee Church and camped there. As the army approached Savannah the country became more marshy, and the roads were obstructed by fallen trees, especially where the roads crossed the swamps on causeways that traverse the low lands, which are overflowed artificially for the culture of rice. When within fifteen miles of the city—the point reached by us on the 9th—the columns were confronted by earthworks and artillery, in addition to the ordinary obstructions of the roads and causeways. But these defenses were easily turned, and on the 10th of December the enemy was driven within the fortifications of Savannah and its investment in great part accomplished. The right and left wings closed in with connected lines near the main defenses of the city. The left of the 20th Corps rested on the Savannah River, and the right of the 14th Corps connected with the left of the 17th Corps beyond the canal near Lawson's plantation, and the 15th Corps was in line on the extreme right. On the 13th General Hazen's 2d Division (15th Corps) assaulted Fort McAllister, carried the works, and opened communication with our fleet in the Ogeechee River.

General Jeff. C. Davis says, in his report, of the movements of our corps:

"During the intervening days between the 12th and 21st, at which time the enemy evacuated his position, my troops were assiduously engaged in skirmishing with the enemy, reconnoitering his position, and making preparations for an attack.

"On the 18th of December General Hardee sent a letter, in answer to one from General Sherman, in which he declined to surrender. With this began preparations for an assault. Our troops prepared torches and awaited orders to charge on the 20th."

The enemy retreated across the Savannah River in the direction of Charleston on the night of the 20th, and our troops took possession early on the 21st. On the 22d our corps marched through the city and encamped upon the north-west side.

During our stay near Savannah the troops began the play known as "The War Game," enjoyed by so many of the lookers-on afterward in our camps at Goldsboro. In one of these games the explosion of loaded canteens and the rattle of blanks from the muskets was loud enough to call out parts of the 20th Corps, they thinking our lines had been attacked.

A change of regimental commanders occurred at Savannah. Lieutenant-Colonel Hutchins went home on leave. Before his return the army was lost in the Carolinas. His vessel put in at Port Royal, S. C., and he was given a command in the operations terminating in the capture of Charleston. He remained in charge of the recruiting service for colored troops in that district until he rejoined for muster-out.

Major Snider, promoted from Company F, assumed command, and was present as the commanding officer during the remaining campaigns of the army up to the muster-out at Washington.

CAMPAIGN OF THE CAROLINAS.

"On the 1st of February, 1865, the army designated for the active campaign from Savannah northward was composed of two wings, commanded respectively by Majors-General Howard and Slocum, and was substantially the same that had marched from Atlanta to Savannah. General Logan reached the army at Savannah, and resumed command of the 15th Corps. The right wing, less General Corse's division of the 15th Corps, was grouped at or near Pocotaligo, South Carolina, with its wagons filled with food, ammunition, and forage, all ready to start, and only waiting for the left wing, which was detained by the flood in Savannah River.

"The actual strength of the army at this time was sixty thousand and seventy-nine men, and sixty-eight guns. The trains were made up of about twenty-five hundred wagons, with six mules to each wagon, and about six hundred ambulances, with two horses each. The contents of the wagons embraced an ample supply of ammunition for a great battle, forage for about seven days, and provisions for twenty days, mostly of bread, sugar, coffee, and salt, depending largely for fresh meat on beeves driven on the hoof, and such cattle, hogs, and poultry as we expected to gather along our line of march."

On the 26th of January, 1865, the 14th Corps marched from Savannah, on the Louisville road, toward Sister's Ferry, to get across for the march north. We reached the ferry forty miles above the city, and began to cross over about the 4th of February. The river was so swollen by the heavy rains that even at this distance above Savannah the bottom was three miles wide, so that it was only on the 7th of February, and with great difficulty and labor, that the crossing was completed, and the left wing concentrated, and in full march for the Charleston and Augusta Railway. The real objective was Goldsboro, distant four hundred and fifty miles, while the movements of the wings at starting were intended to confuse the enemy and lead to the belief that the army would turn up at Charleston. The disposition of the army from Sister's Ferry to Pocotaligo menaced equally Charleston, Columbia, and Augusta; and which was General Sherman's immediate objective the Confederate generals could not discern with certainty.

General Sherman tells a story of the capture of this railway: "As a matter of course I expected some resistance at the railroad, for its loss would sever all the communications of the enemy in Charleston with those of Augusta. General Howard told me a good story concerning this, which will bear repeating. He was with the 17th Corps, marching straight for Midway, and when about five miles distant he began to deploy the leading division so as to be ready for battle. Sitting on his horse by the roadside while the deployment was making, he saw a man coming down the road, riding as hard as he could, and, on his approach, recognized him as one of his own foragers mounted on a white horse, with a rope bridle and a blanket for a saddle. As he came near he called out: 'Hurry up, General; we have got the railroad.' So while we, the generals, were proceeding deliberately to prepare for a serious battle, a party of our foragers in search of plunder had got ahead and actually captured the South Carolina Railroad, a line of vital importance to the rebel government."

The 14th Corps reached Blackville on the 10th, and aided in the destruction of the railway. The whole army was on the line of the road, and, following General Sherman's instructions, it was completely destroyed for about fifty miles, or from the Edisto River on the east to Windsor on the west. From the line of railway the army began the march for Columbia on the 11th, crossing the South Edisto River. On the 12th our corps moved to a position on the Orangeburg and Edgefield road, awaiting movements of the right wing. On the 14th the North Edisto was crossed by our corps at Horsey's Bridge. The heads of the columns united at and below Lexington, and turned toward Columbia. On the 16th, when within two miles of the city, the head of the column was directed to the left toward Winnsboro. The Saluda River was crossed, and, marching by Oakville and Rockville, the left wing reached the Broad River at Alston on the 17th. Encamping here on the 18th and 19th, our wing crossed the Broad near Alston, and began breaking up the railways near that place. The Spartansburg Railway was destroyed for fourteen miles to the northward of Alston, as far as and including the bridge over Broad River. The march was resumed on the 20th, crossing Little River, and on the 21st we reached Winnsboro.

From Winnsboro our march was continued toward Charlotte, the left wing thoroughly destroying the railroad as far as Blackstock, fifteen miles from Winnsboro; then, turning to the east, marched for the Catawba River, reaching it that night (22d) at Rocky Mount.

On the 23d and on to the 26th there was heavy rain. The roads were rendered almost impassable, and the river increased in size until the pontoons were swept away, leaving our 14th Corps on the west bank. Our corps was delayed here nearly a week on account of the difficulty found in rebuilding the bridge. The crossing was made on the 27th, and the general march resumed on to Cheraw. On the 1st of March the left wing was again united, and moved to Horton's Ferry, on Lynch's Creek, and in the direction of Chesterfield.

March 5th our left wing began the crossing of the Great Pedee River. On the 6th our corps, taking the right of the left wing, moved toward Fayetteville by way of Love's Bridge, over Lumber River. We crossed on the 7th, and on the 9th were encamped within twenty miles of the place. We closed up to within ten miles on the 10th, and on the 11th entered Fayetteville, engaging Wade Hampton's cavalry with our skirmishers. He was covering the retreat of Hardee's corps, and succeeding in burning the bridge over the Cape Fear River. The 12th, 13th, and 14th were passed by our army at Fayetteville. On the 15th the entire army was across the river, and at once began its march for Goldsboro. The left wing followed a road along Cape Fear River north, and met with pretty stubborn resistance from Hardee's corps on the road in the direction of Averysboro.

The next day, the 16th, Hardee took a position near Averysboro, which engaged Kilpatrick and two divisions of our 20th Corps. After a severe fight and some flank movements, the enemy gave up his trenches, and was in full retreat on the 17th toward Smithfield. From Averysboro the left wing turned east toward Goldsboro, the 14th Corps leading. On the night of the 18th our corps halted when we were twenty-seven miles from Goldsboro, and five from Bentonville.

BENTONVILLE.

"Up to this time General Sherman had anticipated an attack upon his left flank, but he was now led to believe that General Johnston would not attack, as it was supposed that he had retreated to Smithfield, and he gave orders for the two columns to move upon Goldsboro—General Howard on the new Goldsboro road, by Falling Creek Church, to give the direct road to General Slocum. His object was to concentrate his forces at Goldsboro, as soon as practicable, and he moved to General Howard's head of column to open communications with Generals Schofield and Terry.

"It was not known that General Johnston's whole army was in immediate proximity, but it was supposed that only cavalry would be met on the way to Goldsboro.

"On the morning of the 19th of March the Ninety-fourth led Carlin's division, the advance of the left wing, on the road to Goldsboro. The regiment was directed to march 'left in front,' and when fairly on the way, Captain Heywood was ordered to deploy Company B in advance of the regiment. This done, the line of skirmishers advanced to take the place of the 'Bummers,' and, meeting a rebel skirmish line, opened the battle of Bentonville.

"Soon after, the entire regiment was deployed upon this line in the effort to drive the rebel cavalry, whose stubborn resistance indicated that there was support, or that its courage had given a new type to the conflict of cavalry with infantry.

"At length the whole of the 1st Brigade (General H. C. Hobart's) was deployed and pushed vigorously forward; but still the resistance of the enemy was determined and the advance slow. It began to be evident that they had some reason for this unusual opposition. The 2d Brigade (Colonel George P. Buell's) and the 3d (Lieutenant-Colonel Miles') were soon deployed on the right and left and hotly engaged. Everywhere the enemy was found in front, strong and stubborn. The right and left of our line were ordered to advance right gallantly, but they soon encountered a strong line of infantry. This was pressed back several hundred yards after severe fighting, and our men dashed, all unprepared, against a line of earthworks, manned with infantry, and strengthened with artillery. The enemy opened upon them such a destructive fire that they were compelled to fall back, with severe loss. Many men and officers and two regimental commanders had fallen, and the whole line was severely shattered.

"As resistance increased General Morgan's 2d Division was directed to move to the right of Carlin in support. General Mitchell's brigade went to the right of Miles' brigade and the road, and General Fearing's to the right and rear of Mitchell—both in double lines. Under this stronger formation both division generals were directed to press the enemy closely and compel him to reveal his position and strength.

"General Slocum soon became convinced that he had before him a force more formidable than a division of cavalry. While still in doubt as to the strength of the enemy, a deserter who had been a National soldier was sent to him by General Carlin. This man gave information that General Johnston had, by forced marches, massed his entire army before the left wing. This news had come none too soon, for our little command, in all less than ten thousand men, was again preparing to attack, face to face with an overwhelming force of the enemy, who had chosen their own ground, strengthened it with fieldworks, and placed their artillery in position. Confident and prepared, they awaited the order to advance, while we were deceived and surprised. General Slocum, who had shared Sherman's belief, was now undeceived and went energetically to work to prepare for the most vigorous defensive fighting possible. Our men were set to work throwing up hasty fieldworks, when the attack came upon them like a whirlwind. The onward sweep of the rebel lines was like the waves of the ocean—resistless. Carlin's thin line, decimated by fighting already done, and posted on the theory that it was driving back a division of cavalry, was forced back. Morgan, although heavily assailed, held his position, being better posted.

"When the left was falling back and the rebel line in hot pursuit, Fearing's brigade of reserves, not yet engaged, was maneuvered upon the enemy's flank, and animated by General Davis' words went in at a rattling pace, shouting back: 'Hurrah for old Jeff! We'll whip 'em yet!' They struck the enemy with resistless impetuosity, and were quickly engaged in a desperate conflict. Upon this movement, in all probability, turned the fortunes of the day. It was the right thing, done at the right time. Coggswell's fine brigade of the 20th Corps had been hurried up, and at once, upon reaching the field, moved in upon Fearing's right, supporting him. It was splendidly done, the men seeming to realize how much depended and devolved upon them. After a fierce and bloody contest the flushed and victorious enemy, taken in the flank, gave way, and in turn fell back in confusion, their whole line withdrawing from all the ground they had gained and apparently reëntering their works.

"And now there was a lull along the whole front, which gave invaluable time for the re-formation of our shattered lines. More of the 20th Corps came up, and were advantageously posted. The center of the line rested upon an elevation, with open fields in front, across which the enemy must advance to a second attack. Here several batteries were massed, and, as the long lines of the enemy were seen advancing, about five o'clock, opened upon them with most destructive effect. Attack after attack was gallantly met and repulsed, and their golden opportunity upon our left was lost."

The following extract from a paper on "The March Through the Carolinas," by General Slocum, in the October *Century*, 1887, contains so much of interest to the members of the division that it is copied here, even at the risk that something relating to the movement of troops at Bentonville may be repeated.

The deserter spoken of said to General Slocum: "'There is a very large force immediately in your front, all under command of General Joe Johnston.' While he was making his statement General Carlin's division became engaged with the enemy. A line for defense was at once selected, and as the troops came up they were placed in position and ordered to collect fence-rails and everything else available for barricades. The men used their tin-cups and hands as shovels, and needed no urging to induce them to work.

"I regretted that I had sent the message to General Sherman assuring him I needed no help, and saw the necessity of giving him information at once as to the situation. This information was carried to General Sherman by a young man not then twenty years of age, but who was full of energy and activity, and was always reliable. He was then the youngest member of my staff. He is now Governor of Ohio, Joseph B. Foraker. His work on this day secured his promotion to the rank of Captain."

Going back to the opening of the fight, he says: "General Carlin's division of the 14th Corps had the advance, and, as the enemy exhibited more than usual strength, he had deployed his division and advanced to develop the enemy. Morgan's division of the same corps had been deployed on Carlin's right. Colonel Litchfield, Inspector-General of the corps, had accompanied these troops. I was consulting with General Jeff. C. Davis, who commanded the 14th Corps, when Colonel Litchfied rode up, and in reply to my inquiry as to what he had found in front he said: 'Well, General, I have found something more than Dibrell's cavalry. I find infantry intrenched along our whole front, and enough of them to give us all the amusement we shall want for the rest of the day.'

"Foraker had not been gone half an hour when the enemy advanced in force, compelling Carlin's division to fall back. They were handled with skill and fell back without panic or demoralization, taking places in the line established. The 20th Corps held the left of our line with orders to connect with the 14th.

"A space between the two corps had been left uncovered, and Coggswell's brigade of the 20th Corps, ordered to report to General Davis, filled the gap just before the enemy reached our line.

"The enemy fought bravely, but their line had become somewhat broken in advancing through the woods, and when they came up to our line, posted behind slight intrenchments, they received a fire which compelled them to fall back.

"The assaults were repeated over and over again until a late hour, each assault finding us better prepared for resistance. . . . The plans of the enemy to surprise us and destroy our army in detail were well formed and well executed, and would have been more successful had not the men of the 14th and 20th Corps been veterans who had passed the days when they were liable to become panic-stricken. They were soldiers who had passed through many hard-fought battles, and were the equals in courage and endurance of any soldiers of this or any other country.

"To the enemy the issue must have been dispiriting in the extreme. Sadly and hopelessly must the Confederate chieftain have witnessed the failure of his initiative in destroying General Sherman's corps consecutively in their isolation. He had constructed his fortifications, which were strong and elaborate, to accomplish this object. His intrenchments crossed the main Goldsboro road at right angles, then extended to the west one mile, then crossed more than two miles to the west-north-west nearly parallel to the road, but concealed by distance and forests.

"He then resisted strongly on the Bentonville road to conceal his fortifications at that point, that he might throw his whole army around the 14th Corps and interpose between it and the 20th, which at the first was nearly ten miles in the rear and restrained from swift motion by exceedingly boggy roads, made almost impassable by the wagons and artillery of the 14th Corps.

"The failure of the initiative of this elaborate plan was therefore entirely unexpected to General Johnston, and was doubtless as much a surprise to himself as was the presence of his army at Bentonville to General Sherman, who scattered his columns the morning before the battle, believing that the Confederate army was far to the north, having abandoned the purpose of offering further resistance to his advance to Goldsboro.

"On the morning of the 20th Generals Baird and Geary, each with two brigades, and General Hazen, with his entire division, arrived on the field. General Hazen, by direction of General Slocum, formed his command on the right of General Morgan's 2d Division, and General Baird moved out in front of the line of battle of the day before. These three generals received orders to press the enemy, and General Morgan gained a portion of his line on the right." (*History of Army of the Cumberland.*)

General Sherman says of the movements of the right wing:

"Early on the morning of the 20th the 15th Corps, General Charles R. Wood's division leading, closed down on Bentonville, near which it was brought up by encountering a line of fresh parapet crossing the road and extending north towards Mill Creek. After deploying, I ordered General Howard to proceed with due caution, using skirmishers alone until he made a junction with General Slocum's left wing on his left.

"These deployments occupied all day, during which two divisions of the 17th also got up. At that time General Johnston's army occupied the form of a V, the angle reaching the road leading from Averysboro to Goldsboro, and the flanks resting on Mill Creek, his lines embracing the village of Bentonville. General Slocum's wing faced one of these lines, and General Howard's the other; and, in the uncertainty of General Johnston's strength, I did not feel disposed to invite a general battle, for we had been out from Savannah since the latter part of January, and our wagon-trains contained but little food.

"During the 20th we simply held our ground, and started our trains back to Kingston for provisions, which would be needed in the event of being forced to fight a general battle at Bentonville." (*Sherman's Memoirs.*)

On the 21st General Sherman gave orders to press the enemy with skirmishers, use artillery freely, but not give battle unless at an advantage. During the day General Mower's division of the 17th Corps worked around the enemy's left flank, and nearly reached the bridge, so essential to General Johnston.

This movement and the approach of Generals Schofield and Terry induced General Johnston to abandon his position during the night.

General Johnston, in this case, as in all others during the war, made a safe retreat. He sacrificed his pickets, left his wounded in hospitals, but lost nothing of value beside.

The loss in the left wing, as reported by General Slocum, was: 9 officers and 145 men killed, 816 wounded, and 226 missing. He reported having buried of the rebel dead 167, and captured 338. The loss of the right wing was: 2 officers and 35 men killed, 12 officers and 289 wounded, and 70 missing. Aggregate loss: 1,604.

General Johnston states his loss at 2,343; he puts his missing at 653.

General Slocum accounts for 338 prisoners captured; General Howard for 1,287—1,625 in all to Johnston's 653—a difference of 872.

The loss in the Ninety-fourth can not be fixed positively now. The following appear on the rolls among the killed and wounded on that day:

[It is believed that the deployment of the regiment as skirmishers at the opening of the battle, and again when moved to the left, and re-formed with the brigade in line in the advance on the enemy's works, reduced the loss as compared with a regiment in line of battle.]

Killed and died of wounds:
        JOHN DUTRO, Corporal WILLIAM HILL, Co. G.
        CHRISTIAN VANHORN, Co. H.
Wounded: First Sergeant GEORGE ELDER, ADAM R. WITMYER, Co. A.
        THOMAS J. ROSS, Co. B.
        JAMES H. KYLE, Co. H.
        Corporal WILLIAM ROHR, Co. I.
        AUGUSTUS GOUBEAU, Co. K.

On the 22d it was found that the enemy had retreated in the direction of Smithfield. The roads being clear, our army moved to Goldsboro.

FROM GOLDSBORO TO WASHINGTON.

Our army started upon the last campaign, from Goldsboro, on Monday, April 10th, 1865. While at Goldsboro changes in the army resulted in the formation of three distinct armies. The left wing secured the title of the "Army of Georgia," and continued under the command of General Slocum, with the 14th Corps commanded by General Jeff. C. Davis, and the 20th Corps commanded by General Joseph A. Mower. The 10th and 23d constituted the Army of Ohio, under command of General Schofield, and the right wing retained the title of the Army of the Tennessee, and consisted of the 15th and 17th Corps, under command of General Howard.

The strength of the Army of Georgia, as reported April 10th, 1865, was 28,063 officers and enlisted men. Of this number 15,098 belonged to the 14th Corps, and 12,965 to the 20th.

The movement began with an advance on Smithfield, the Army of Georgia moving on two direct roads toward Raleigh, distant fifty miles. Smithfield was found abandoned by the enemy, who retreated hastily after burning the bridges. General Kilpatrick's division of cavalry drove Wade Hampton's before the advance. The 1st Division was kept in the rear and marched with the trains. The troops encamped for the night, after marching twelve miles.

Tuesday, April 11th. The rain prevented rapid movement this day. At 11 o'clock the 1st Division went to the advance, and at the close of the march, at 10 o'clock that night, encamped eight miles from the place of starting. The 12th our camps were aroused at daybreak and the troops on the march, the 3d Division in the lead, the 1st Division next. The advance skirmished with the "Johnnies" all day, receiving but small loss in wounded. While in camp at Gulley's, sixteen miles from the place of starting, a locomotive came into camp from Raleigh under a flag of truce. Four men came bearing a message from Governor Vance asking protection for the people of Raleigh.

April 13th. Reveille at 4:00 A. M., and the column on the way while yet dark. Hobart's brigade led the way, with the Ninety-fourth at the head of the division and corps. The drums of the

20th Corps helped arouse the men, and, learning that this corps encamped upon a road to our left, the regiment led off rapidly from the start, determined to reach Raleigh before they could do so. The 1st Division passed the junction of roads a few miles from the city before the head of the 20th Corps appeared in sight. At 10:00 o'clock the regiment was halted for a short time at the edge of the city to allow General Kilpatrick to go on in pursuit of Wade Hampton and Butler's cavalry. The brigade then marched up the avenue and took possession of the city. The regiments of the brigade following the Ninety-fourth entered the Capitol grounds, stacked arms, and from there were distributed over the city for provost duty and safeguards. The remainder of the corps, with the 20th corps, passed through that day and encamped beyond in the direction of Holly Springs.

The march from Gulley's to Raleigh—fifteen miles—was completed by the brigade before 10:00 o'clock that day. The troops kept closed up, and were in good condition at the halt. This beat our record for rapid marching.

Friday, April 14th. The brigade was relieved by troops from the 23d Corps at 2:30 P. M. The men were again assembled in the Capitol grounds, and then began the march toward Cape Fear River and to rejoin the corps. The first halt was made when about eight miles from Raleigh. The entire division continued the advance during the 15th and 16th, passing beyond Holly Springs, and were encamped in the order of battle about Martha's Vineyard pending the negotiations for the surrender of Johnston's army.

The brigade was placed within four miles of Avon's Ford, Cape Fear River, with one regiment at and beyond the river at the ferry. The 2d and 3d Divisions were encamped within easy supporting distance in the vicinity of Holly Springs. The regiment made one expedition for forage while here that will be remembered by all present. The advance reached a little town called Haywood, some distance beyond the river, and returned with plenty of corn, tobacco, chickens, etc. The position of all our troops remained the same until the surrender of Johnston's army. The final agreement was completed on the 26th of April. General orders from headquarters of the department, dated April 27th, directed the order of march northward. The order to march was received in our brigade at about 2:00 A. M. of the 28th, and, owing to a sentence attached at General Walcutt's headquarters, saying, "Make all the noise you like," the entire division turned out at the reading of the order, and began firing from the sixty rounds in their boxes and knapsacks; soon after the battery attached began its salute, and, judging by sound alone, the 1st Division engaged in its greatest conflict. The alarm in the 2d and 3d Divisions can be imagined—both were marched toward our camps, much of the distance at double-quick. The lines deployed, intrenched, and a skirmish line advanced to engage the enemy surrounding the 1st Division. These skirmishers were told as they came into the camp of the 79th Pennsylvania, "The war is over, and Charley Walcutt said make as much noise as you please." The troops that put in the morning coming to the relief of the 1st Division were in ill humor all of that day, and did not appreciate the joke at all.

At six o'clock the morning of the 28th the division started in the direction of Raleigh. The usual details were sent out for forage, and, owing to some insults offered our troops during the stay at Martha's Vineyard, the house occupied as headquarters of the division was burned just after General Walcutt rode to the head of the column. The distance marched was eighteen miles.

Saturday, April 29th. At 6:30 A. M. the Ninety-fourth led the division. At 10 o'clock the troops encamped, with the exception of the train and our regiment as guard. The regiment turned toward Raleigh, and after a march of eighteen miles halted for the night in the grounds of a young ladies' seminary, near the city. The train went into town that night for loads of supplies for the march home.

Sunday, April 30th. The march began in earnest this day. The regiment and train reached the division at noon, and had barely time to cook dinner before all of the corps were on the march toward Richmond. The Army of the Tennessee followed roads leading through Petersburgh. The Army of Georgia started on roads farther west. The 14th and 20th Corps were directed to march on parallel roads *via* Oxford, Boydton, and Nottoway Court-House. With this day's march began the friendly race to Richmond. The march for the corps for this day, from noon until eleven o'clock that night, was twenty miles; for the Ninety-fourth, including the forenoon march from Raleigh, it was *thirty-eight to forty miles.*

Monday, May 1st, 1865. The column passed through the town of Oxford, and the troops were encamped in that vicinity, after a march of twenty-seven miles from the camp of last night. The soldiers of Lee and Johnston met us here. Large numbers sat by the camp-fires of Sherman's army, and shared their rations, as they journeyed to their homes in the States below us.

At 6:00 A. M. of the 2d the corps was on the march for Roanoke River. According to rumor, the 20th Corps would crowd forward and secure the crossing. The column moved rapidly all day, passing through two small towns called Little William and Henderson. At 5:00 P. M. our columns halted within a half mile of the Roanoke to await the completion of the bridge. The distance traveled was twenty-six miles.

Wednesday, May 3d. After crossing the river our bands led the way, playing patriotic airs. The colors were unfurled and the ranks closed up while passing through the town of Boydton.

Thursday, May 4th. The Ninety-fourth led the corps this day. At the head of the column the regiment and brigade marched rapidly without a halt for one hour, then a rest of ten minutes. This was kept up until sundown, when the advance stacked arms at a dam on a branch of the Appomattox River, at least thirty-six miles from the place of starting. The men of the regiment robbed an ice house upon the banks of the stream, and many took a bath in the stream near by. This was the great day of the march. The horses of the corps commander (Jeff. C. Davis) and staff were exchanged at noon for fresh ones.

Friday, May 5th. Reports came to the column this day that the 20th Corps was about to pass our troops. The same plan was adopted as that used yesterday—the march kept up for an hour, then a rest of ten minutes, with three-quarters of an hour for dinner. The distance marched was thirty miles.

May 6th. There was some delay at the crossing of the Appomattox River on account of the pontoon train. After crossing, the march was kept up until within ten miles of Richmond.

Sunday, May 7th. The columns of all our divisions pushed into Manchester, opposite Richmond. Determined that the 20th Corps should not find room near the town, at nine o'clock that morning the troops of the 14th Corps covered the country about the town. A little later the corps moved up the river and encamped on high ground about four miles from Richmond. The 20th Corps did not reach the vicinity of Richmond until after marching another day and a half. The Richmond papers of the next day said this was the greatest march ever made by a corps of any army. It was an average of more than thirty-one miles a day for the entire corps—six and one-half days from a point west of Raleigh.

The History of the 74th O. V. I. (in the 3d Brigade, 1st Division) says of the march: "It was the most wonderful march on record, and exhibited in these veterans of many battles unparalleled powers of endurance in marching."

The corps remained in camp on the James River until the 11th of May. On the morning of the 11th our troops filed out of our camps through Manchester, passing the 1st Division of the 24th Corps standing in line with arms presented. After crossing the James, the route led past the Capitol, Castle Thunder, and Libby Prison. General Hobart halted the brigade at Libby for a better view of the place, inside and out.

After leaving Richmond the march was kept up for thirteen miles to the north-east. Soon after halting that day, a rain-storm came up, filling the camp with water, and leveling the tents in many places.

Friday, May 12th. The regiments near ours moved out of the mud and water, awaiting the order to march. At 2:00 P. M. that day the march began, leading through Hanover Court-House. The Pamunky River was reached about dark. The troops halted in bivouac while the trains passed over. At about 2:00 A. M. the troops began moving, and by daybreak of the 13th were all over. At 10:00 A. M. the march was continued for eighteen miles.

Sunday, May 14th. Our regiment marched at the head of the division toward the north-west, passing through Chilesburg and Newmarket. North of the Pamunky we found a better country than the vicinity of Richmond. Distance marched, twenty miles.

Monday, May 15th. The column passed through a portion of the Wilderness; from all we could learn, our march led through Chancellorsville, rather than the battle-field of the Wilderness. Spottsylvania Court-House was eight miles to the right. In the country passed over were found traces of earthworks, graves, and bullet-marks, showing some traces of Chancellorsville in 1862.

After leaving the trenches about Atlanta, and knowing something of the defenses about that city, it was a surprise to the troops of Sherman's army to pass over country surrounding Richmond that did not show even a line of skirmish pits. In the country facing McClellan's army, especially in the region of Mechanicsville and Gaines' Mill, in the seven days' fighting of May and June, 1862, there was nothing like a line of earthworks facing the Union Army—not a sign of a fort—the country open and well adapted for the movements of troops of all arms.

Tuesday, May 16th. The march began at 6:00 A. M. The Rapidan River was reached at 9:00 A. M. The column halted a time for the completion of the pontoon bridge. The bridge gave way with the head of the brigade; the remainder stripped and waded the stream. The crossing was at Raccoon Ford. The battle-field of Cedar Mountain could be seen from the north bank of the Rapidan. After crossing, the column passed through Stevensburg, and left Culpepper Court-House, five miles west of the route. The country was found stripped—fences, chickens, pigs, all gone—nothing familiar except old camps, bunk poles, chimneys, and roads in every direction.

May 17th. The march continued at 6:30 A. M. The Rappahannock was crossed at Kelly's Ford, and then on through the town of Kellysville, on the banks of the river. The camp was located that night on Cedar Run, about fifteen miles from the camp of the day before.

Thursday, May 18th. The troops began to move at 5:30 A. M. After reaching the Orange and Alexandria Railroad, they followed the line of the railroad to Manassas Junction; from here the column crossed, and remained on the left, and came on through a portion of the battle-field of Groveton, passing near the monument. Later in the day we reached the battle-field of Bull Run, halting for dinner near the run, and crossing soon afterward.

The march ended next day, May 19th, 1865. After passing through Fairfax Court-House, the corps continued on in the direction of Washington, and were placed in camps on Arlington Heights, south of Alexandria, and seven miles from the Capitol. This march was estimated at one hundred and eighty-seven miles by the route followed by the Army of Georgia. The men were so accustomed to the march that this was regarded an easy task. The health of the men was perfect.

FROM WASHINGTON TO OHIO.

The whole of Sherman's army encamped on the south side of the Potomac not far from our position, in the rear of Alexandria, until after the review.

During the afternoon and night of the 23d of May the 15th, 17th, and 20th Corps crossed the Long Bridge and bivouacked in the streets of the Capitol, and our 14th Corps closed up to the bridge.

The army was closed in around the Capitol early on the morning of the 24th, the regiments standing or resting, with arms stacked, in the open grounds in closed division columns.

Promptly at a signal the column began to move out. The Ninety-fourth had nine companies present, equalized as eight—Company C marching at the head of the division as provost guards—all in better trim and showing a better manual than ever before at review. General Sherman says of the review of his army that day after he entered the stand: "I took my post on the left of the President, and for six hours and a half stood while the army passed in the order of the 15th, 17th, 20th, and 14th Corps. It was in my judgment the most magnificent army in existence—sixty-five thousand men, in splendid physique, who had just completed a march of nearly two thousand miles in a hostile country, in good drill, and who realized that they were being closely scrutinized by thousands of their fellow-countrymen and by foreigners. Division after division passed, each commander of an army corps or division coming on the stand, during the passage of his command, to be presented to the President, Cabinet, and spectators. The steadiness and firmness of the tread, the careful dress on the guides, the uniform intervals between the companies, all eyes directly to the front, and the tattered and bullet-riven battle-flags, festooned with flowers, all attracted universal notice. Many good people, up to that time, had looked upon our Western army as a sort of mob; but the world then saw, and recognized the fact, that it was an army in the proper sense, well organized, well commanded and disciplined; and there was no wonder that it swept through the South like a tornado. For six hours and a half that strong tread of the Army of the West resounded along Pennsylvania Avenue. Not a soul of that vast crowd of spectators left his place, and when the rear of the column had passed by thousands of the spectators still lingered to express their sense of confidence in the strength of a Government which could claim such an army.

"Some little scenes enlivened the day, and called for the laughter and cheers of the crowd. Each division was followed by six ambulances as a representative of its baggage train. Some of the division commanders had added, by way of variety, goats, milch cows, and pack mules, whose loads consisted of game-cocks, poultry, hams, etc., and some of them had the families of freed slaves along, with women leading their children. Each division was preceded by its corps of black pioneers, armed with picks and spades. These marched abreast in double ranks, keeping perfect dress and step, and added much to the interest of the occasion. On the whole, the grand review was a splendid success, and was a fitting conclusion to the campaign and the war."

Our brigade was halted for a few minutes during the passage in review, our regiment occupying the street directly before the reviewing stand. The position of the men in ranks and portions of the manual used for standing at an order brought out much applause from the persons on the stand. We were the last brigade in the army, and the afternoon was well advanced before we reached the reviewing stand — probably half-past four. The column turned north through Georgetown, and recrossed the Potomac over the Chain Bridge, making a march of twenty miles from our camps until we reached them again at night.

Two days afterward, May 26th, our corps moved through Washington, and we were placed in camps about the Soldiers' Home.

The last review was tendered General Thomas. About this time he came on from Nashville, and asked to see his corps again before it was broken and the regiments sent to their homes.

The corps turned out to the man to see our old commander. As he came to our regiment, followed by General Jeff. C. Davis' staff, General Walcutt and General Hobart and their staffs, Major Snider presented the regiment, as usual. General Thomas then came close to the regiment with Major Snider and spoke words of praise for the gallantry displayed in his presence at Stone River and the honorable record made by the regiment during its term of service.

The last foraging was performed at our camp here on General

Hunter's farm. Our regiment was directed to guard a large patch of cabbage. The work was well done. The markets in the city were supplied every morning, and each mess in our regiment supplied with the same regularity, yet never a word of complaint was spoken by the owners.

Our rolls were made out here, and discharges dated the 5th of June, 1865. Within a day or two after, the regiment was formed and marched to the Baltimore and Ohio tracks to find transportation to Ohio. This secured, our regiment, with the recruits enlisted in 1862 in the 21st, 33d, 69th, and 74th Ohio Regiments in the 1st Division, were placed upon a train of forty freight cars, containing besides the 16th Maine Volunteers and 119th Pennsylvania Volunteers from the Army of the Potomac. At the Relay House we parted, our Western half following the Baltimore and Ohio route through Virginia, crossing the Ohio at Bellaire, and on to Columbus. We left our cars just in time to fall in behind the 52d Ohio, that came one day in advance from Washington. We were marched to the Capitol, and stacked arms, facing the west entrance. After an address of welcome here from Lieutenant-Governor Anderson we had a march to Goodale Park, a reception and speeches from Governor Tod and others, and dinner served by the people of Columbus.

We made a short stop in Tod Barracks during the day, but at night we were again in camp four miles out at Camp Chase. We remained here with the 52d for six days longer. Finally, on the 14th of June, our companies were assembled for the last time, marched to the Paymaster, received their pay and discharges; the men dispersed to their homes, and the gallant Ninety-fourth Regiment ceased to exist as a military organization.

RECORD

OF THE

NINETY-FOURTH REGIMENT, O. V. I.

IN THE

SERVICE OF THE UNITED STATES.

COMPANIES B, C, F, G, and I were mustered in on Saturday, August 23d, and Companies A, D, E, H, and K on Sunday, August 24th, 1862, at Camp Piqua, Ohio, by Captain ALEXANDER E. DRAKE, 2d Infantry, U. S. A. The regiment was mustered out at Washington, D. C., June 5th, 1865, by Captain GEORGE W. TRACY, 15th Infantry, U. S. A.

FIELD AND STAFF.

COLONELS.

JOSEPH W. FRIZELL.
    Lieutenant-Colonel 11th O. V. I. April 20, 1861, to Dec. 29, 1861. Appointed Colonel 94th O. V. I. July 21, 1862. Wounded at Stone River, Tenn., Dec. 31, 1862. Resigned Feb. 22, 1863. Brevet Brigadier-General Volunteers March 13, 1865. Died at Greenville, O., 1874.

STEVEN A. BASSFORD.
    Captain 74th O. V. I. Dec. 5, 1861, to July, 1862. Appointed Lieutenant-Colonel 94th O. V. I. July 21, 1862. Promoted to Colonel Feb. 22, 1863. Resigned April 16, 1864. New York.

LIEUTENANT-COLONELS.

DAVID KING.
    First Lieutenant and Captain 2d O. V. I. April 17, 1861, to August, 1861. Appointed Major 94th O. V. I. July 21, 1862; Lieutenant-Colonel Feb. 22, 1863. Resigned Oct. 8, 1863. Springfield, O.

RUE P. HUTCHINS.
    Appointed Captain Co. D July 22, 1862. Promoted to Major Feb. 22, 1863; Lieutenant-Colonel Oct. 8, 1863; Brevet Brigadier-General March 13, 1865. Mustered out with regiment. Topeka, Kan.

MAJORS.

CHARLES C. GIBSON.
    Private and Sergeant-Major 74th O. V. I. 1861. Appointed Captain Co. G, 94th O. V. I., Aug. 7, 1862; Major Jan. 10, 1864. Resigned Dec. 18, 1864.

WILLIAM H. SNIDER.
    Appointed First Lieutenant Co. F, 94th O. V. I., July 26, 1862. Promoted to Captain Jan. 23, 1863; Major Jan. 6, 1865; Brevet Lieutenant-Colonel March 13, 1865. Mustered out with regiment. Logansport, Ind.

(103)

THE NINETY-FOURTH OHIO.

SURGEONS.

EDWIN SINNET.
 Assistant Surgeon 17th O. V. I. September, 1861, to Jan. 18, 1862; Surgeon 94th O. V. I. Aug. 26, 1862. Resigned Sept. 19, 1863. Granville, O.

WILLIAM B. GIBSON.
 Appointed Assistant Surgeon Aug. 19, 1862. Promoted to Surgeon Sept. 19, 1863. Mustered out with regiment. Topeka, Kan.

ASSISTANT SURGEONS.

LOUIS C. FOUTS.
 Appointed Assistant Surgeon July 20, 1862. Resigned April 18, 1863. Died.

DANIEL HUMFREVILLE.
 Appointed Assistant Surgeon April 7, 1864. Mustered out with regiment. Waterville, Kansas.

CHAPLAIN.

WILLIAM ALLINGTON.
 Appointed Chaplain Sept. 14, 1862. Mustered out with regiment. Richmond, Macomb County, Mich.

ADJUTANTS.

JOSHUA H. HORTON.
 Second Lieutenant, First Lieutenant, and Adjutant 11th O. V. I. April, 1861, to June, 1862. Appointed Adjutant 94th O. V. I. July 21, 1862. Resigned Feb. 16, 1863. Cincinnati, Ohio.

FRANK DINWIDDIE.
 Enrolled as private, Co. H, June 23, 1862. Appointed Sergeant-Major Sept. 23, 1864. Promoted to First Lieutenant Jan. 6, 1865. Appointed Adjutant Jan. 24, 1865. Mustered out with regiment. Bell Brook, Greene Co., O.

QUARTERMASTER.

B. F. COOLEDGE.
 Appointed First Lieutenant and Quartermaster July 20, 1862. Detached on General W. T. Ward's staff as Acting Assistant Quartermaster Sept. 16, 1862. Mustered out at the close of the war. Died September, 1887.

COMPANY A.

CAPTAINS.

PERRY STEWART.
Appointed July 15, 1862. Captured near Lexington, Ky., Sept. 1, 1862. Rejoined Jan. 17, 1863. Resigned Nov. 9, 1863. Springfield, O.

AMAZIAH WINGER.
Appointed Second Lieutenant July 15, 1862. Promoted to First Lieutenant Dec. 25, 1862; Captain Feb. 18, 1864. Mustered out with regiment. Springfield, O.

FIRST LIEUTENANTS.

HEZEKIAH KERSHNER.
Appointed July 15, 1862. Resigned Dec. 25, 1862. Springfield, O.

HENRY C. CUSHMAN.
Enrolled July 26, 1862. Appointed First Sergeant at muster-in. Wounded at Tate's Ferry, Kentucky River, Aug. 31. 1862. Captured near Lexington, Ky., Sept. 1, 1862. Promoted to Second Lieutenant Dec. 25, 1862. Rejoined Jan. 17, 1863. Wounded at Chickamauga, Ga., Sept. 19, 1863. Promoted to First Lieutenant Feb. 18, 1864. Mustered out with regiment. Logansport, Ind.

ENLISTED MEN.

LEMUEL ALBIN.
Private; enrolled Aug. 11, 1862. Wounded at Chickamauga, Ga., Sept. 19, 1863. Returned to duty. Killed in battle of Resaca, Ga., May 14, 1864.

WILLIAM J. ALEXANDER.
Private; enrolled July 25, 1862. Discharged on Surgeon's certificate at Columbus, O., March 13, 1863. Re-enlisted in 17th Ohio Independent Battery.

WILLIAM ARBOGAST.
Enrolled Aug. 2, 1862. Appointed Sergeant at muster-in. Detailed as color bearer (National color). Mustered out with regiment. Springfield, O.

PETER BABB.
Private; enrolled Sept. 1, 1863. Killed in battle of Resaca, Ga., May 14, 1864.

JACOB S. BABB.
Private; enrolled July 28, 1862. Mustered out with regiment. Died.

WILLIAM C. BAKER.
Private; enrolled Aug. 9, 1862. Captured near Lexington, Ky., Sept. 1, 1862. Returned to duty Jan. 17, 1863. Missing in battle of Chickamauga, Ga., Sept. 20, 1863. Prisoner of war. Died at Andersonville, Ga., Sep. 19, 1864.

RUDOLPH BAKER.
Private; enrolled Aug. 6, 1862. Mustered out with regiment. Springfield, O.

FREDERICK BAUGH.
Musician; enrolled July 25, 1862. Mustered out with regiment. Died at Springfield, O.

LUCIUS Q. BENNETT.
Private; enrolled Aug. 5, 1862. Sick in hospital at Nashville, Tenn., March 1, 1864. Returned to regiment. Wounded in battle of Peachtree Creek, Ga., July 20, 1864. Mustered out with regiment. Died at Jackson Center, Shelby Co., O.

ADAM BRUNER.
Private; enrolled Aug. 5, 1862. Captured near Lexington, Ky., Sept. 1, 1862. Discharged on Surgeon's certificate of disability at Columbus, O., Dec. 19, 1862. Springfield, O.

JOHN BRUNER.
Private; enrolled Aug. 6, 1862.

ANDREW J. CLACE.
Enrolled July 26, 1862. Appointed Corporal at muster-in. Wounded in battle of Stone River, Tenn., Dec. 31, 1862. Mustered out with regiment. Died at Springfield, O., 1871.

GEORGE CLUMB.
Private; enrolled Aug. 13, 1862. Transferred to Veteran Reserve Corps Sept. 26, 1863. Mustered out. Thornville, Perry Co., O.

JOHN S. COLLIS.
Private; enrolled Aug. 11, 1862. Mustered out with regiment. Springfield, O.

ISAAC M. COLLISON.
Private; enrolled Nov. 28, 1863. Discharged at Camp Dennison, O., Oct. 28, 1864, on account of wounds received at Resaca, Ga., May 14, 1864. Springfield, O.

SAMUEL R. COLLISON.
Private; enrolled Oct. 5, 1863. Wounded at Atlanta, Ga., Aug. 10, 1864. Discharged at Louisville, Ky., June 14, 1865. Died 1872.

GEORGE W. CONRAD.
Private; enrolled July 31, 1862. Captured near Lexington, Ky., Sept. 1, 1862. Returned to duty. Mustered out with regiment. Donnelsville, Clarke Co., O.

DAVID J. CONKLIN.
Private; enrolled Aug. 13, 1862. Detached to headquarters 1st Division, 14th Army Corps, on special duty. Mustered out with regiment. Thornville, Perry Co., O.

SAMUEL S. COWAN.
Private; enrolled Aug. 1, 1862. Captured near Lexington, Ky., Sept. 1, 1862. Returned to regiment. Wounded at Chickamauga, Ga., Sept. 19, 1883. Transferred to Veteran Reserve Corps 1864. Butler, Bates Co., Mo.

CHARLES A. CRANE.
Private; enrolled Aug. 14, 1862. Captured near Lexington, Ky., Sept. 1, 1862. Returned to regiment. In hospital at Murfreesboro, Tenn. Discharged May 20, 1865. Wilmington, Ohio.

JOHN DESSENBERG.
Private; enrolled Aug. 8, 1862. Wounded at Lookout Mountain, Tenn., Nov. 24, 1863. Mustered out with regiment.

GEORGE DETRICH.
Private; enrolled July 17, 1862. Captured near Lexington, Ky., Sept. 1, 1862. Returned to regiment Jan. 17, 1863. Transferred to Veteran Reserve Corps Sept. 26, 1863, by general order of War Department. Springfield, O.

SAMUEL DETRICH.
Private; enrolled Aug. 9, 1862. Sick in hospital at Nashville June 24, 1864, Discharged at Murfreesboro, Tenn., May 20, 1865. Donnelsville, Clarke Co., O.

THOMAS DOYLE.
Private; enrolled July 21, 1862. Mustered out with regiment. Springfield, O.

NATHAN T. DUDLEY.
Private; enrolled August 9, 1862. Mustered out with regiment. Decatur, Ill.

GEORGE ELDER.
Enrolled Aug. 11, 1862. Appointed Sergeant at muster-in. Captured at Stone River, Dec. 31, 1862. Returned to regiment October, 1863. Appointed First Sergeant May 1, 1863. Wounded in battle of Bentonville, N. C., March 19, 1865. Mustered out with regiment. Clifton, Greene Co., O.

ROBERT N. ELDER.
Private; enrolled Aug. 13, 1862. Missing on the march near Lexington, Ky., Sept. 1, 1862. Prisoner of war at Camp Chase, O. Returned to duty Jan. 17, 1863. Appointed Corporal Nov. 1, 1863. Mustered out with regiment. Selma, Clarke Co., O.

WILLIAM ELDER.
Private; enrolled Aug. 13, 1862. Absent on recruiting service since Feb. 8, 1864. Mustered out at Columbus, O., June 10, 1865. Pitchin, Clarke Co., O.

JAMES D. FAUX.
Private; enrolled Aug. 6, 1862. Mustered out with regiment. Springfield, O.

RECORD OF COMPANY A. 107

JACOB FAUX.
Private; enrolled Aug. 11, 1862. Discharged on Surgeon's certificate at Bowling Green, Ky., Jan. 21, 1863. Springfield, O.

WILLIAM FELL.
Private; enrolled Aug. 12, 1862. Transferred Dec. 25, 1862. Claimed as a deserter from 11th Mich. Volunteers.

JACOB C. FILBERT.
Private; enrolled Oct. 8, 1863. Transferred to 74th O. V. V. I. at muster-out of regiment.

THOMAS. J. FILBERT.
Private; enrolled Oct. 8, 1863. Killed in action at Resaca, Ga., May 14, 1864.

VALERIUS C. GELWICK.
Musician; enrolled Aug. 5, 1862. Captured near Versailles, Ky., Sept. 2, 1862. Returned to regiment Jan. 17, 1863. Mustered out with regiment. Cincinnati, O.

OLLY GORDON.
Private; enrolled July 17, 1862. Killed in action at Resaca, Ga., May 14, 1864.

JOSEPH GRAM.
Private; enrolled Aug. 8, 1862. Mustered out with regiment. Springfield, O.

GILES G. GUY.
Private; enrolled Aug. 11, 1862. Deserted at battle of Stone River.

GEORGE GRISSO.
Private; enrolled Aug. 9, 1862. Captured near Lexington, Sept. 1, 1862. Returned to regiment Jan. 17, 1863. Discharged on Surgeon's certificate of disability at Columbus, O., April 9, 1863.

AUGUSTUS HAGAN.
Private; enrolled Aug. 1, 1862. Discharged on Surgeon's certificate at Gallatin, Tenn., May 12, 1863. Troy, O.

WILLIAM H. HAIN.
Private; enrolled Aug. 9, 1862. Wounded at Stone River, Tenn., Dec. 31, 1862. Returned to duty. Mustered out with regiment. Fairfield, Greene Co., O.

MILTON HARDACRE.
Private; enrolled July 28, 1862. Captured near Lexington, Ky., Sept. 1, 1862. Returned to regiment Jan. 17, 1863. Killed in action at Buzzard's Roost, Ga., May 10, 1864.

GEORGE W. HARDACRE.
Enrolled July 28, 1862. Appointed Sergeant at muster-in. Transferred to Veteran Reserve Corps, by general order of War Department, Nov. 28, 1863.

JOHN HARRINGTON.
Private; enrolled Aug. 6, 1862. Captured Sept. 1, 1862, near Lexington, Ky. Returned to duty. Mustered out with regiment. Killed by a railway train at Springfield, O., 1875.

SAMUEL HARRIS.
Private; enrolled Aug. 13, 1862. Discharged on Surgeon's certificate of disability at Nashville, Tenn., Feb. 18, 1864. Pitchin, Clarke Co., O.

CHARLES HEFFLEY.
Private; enrolled Aug. 8, 1862.

WILLIAM H. HERMAN.
Private; enrolled Aug. 11, 1862. Died at Nashville, Tenn., Jan. 28, 1863.

PETER H. HENSLEE.
Private; enrolled Oct. 2, 1863. Discharged on Surgeon's certificate of disability at Richmond, Va., May 8, 1865. Springfield, O.

ADAM HENSLEE.
Private; enrolled July 29, 1862. Transferred to Veteran Reserve Corps Aug. 9, 1863, by General Order No. 271, War Department. Minear, Tazwell Co., Ill.

CLARK HENKLE.
Private; enrolled Aug. 14, 1862. Mustered out with regiment. Greenville, O.

JACOB A. HENKLE.
Enrolled Aug. 9, 1862. Appointed Corporal at muster-in. Mustered out with regiment. La Rue, O.

THOMAS C. HIRST.
Enrolled Aug. 6, 1862. Appointed Corporal at muster-in. Discharged on Surgeon's certificate at Louisville, Ky., Nov. 24, 1862. Enlisted in Co. I, 128th O. V. I., Dec. 24, 1863; Appointed Sergeant. Promoted to 1st Lieutenant 180th O. V. I. Sept. 30, 1864. Wounded in action at Wise's Fork, N. C., March 8, 1865. Mustered out on account of wounds June 16, 1865. Yellow Springs, O.

JOHN HERR.
Private; enrolled Aug. 8, 1862. Appointed Corporal May 1, 1863. Mustered out with regiment. Donnelsville, Clarke Co., O.

MICHAEL HOOVER.
Private; enrolled July 17, 1862. Transferred to Veteran Reserve Corps Aug. 9, 1863, by General Order No. 271, War Department. Paris, Ill.

PETER E. HUFFMAN.
Private; enrolled July 28, 1862. Detached as teamster. Mustered out with regiment. Northampton, Clarke Co., O.

MARTIN C. HOFFMAN.
Private; enrolled Aug. 9, 1862. Mustered out with regiment. Died near Springfield, O., July 4, 1884.

PATRICK HUGHES.
Private; enrolled July 30, 1862. Mustered out with regiment. Springfield, O.

DAVID JENKINS.
Private; enrolled Aug. 13, 1862. Wounded at Stone River, Tenn., Dec. 31, 1862. Discharged April 29, 1863, on account of wounds.

ABRAHAM KAUFFMAN.
Private; enrolled Aug. 23, 1862.

SAMUEL B. KINGORE.
Private; enrolled July 26, 1862. Appointed Corporal May 1, 1863; Sergeant May 1, 1864. Mustered out with regiment. Donnelsville, O.

EDWIN N. KITCHEN.
Private; enrolled Aug. 13, 1862. Wounded in action at Chickamauga, Ga., Sept. 19, 1863. Transferred to Veteran Reserve Corps by Transfer No. 173, 1864. Mount Pleasant, Iowa.

LEVI KOLP.
Enrolled Aug. 7, 1862. Appointed Sergeant at muster-in. Captured near Lexington, Ky., Sept. 1, 1862. Transferred to Veteran Reserve Corps Nov. 23, 1863, by General Order No. 365, War Department. Springfield, O.

RICHARD LEEDLE.
Private; enrolled Aug. 8, 1862. Captured near Lexington, Ky., Sept. 1, 1862. Returned to duty Jan. 17, 1863. Appointed Corporal May 1, 1863. Mustered out with regiment. Springfield, O.

GEORGE LOHNES.
Private; enrolled Aug. 11, 1862. Killed in action at Chickamauga, Ga., Sept. 19, 1863.

SAMUEL MILLER.
Private; enrolled Aug. 8, 1862. Mustered out with regiment. Columbia City, Whiteley County, Indiana.

THOMAS D. MILLS.
Private; enrolled Aug. 9, 1862. Transferred to Veteran Reserve Corps by Transfer No. 3, 1865. Springfield, O.

JOHN L. MINNICH.
Private; enrolled Aug. 7, 1862. Captured Sept. 1, 1862, near Lexington. Ky. Returned to regiment Jan. 17, 1863. Mustered out with regiment. Springfield, O.

JOSEPH MEENACH.
Private; enrolled Aug. 9, 1862. Captured near Lexington, Ky., Sept, 1, 1862. Discharged on Surgeon's certificate at Columbus, O., Feb. 19, 1863. Springfield, O,

DAVID E. McKINLEY.
Private; enrolled Aug. 9, 1862. Mustered out with regiment. National Military Home, Dayton, O.

RECORD OF COMPANY A.

TULLY McKINNEY.
  Private; enrolled Aug. 11, 1862. Captured at battle of Chickamauga, Ga., Sept. 19, 1863. Returned to duty. Mustered out with regiment. Mechanicsburg, O.

WILLIAM MOORE.
  Private; enrolled July 25, 1862, Mustered out with regiment. Springfield, O.

CHARLES PARK.
  Private; enrolled Aug. 8, 1862. Deserted from Camp Piqua Aug. 27, 1862.

DAVID PATTERSON.
  Private; enrolled Aug. 22, 1862. Transferred to 74th O. V. I. at muster-out of regiment. Mustered out from hospital at Troy, N. Y., June 16, 1865.

ROSWELL A. POOLE.
  Private; enrolled Aug. 11, 1862. Mustered out with regiment. Killed by a blast in a quarry near Springfield, O., 1874.

JOHN V. PURSELL.
  Enrolled July 17, 1862. Appointed Corporal at muster-in. Promoted to Sergeant May 1, 1863. Wounded in action at Resaca, Ga., May 14, 1864. Discharged at Camp Dennison, Ohio, May 24, 1865. Donnelsville, Clarke, Co., O.

CYRUS RHODES.
  Wagoner. Enrolled Aug. 5, 1862. Mustered out with regiment.

ROBERT RICKET.
  Private; enrolled Aug. 6, 1862. Killed in action at Peachtree Creek, Ga., July 20, 1864.

WILLIAM A. ROBERTS.
  Enrolled Aug. 5, 1862. Appointed Corporal at muster-in. Captured near Lexington, Ky., Sept. 1, 1862. Discharged on Surgeon's certificate at Columbus, O., Feb. 19, 1863. Osborne, Greene Co., O.

JOSEPH W. SCHAEFFER.
  Private; enrolled Aug. 6, 1862. Discharged on Surgeon's certificate at Louisville, Ky., April 30, 1863. Died.

TIMOTHY SCHAE.
  Private; enrolled Aug. 8, 1862. Mustered out with regiment. Springfield, O.

SAMUEL SHELLABARGER.
  Enrolled Aug. 14, 1862. Appointed Corporal at muster-in. Died in hospital at Murfreesboro, Tenn., March 4, 1863.

JOSEPH S. SHUMAN.
  Private; enrolled Aug. 6, 1862. Mustered out with regiment. Springfield, O.

WILLIAM SHRADER.
  Private; enrolled July 25, 1862. Died at General Headquarters at Nashville, Tenn., Nov. 27, 1863.

JOHN SIDENSTICK.
  Private; enrolled July 31, 1862. Killed in battle of Resaca, Ga., May 14, 1864.

DANIEL SIDENSTICK.
  Private; enrolled Aug. 1, 1862. Absent, sick in hospital at Murfreesboro, Tenn., March 1, 1864, Returned to duty. Mustered out with regiment.

JOHN SYMMONDS.
  Enrolled Aug. 5, 1862. Appointed Corporal at muster-in. Promoted to Sergeant May 1, 1863. Killed in battle of Resaca, Ga., May 14, 1864.

GEORGE SINTZ.
  Private; enrolled Aug. 14, 1862. Discharged on Surgeon's certificate at Nashville, Tenn., Dec. 9, 1862. Re-enlisted in 16th Ohio Independent Battery March 20, 1864. Mustered out Aug. 2, 1865. Springfield, O.

GEORGE SIMPSON.
  Private; enrolled July 26, 1862. Captured near Lexington, Ky., Sept. 1, 1862. Returned to duty Jan. 17, 1863. Mustered out with regiment. Died at Springfield, O., Nov. 27, 1887.

ANDREW J. SPAHR.
  Private; enrolled Aug. 22, 1862. Transferred to Veteran Reserve Corps April 1, 1865.

JAMES STEWART.
  Private; enrolled Aug. 13, 1862. Captured near Lexington, Ky., Sept. 1, 1862. Returned to regiment Jan. 17, 1863. Discharged on Surgeon's certificate at Nashville, Tenn., Jan. 12, 1865. Died 1882, at Kansas City, Mo.
SOLOMON SWABB.
  Private; enrolled Aug. 13, 1862. Mustered out with regiment.
ELIJAH TAYLOR.
  Private; enrolled Aug, 1, 1862. Discharged on Surgeon's certificate at Nashville, Tenn., Dec. 16, 1862.
GEORGE W. TWIST.
  Private; enrolled Aug. 13, 1862. Appointed Corporal May 1, 1863. Wounded at battle of Chickamauga, Ga., Sept. 19, 1863. Promoted to Sergeant Jan. 1, 1864. Mustered out with regiment.
JOHN P. VARVEL.
  Private; enrolled Aug. 11, 1862. Mustered out with regiment. Kenton, O.
JACOB VOLMER.
  Enrolled Aug. 11, 1862. Appointed Corporal at muster-in. Captured at the battle of Chickamauga, Ga., Sept. 19, 1863. Prisoner of war. Mustered out from Columbus, O., June 16, 1865. Springfield, O.
ROBERT J. WALKER.
  Private; enrolled Aug. 11, 1862. Mustered out with regiment.
JOSEPH S. WALKER.
  Private; enrolled July 19, 1862. Died of wounds at Louisville, Ky., Sept. 13, 1862.
TIMOTHY WARD.
  Private; enrolled July 21, 1862. Discharged on Surgeon's certificate at Louisville, Ky., Oct. 16, 1862. Springfield, O.
BENJAMIN F. WINGER.
  Private; enrolled Aug. 10, 1862. Died at Bowling Green, Ky., Dec. 3, 1862.
GRANVILLE WINGER.
  Private; enrolled Aug. 11, 1862. Discharged on Surgeon's certificate at Murfreesboro, Tenn., March 31, 1863. Springfield, O.
ADAM R. WITMYER.
  Private; enrolled Aug. 14, 1862. Wounded at Bentonville, N. C., March 19, 1865. Discharged at Camp Dennison, O., May 24, 1865. York, Pa.
SAMUEL WOOLEY.
  Private; enrolled Aug. 6, 1862. Mustered out with regimennt. Tawawa, Shelby, Co., O.
MALCOLM YOUNG.
  Private; enrolled Aug. 12, 1862. Appointed Quartermaster-Sergeant March 1, 1864. Mustered out with regiment. Springfield, O.
DANIEL D. YOUNG.
  Private; enrolled Aug. 9, 1862. Discharged, on Surgeon's certificate at Columbus, O., May 9, 1863. New Carlisle, O.

COMPANY B.

CAPTAINS.
JOHN C. DRURY.
Captain 11th O. V. I. April, 1861, to December, 1861. Captain 94th O. V. I July 22, 1862. Killed in action at Perryville, Ky., Oct. 8, 1862.

DIXON G. McLAUGHLIN.
Appointed First Lieutenant July 22, 1862. Promoted Captain, to date from Oct. 8, 1862. Wounded at Missionary Ridge November 25, 1863. Returned to duty. Resigned Sept. 26, 1864. Died.

ALEXANDER M. HEYWOOD.
Sergeant Co. H, 11th O. V. I., April, 1861, to June 20, 1861. Enrolled as private, Co. B, 94th O. V. I., Aug. 5, 1862. Appointed First Sergeant at muster-in. Promoted to Second Lieutenant, to date from Oct. 8, 1862; First Lieutenant May 23, 1863; Captain Jan. 6, 1865. Mustered out with regiment. Troy, O.

FIRST LIEUTENANT.
FREDERICK B. McNEAL.
Appointed Second Lieutenant July 22, 1862. Promoted to First Lieutenant with rank from Oct. 8, 1862. Resigned March 19, 1863. New Carlisle, O.

SECOND LIEUTENANT.
MARTIN V. DICKEY.
Enrolled Aug. 9, 1862. Appointed Corporal Aug. 29, 1862; First Sergeant Feb. 25, 1863. Promoted to Second Lieutenant May 23, 1863. Missing in battle of Chicamauga, Ga., Sept. 19, 1863. Prisoner of war at Richmond, Va. Mustered out, to date from May 15, 1865, General Order No. 241, War Department. Died at Franklin, O.

ENLISTED MEN.
WILLIAM L. ANDERSON.
Private; enrolled Aug. 5, 1862. Discharged on Surgeon's certificate, July 13, 1863.

JOHN BARNHART.
Private; enrolled Aug. 7, 1862. Died at Bowling Green, Ky., November, 1862.

DAVID BOTTORFF.
Private; enrolled Aug. 7, 1862. Absent sick in hospital. Returned to duty. Mustered out with regiment. Piqua, O.

JOHN M. BRADLEY.
Private; enrolled Aug. 9, 1862. Mustered out with regiment. Tippecanoe City, O.

JOHN BRANDON.
Private; enrolled Aug. 20, 1862. Mustered out with regiment. Osgood, Darke Co., O.

ISAAC W. CABLE.
Enrolled Aug. 8, 1862. Appointed Sergeant at muster-in. Discharged on Surgeon's certificate from hospital at Nashville, Tenn., by order General Rosecrans, Feb. 12, 1863. Died at Pleasant Hill, O., Apr. 17, 1883.

JOHN L. CARPENTER.
Private; enrolled Aug. 6, 1862. Detailed to Pioneers. Transferred to 1st Regiment Veteran Volunteer Engineers July 24, 1864, by S. F. O. No. 77, Department Cumberland. Lafayette, Ind.

SAMUEL CHROWL.
Private; enrolled Aug. 7, 1862. Sent to hospital. Died at Covington, O., March 15, 1863.

JACOB CHROWL,
Private; enrolled Aug. 7, 1862. Discharged on Surgeon's certificate April 27, 1863, at Louisville, Ky. Bradford Junction, O.

DAVID L. CORBIN.
Private; enrolled Aug. 7, 1862. Left sick at Nolensville, Tenn., Dec. 28, 1862. Prisoner of war at Camp Chase, O. Returned to duty. Sick in hospital at Camp Dennison, O. Discharged May 24, 1865. Van Wert, O.

WILLIAM CORSE.
Private; enrolled Aug. 7, 1862. Died in hospital at Murfreesboro, Tenn., March 29, 1863.

ALBERT DAVENPORT.
Private; enrolled Aug. 7, 1862. Died in camp near Murfreesboro, Tenn., March 15, 1863.

DAVID S. DEETER.
Private; enrolled Aug. 7, 1862. Died in Regimental Hospital at Murfreesboro, Tenn. March 25, 1863.

WILLIAM Mc. DELAP.
Private; enrolled Aug. 12, 1862. Mustered out with regiment. Piqua, O.

HENRY W. DEWEESE.
Private; enrolled Aug. 18, 1862. Missing near Lexington, Ky., Sept. 1, 1862. Prisoner of war. Returned to Regiment February, 1863. Mustered out with regiment. Died near Casstown, O., Oct. 14, 1868.

WILLIAM DILTZ.
Private; enrolled Aug. 7, 1862. Appointed Commissary Sergeant at muster-in. Left sick at Nolensville, Tenn. Prisoner of war at Camp Chase, O. Discharged on Surgeon's certificate at Columbus, O., May 13, 1863. Commissary Sergeant 194th O. V. I. March, 1865. Appointed First Lieutenant and Quartermaster. Mustered out October, 1865.

GEORGE S. DOLLINGER.
Enrolled Aug. 7, 1862. Appointed Corporal at muster-in. Wounded at battle of Stone River, Tenn., Dec. 31, 1862. Returned to duty. Mustered out with regiment. Covington, Ohio.

MATTHIAS DYE.
Private; enrolled Aug, 18, 1862. Wounded at Chickamauga, Ga., Sept. 19, 1863. Provision made for discharge in General Order 77, War Department, series of 1865. Sidney, O.

ELI DYE.
Private; enrolled Aug. 1, 1862. Died at Murfreesboro, Tenn., Feb. 9, 1863.

JAMES DUNCAN.
Private; enrolled Aug. 7, 1862. Transferred to 1st Regiment Veteran Volunteer Engineers July 24, 1864, by S. F. O. 77, Department of Cumberland.

MARTIN ELIFRITZ.
Private; enrolled Aug. 9, 1862. Died at Nashville, Tenn., Jan. 3, 1863.

WILLIAM FAGER.
Private; enrolled Aug. 7, 1862. Left sick at Bowling Green, Ky., Nov. 12, 1862. Discharged on Surgeon's certificate at Louisville, Ky., Dec. 12, 1862.

LEVI FALKNOR.
Private; enrolled Aug. 7, 1862. Wounded near Lexington, Ky., Sept. 1, 1862. Prisoner of war. Discharged, on account of wounds, at Columbus, O., Sept. 12, 1862. Covington, Ohio.

SIMEON FINE.
Enrolled Aug. 7, 1862. Appointed Corporal at muster-in. Died in hospital at Murfreesboro, Tenn., Feb. 15, 1863.

DAVID W. FLEMING.
Private; enrolled Aug. 2, 1862. Absent sick in hospital. Returned to duty. Mustered out with regiment.

MORRIS FRAZEE.
Private; enrolled Aug. 9, 1862. Mustered out with regiment. Lena, O.

JOHN GINN.
Private; enrolled Aug. 13, 1862. Mustered out with regiment. Houston, Shelby Co., O.

GRIFFITH M. D. GIRARD.
Private; enrolled Aug. 10, 1862. Wounded at battle of Perryville, Ky., Oct. 8, 1862. Returned to duty. Mustered out with regiment. Shelbyville, Ind.

RECORD OF COMPANY B.   113

GEORGE GORMAN.
    Private; enrolled Aug. 7, 1862. Mustered out with regiment. Died at Covington, O.

JOSEPH E. HARRISON.
    Private; enrolled Aug. 7, 1862. Killed in battle of Perryville, Ky., Oct. 8, 1862.

DAVID M. HARRISON.
    Private; enrolled Aug. 7, 1862. Wounded at battle of Resaca, Ga., May 14, 1864. Died in hospital at Nashville, Tenn, July 2, 1864.

CHARLES C. HARKER.
    Enrolled Aug. 5, 1862. Appointed Corporal at muster-in. Discharged on Surgeon's certificate by order of General Rosecrans May 30, 1863. Troy, O.

GEORGE W. HAWN.
    Private; enrolled Aug. 10, 1862. Died in hospital at Nashville, Tenn., April 3, 1863.

JACOB HOEFFER.
    Private; enrolled Aug. 8, 1862. Died in hospital at Nashville, Tenn., Jan. 24, 1863.

ABRAHAM B. HUSTON.
    Enrolled Aug. 10, 1862. Appointed Sergeant at muster-in. Wounded at battle of Perryville, Ky., Oct. 8, 1862. Discharged on Surgeon's certificate from Columbus, O., April 15, 1863. Paris, Ills.

HARRY J. HUSTON.
    Private; enrolled Aug. 10, 1862. Missing near Lexington, Ky., Sept. 1, 1862. Prisoner of war at Camp Chase, O. Returned to duty. Mustered out with regiment. Evansville, Indiana.

WASHINGTON INGLE.
    Private; enrolled Aug. 7, 1862. Transferred to Veteran Reserve Corps March 24, 1864, by General Order No. 21, War Department. Covington, O.

WILLIAM INGLE.
    Private; enrolled Aug. 7, 1862. Mustered out with regiment. Covington, O.

JOSHUA JACOBS.
    Private; enrolled Aug. 8, 1862. Discharged on Surgeon's certificate at Murfreesboro, Tenn., March 23, 1863.

MADISON KENDALL.
    Private; enrolled Aug. 7, 1862. Missing in action at Chickamauga, Ga., Sept. 19, 1863. Prisoner of war at Andersonville, Ga. Declared exchanged May 6, 1865. Mustered out at Camp Chase, O., May 25, 1865. Covington, O.

LEWIS KENDIG.
    Private; enrolled Aug. 7, 1862. Sent to hospital at Murfreesboro, Tenn., May 21, 1863. Provision for discharge under General Order No. 77, War Department. Versailles, O.

SAMUEL B. KEPNER.
    Private; enrolled Aug. 7, 1862. Mustered out with regiment. Covington, O.

BENJAMIN M. KEPNER.
    Enrolled Aug. 7, 1862. Appointed Corporal at muster-in. Wounded in action at Resaca, Ga., May 14, 1864. Discharged on Surgeon's certificate Dec. 2, 1864.

JOSEPH KITCHEN.
    Musician; enrolled Aug. 14, 1862. Discharged on Surgeon's certificate Jan. 18, 1865, at Savannah, Ga. Kalida, O.

REUBEN G. KREIDER.
    Private; enrolled Aug. 10, 1862. Captured near Lexington, Ky., Sept. 1. 1862. Prisoner of war. Discharged on Surgeon's certificate at Columbus, O., Dec. 16, 1862, Indianapolis, Indiana.

JOHN J. LEHMAN.
    Private; enrolled Nov. 27, 1863. Transferred to 74th O. V. I. at muster-out of regiment. Topeka, Kan.

JOSEPH LEWIS.
    Private; enrolled Aug. 7, 1862. Detailed to brigade train Sept. 10, 1862, General W. T. Ward. Returned to duty with company. Wounded in action at Resaca, Ga., May 14, 1864. Mustered out with regiment. Troy, O.

JOHN LEE.
   Private; enrolled July 30, 1862. Mustered out with regiment. Dayton, O.
JAMES L. LONG.
   Private; enrolled Aug. 10, 1862. Detailed to Ambulance Corps Feb. 6, 1864, by General Order No. 30, Army of the Cumberland. Mustered out with regiment. Died near Casstown, O., March 21, 1867.
JOHN A. LONG.
   Private; enrolled Aug. 5, 1862. Died at Nashville, Tenn., Feb. 8, 1883.
MICHAEL LONGNECKER.
   Private; enrolled Aug. 7, 1862. Captured near Lexington, Ky., Sept. 1, 1862. Prisoner of war at Camp Chase, O. Returned to duty. Mustered out with regiment. Springport, Henry Co., Ind.
ELIJAH MAGEE.
   Private; enrolled Aug. 8, 1862. Died on board steamboat "General Buell," on the way to Cincinnati, O., May 19, 1863.
ANDREW G. MARTIN.
   Enrolled Aug. 7, 1862. Appointed Corporal at muster-in. Died in hospital at Nashville, Tenn., April 12, 1863.
JOHN MATTHEWS.
   Private; enrolled Aug. 7, 1862. Killed in battle of Chickamauga, Ga., Sept. 19, 1863.
JOHN D. MAURER.
   Private; enrolled Aug. 7, 1862. Left sick at Nolensville, Dec. 28, 1862. Prisoner of war. Returned to duty. Mustered out with regiment. Torrence, Kan.
JOSEPH MITCHELL.
   Private; enrolled Aug. 15, 1862. Transferred to Veteran Reserve Corps by General Order No. 158, War Department, May 10, 1864. Muncie, Ind.
THOMAS O. McCAIN.
   Private; enrolled Aug. 5, 1862. Discharged on Surgeon's certificate at Nashville, Tenn. Feb. 27, 1863. Covington, O.
WILLIAM McCOOLE.
   Private; enrolled Aug. 4, 1862. Detailed to headquarters 1st Division 14th Army Corps. Mustered out with regiment. Died near Troy, O., Sept. 28, 1887.
MICHAEL McDANIEL.
   Enrolled Aug. 12, 1862. Appointed Sergeant at muster-in. Promoted to Third Sergeant Feb. 12, 1863. Mustered out with regiment. Celina, O.
JOHN McKNIGHT.
   Private; enrolled Aug. 13, 1862. Missing near Lexington Ky., Sept, 1, 1862. Prisoner of war at Camp Chase, O. Discharged at Columbus, O., Dec. 31, 1862. Troy, O.
WALTER NEFF.
   Private; enrolled Aug. 10, 1862. Discharged on Surgeon's certificate at Nashville, Tenn., December, 1862.
JACOB NETH.
   Private; enrolled Aug. 10, 1862. Missing near Battle Creek, Tenn. Prisoner of war Oct. 2, 1863. Returned to duty. Mustered out with regiment. Died in Illinois, 1886.
DAVID NICHOLS.
   Private; enrolled Aug. 22, 1862. Transferred to Veteran Reserve Corps Nov. 11, 1863, by General Order No. 271, War Department.
HARRISON NICODEMUS.
   Private; enrolled Aug. 8, 1862. Captured near Lexington, Ky., Sept. 1, 1862. Returned to duty. Wounded in action near Atlanta, Ga., July 22, 1864. Discharged on account of wound Nov. 29, 1864. Covington, O.
SAMUEL B. NISLEY.
   Private; enrolled Aug. 22, 1862. Died in camp near Murfreesboro, Tenn., March 15, 1863.
CHARLES O'DONNELL.
   Private; enrolled Aug. 10, 1862. Deserted from Lexington, Ky., Sept. 1, 1862.

RECORD OF COMPANY B.

BENJAMIN F. PROCTOR.
    Private; enrolled Aug. 9, 1862. Missing near Lexington, Sept. 1, 1862. Prisoner of war at Camp Chase. Returned to duty Jan. 22, 1863. Mustered out with regiment. Casstown, Miami Co., O.

JACOB RANKIN.
    Private; enrolled Aug. 12. 1862. Wounded at battle of Resaca, Ga., May 14, 1864. Detailed on special duty at Columbus, O. Returned to duty with company. Mustered out with regiment. Died near Elkhart, Ind.

ELIJAH M. RAPP.
    Private; enrolled Aug. 9, 1862. Captured at Lexington, Ky., Sept. 1, 1862. Returned to duty April 1, 1863. Disabled by accidental discharge of rifle April 23, 1863. Transferred to Veteran Reserve Corps by General Order No. 320, War Department Dec. 12, 1863. Mustered out at Louisville, Ky., August, 1865. Fletcher, O.

OLIVER B. RAPP.
    Private; enrolled Aug. 9. 1862. Captured at Lexington, Ky., Sept., 1, 1862. Prisoner of war. Returned to duty Jan. 22, 1863. Transferred to Veteran Reserve Corps March 24, 1864, by General Order No. 11, War Department. Troy, O.

JACOB G. RITTER.
    Enrolled Aug. 8, 1862. Appointed Corporal at muster-in. Sent to hospital on the march from Raleigh, N. C., May 4, 1865. Mustered out from Mower General Hospital Philadelphia, Pa.. June 20, 1865. Versailles, O.

THOMAS J. ROSS.
    Private; enrolled Aug. 8, 1862. Wounded at battle of Bentonville, N. C., March 19, 1865. Mustered out at Camp Dennison, O., May 24, 1865. Hersey, St. Croix Co., Wis.

WILLIAM ROSS.
    Private; enrolled Aug. 9, 1862. Mustered out with regiment. Died near Pleasant Hill, Ohio.

ISAAC ROYER.
    Private; enrolled Aug. 7, 1862. Sick in hospital at Louisville, Ky., Oct. 1, 1862. Re-enlisted in Co. G 92d Illinois Volunteers 1864. Mustered out at close of the war. Hardy, Nebraska.

DAVID RUSK.
    Private; enrolled Aug. 12, 1862. Captured near Lexington, Ky., Sept. 1, 1862. Discharged on Surgeon's certificate at Columbus, O., Oct. 13, 1862. Troy, O.

JAMES RYAN.
    Private; enrolled Oct. 26, 1863. Transferred to 74th O. V. I. at muster-out of regiment.

NATHAN SCHARFF.
    Private; enrolled Aug. 12, 1862. Captured near Lexington, Ky., Sept. 1, 1862. Discharged on Surgeon's certificate at Columbus, O., May 16, 1863. Indianapolis, Ind.

JOSEPH SHAFFER.
    Private; enrolled Aug. 7, 1862. Sent to hospital at Chattanooga, Tenn. Dec., 1863. Transferred to Veteran Reserve Corps April 6, 1864. Mustered out at close of the war. Pleasant Hill, Ohio.

JAMES E. SHELLENBERGER.
    Musician; enrolled Aug. 22, 1862. Detailed to Regimental Band Dec. 29, 1862. Mustered out with regiment. Piqua, Ohio.

AUGUSTUS F. SMITH.
    Private; enrolled Aug. 9, 1862. Captured on the march near Lexington, Ky., Sept. 1, 1862. Returned to duty Jan. 22, 1863. Died in hospital near Murfreesboro, Tenn., March 24, 1863.

SAMUEL SHUPP.
    Private; enrolled Aug. 7, 1862. Mustered out with regiment.

EDGAR G. SPAID.
    Enrolled Aug. 7, 1862. Appointed Corporal at muster-in. Sent to hospital at Murfreesboro, Tenn., Feb. 28, 1863. Provision made for discharge by General Order 77, War Department, Series 1865. Troy, O.

CHARLES SPROSS.
  Private; enrolled Nov. 27. 1863. Transferred to 74th O. V. I. at muster-out of regiment.
PETER SCHULER.
  Private; enrolled Aug. 9, 1862. Died in quarters near Murfreesboro, Tenn., March 15, 1863.
WILLIAM H. STANNAH.
  Private; enrolled Aug. 10, 1862. Mustered out with regiment. Denver, Col.
LEVI D. STARRY.
  Private; enrolled July 27, 1862. Discharged on Surgeon's certificate at Nashville, Tenn., Jan. 22, 1863. Piqua, O.
WILLIAM W. STEVENSON.
  Private; enrolled Aug. 10, 1862. Died at Louisville, Ky., Dec. 30, 1863.
GABRIEL A. SWEARINGEN.
  Private; enrolled July 30, 1862. Appointed Corporal May 20, 1863. Mustered out with regiment. Silver Creek, Madison Co., Ky.
BENNETT SOUTH.
  Private; enrolled Aug. 9, 1862. Sent to hospital at Murfreesboro, Tenn., June 23, 1863. Returned to duty. Mustered out with regiment. Conover, Miami Co., O.
JACOB TOBIAS.
  Private; enrolled Aug. 7, 1862. Appointed Corporal Feb. 25, 1863. Slightly wounded at Kenesaw Mountain, Ga. Mustered out with regiment. Bradford Junction, O.
WILLIAM VAN HORN.
  Private; enrolled Aug. 7, 1862. Mustered out with regiment. Piqua, O.
JOHN F. WATSON.
  Private; enrolled Aug. 9, 1862. Mustered out with regiment. Conover, Miami County, Ohio.
JAMES W. WALES.
  Private; enrolled Aug. 8, 1862. Wounded in battle at Perryville, Ky., Oct. 8, 1862. Died at Nashville, Tenn., 1863.
JOHN D. WEBB.
  Private; enrolled Aug. 10, 1862. Died at Mitchellville, Tenn., Nov. 1, 1862.
PLINY C. WILLIAMSON.
  Wagoner; enrolled Aug. 7, 1862. Captured near Edgefield Junction, Tenn., November, 1862. Escaped and returned to duty. Missing in battle at Chickamauga, Ga., Sept. 19, 1863. Prisoner of war at Andersonville. Escaped from Saulsbury, N. C. Returned to duty June 17, 1864. Mustered out with regiment. Covington, O.
PETER WHITMER.
  Private; enrolled Aug. 12, 1862. Disabled by an accidental wound May, 1864. Transferred to Veteran Reserve Corps by general order of War Department March 15, 1885. Oregon, Holt County, Missouri.
JONAS WHITMER.
  Private; enrolled Aug. 7, 1862. Appointed Corporal Feb. 25, 1863. Appointed Sergeant May 20, 1863. First Sergeant July 22, 1863, Mustered out with regiment. Mound City, Holt County, Missouri.
SAMUEL WHITMER.
  Enrolled Aug. 8, 1862. Appointed Sergeant at Muster-in. Left sick at Nolensville, Tenn., Dec. 28, 1862. Prisoner of war. Returned to duty. Promoted Second Sergeant April 15, 1863. Mustered out with regiment. Taylorsville, Ills.
UPTON ZOLL.
  Private; enrolled Aug. 6, 1862. Appointed Corporal Feb. 25, 1863. Mustered out with regiment. Asherville, Stoddard Co., Mo.

COMPANY C.

CAPTAINS.

FRED. W. WALTON.
Appointed July 22, 1862. Resigned Dec. 25, 1862. Died at Piqua, O., June 3, 1887.

JAMES E. EDMONDS.
Enrolled as private July 23, 1862. Appointed First Sergeant at muster-in; Sergeant-Major Sept. 25, 1862. Promoted Second Lieutenant December 26, 1862; First Lieutenant Feb. 14, 1863; Captain March 1, 1863. Detached as Inspector-General 1st Division 14th Army Corps Feb. 29, 1864. Mustered out with regiment. Appointed Assistant Adjutant-General U. S. Volunteers, with rank of Major, June 30, 1865. Mustered out Dec. 8, 1865. Bolivar, Miss.

FIRST LIEUTENANT.

JAMES H. PETTIGREW.
Appointed July 22, 1862. Resigned Nov. 16, 1862. Piqua, O.

SECOND LIEUTENANT.

BURTON C. MITCHELL.
Enrolled as private Aug. 1, 1862. Appointed Sergeant at muster-in; First Sergeant Sept. 26, 1862. Wounded in battle of Stone River, Tenn. Promoted Second Lieutenant Feb. 14, 1863. Resigned Nov. 14, 1863. Richfield, Kas.

ENLISTED MEN.

SAMUEL P. ACHUFF.
Private; enrolled July 28, 1862. Appointed Corporal at muster-in; Sergeant; First Sergeant Feb. 14, 1863; Sergeant-Major January 24, 1865. Mustered out with regiment.

JOHN T. ADAMS.
Private; enrolled July 31, 1862. Discharged on Surgeon's certificate at Evansville, Ind., Jan. 16, 1863.

RICHARD ADAMS.
Private; enrolled Aug. 4, 1862. Discharged on Surgeon's certificate at Louisville, Ky., Aug. 3, 1863. Wilson's, St. Croix Co., Wis.

RICHARD AYERS.
Private; enrolled Aug. 4, 1862. Died in hospital at Murfreesboro, Tenn. June 14, 1863.

AUGUSTUS AYERS.
Private; enrolled Aug. 4, 1862. Captured near Lexington, Ky., Sept. 1, 1862. Prisoner of war at Camp Chase, O. Discharged on Surgeon's certificate at Camp Dennison, O., Sept. 23, 1863. Lena, O.

LAFAYETTE AVERY.
Private; enrolled Aug. 5, 1862. Missing on the march from Lexington, Ky., Sept. 1, 1862. Prisoner of war at Camp Chase, O. Transferred to Veteran Reserve Corps Aug. 25, 1863.

JOSEPH BAKER.
Wagoner; enrolled July 23, 1862. Sick at Louisville, Ky., Aug. 16, 1863. Transferred to Veteran Reserve Corps. Mustered out at Indianapolis, Ind., May 11, 1865. Greenville, O.

JONATHAN BARD.
Private; enrolled July 29, 1862. Discharged at Columbus, O., April 4, 1863. Died at Piqua O., May 9, 1874.

NICHOLAS M. BARR.
Private; enrolled Aug. 5, 1862. Appointed Corporal at muster-in. Discharged on Surgeon's certificate at Nashville, Tenn., Dec. 15, 1862. Piqua, O.

SAMUEL C. BOWMAN.
: Private; enrolled Aug. 5, 1862. Wounded at battle Perryville, Ky., Oct. 8th, 1862. Discharged on account of wounds at Columbus, Feb. 11, 1863. Piqua, O.

JOHN H. BOWMAN.
: Private; enrolled July 26, 1862. Discharged on Surgeon's certificate at Columbus, O., March 18, 1863. Piqua, O.

ALEXANDER BOURQUIN.
: Private; enrolled July 23, 1862. Discharged on Surgeon's certificate at Louisville, Ky., March 27, 1863. New Bremen, O.

PETER BRADFORD.
: Private; enrolled Aug. 4, 1862. Died in hospital at Nashville, Tenn., Jan. 3, 1863.

WILLIAM H. BRAY.
: Private; enrolled Aug. 5, 1862. Left sick at Nolensville, Tenn., Dec. 28, 1862. Prisoner of war. In hospital at Kelly's Island, O., and Stevenson, Ala. Returned to duty. Mustered out with regiment. Brownsburgh, Hendricks Co., Ind.

ELMER C. BRECOUNT.
: Private; enrolled Aug. 5, 1862. Wounded in battle of Perryville, Oct. 8, 1862. Died in hospital on the field, Oct. 13, 1862.

HENRY H. BRECOUNT.
: Enrolled Aug. 5, 1862. Detailed to Pioneers, Dec. 9, 1862. On duty with regiment from Nov. 4, 1863, to Jan. 15, 1864. Returned to company July 29, 1864. Detailed to headquarters 1st Brigade, 1st Division, 14th Army Corps Oct. 9, 1864. Mustered out with regiment. Lena, Miami Co., O.

JOHN T. BRECOUNT.
: Private; enrolled Aug. 5, 1862. Detached on recruiting service to Columbus, O., Feb. 8, 1864. Drowned in Mississippi River Feb. 29, 1864.

JOSEPH CALDWELL.
: Private; enrolled July 24, 1862. Appointed Corporal at muster-in; Sergeant Jan. 24, 1865. Mustered out with regiment. Piqua, O.

ALEXANDER B. CARVER.
: Private; enrolled Aug. 6, 1862. Missing on the march near Lexington, Ky., Sept. 1, 1862. Prisoner of war; exchanged. Returned to duty. Appointed Corporal Nov. 1, 1864. Mustered out with regiment. Sumner, Lawrence Co., Ill.

EDWARD CLARK.
: Private; enrolled July 31, 1862. Appointed Sergeant Jan. 1, 1863. Mustered out with regiment. Celina, O.

VAN BUREN COX.
: Private; enrolled Aug. 5, 1862. Discharged on Surgeon's certificate at Nashville, Tenn., April 6, 1863. Lena, O.

EMORY CHAMBERS.
: Private; enrolled Aug. 5, 1862. Wounded in battle of Stone River, Tenn., Dec. 31, 1862. Transferred to Veteran Reserve Corps by general order of War Department, Oct. 29, 1863.

LEWIS W. COLVIN.
: Private; enrolled Aug. 5, 1862. Missing on the march near Lexington, Ky., Sept. 1, 1862. Prisoner of war. Returned to duty. Mustered out with regiment.

ROBERT DARNOLD.
: Private; enrolled Aug. 2, 1862. Captured near Lexington. Ky., Sept. 1, 1862. Prisoner of war. Discharged to date from Nov. 12, 1862. War Department letter dated Nov. 12, 1886.

CHARLES B. DAVIS.
: Private; enrolled Aug. 5, 1862. Appointed Corporal Jan. 20, 1863. Discharged on Surgeon's certificate at Columbus, O., June 1, 1863.

WILLIAM G. DAVIS.
: Private; enrolled Aug. 5, 1862. Appointed Surgeon at muster-in. Discharged on Surgeon's certificate at Nashville, Tenn., Feb. 24, 1863.

RECORD OF COMPANY C.

JAMES DOOLEY.
Private; enrolled Aug. 5, 1862. Appointed Corporal Jan. 20, 1863. Detailed to colors. Mustered out with regiment.

THOMAS F. DRAKE.
Private; enrolled July 28, 1862. Captured near Lexington, Ky., Sept. 1, 1862. Exchanged. Captured Oct. 13, 1863, while on the way to join the regiment. Returned to duty Nov. 9, 1863. Sick since Oct. 8, 1864. Mustered out at Murfreesboro, Tenn., July 4, 1865.

SAMUEL B. DRAKE.
Private; enrolled Aug. 4, 1862 Sent to hospital at Louisville, Ky., October 17, 1862. Died Nov. 21, 1862.

MICHAEL DUGAN.
Private; enrolled Aug. 5, 1862. Missing in battle of Chickamauga, Ga., Sept. 19, 1863. Prisoner of war at Andersonville, Ga. Exchanged. Returned to duty. Mustered out with regiment. Conover, O.

JOHN A. EDMONDS.
Private; enrolled July 25, 1862. Wounded in battle of Perryville, Ky., Oct. 8, 1862. Appointed Sergeant Jan. 1, 1863. Mustered out with regiment. Died at Piqua, O., May 30, 1885.

ROBERT M. EDMONDS.
Private; enrolled Aug. 5, 1862. Left sick at Nolensville, Tenn., Dec. 28, 1862. Prisoner of war at Camp Chase, O. Discharged on Surgeon's certificate at Columbus, O., March 12, 1863. Died at Piqua, O., July 8, 1873.

JOHN ESKEW.
Private; enrolled Aug. 25, 1862. Missing on the march near Lexington, Ky., Sept. 1, 1862. Prisoner of war. Discharged on Surgeon's certificate at Camp Dennison, O., Nov. 29, 1862.

HENRY FROLIGER.
Private; enrolled Aug. 5, 1862. Missing on the march near Lexington, Ky., Sept. 1, 1862. Prisoner of war at Camp Chase, O. Exchanged. Reported for duty Jan. 17, 1863. Mustered out with regiment. Casstown, Miami Co., O.

CHARLES GARUSEY.
Musician; enrolled July 25, 1862. Discharged on Surgeon's certificate at Columbus, O., March 11, 1863.

DANIEL GEPHART.
Private; enrolled Aug. 1, 1862. Sent to Convalescent Camp, near Murfreesboro, Tenn., June 23, 1863. At Convalescent Barracks, St. Louis, Jan. 19, 1864. Mustered out at Columbus, O., June 22, 1865. Died at Piqua, O.

WILLIAM F. GORDON.
Private; enrolled July 28, 1862. Appointed Corporal at muster-in. Discharged on Surgeon's certificate at Nashville, Tenn., Dec. 24, 1862. Died at Piqua, O., Feb. 1875.

GEORGE D. GRAHAM.
Private; enrolled Aug. 5, 1862. Missing on the march near Lexington, Ky., Sept. 1, 1862; Prisoner of war. Transferred to Veteran Reserve Corps by General Order No. 71, War Department Jan. 3, 1864. Lena, O.

ABEL F. GREENWOOD.
Private; enrolled July 24, 1862. Missing on the march from Kentucky River Sept. 1, 1862. Prisoner of war. Exchanged. Returned to duty Jan. 17, 1863. Transferred to Veteran Reserve Corps by General Order No. 381, War Department, Nov. 28, 1863. Columbus, O.

MARTIN GRIFFIN.
Private; enrolled Aug. 6, 1862. Missing on the march near Lexington, Ky., Sept. 1; 1862. Prisoner of war at Camp Chase, O. Exchanged Dec. 26, 1862. Returned to duty. Sent to Convalescent Camp at Murfreesboro, Tenn., June 23, 1863. Provision for discharge made by General Order 77, series 1865.

ROYAL W. GROSVENOR.
Private; enrolled Aug. 4, 1862. Missing on the march near Lexington, Ky., Sept. 1, 1862. Prisoner of war at Camp Chase, O. Returned to duty with regiment Jan. 19, 1863.

Wounded at battle of Resaca, Ga., May 14, 1864. Transferred to Veteran Reserve Corps by War Department order April 1, 1865, Mustered out July 13, 1865. Cincinnati, O.

SAMUEL HAINES.
Private; enrolled July 28, 1862. Mustered out with regiment. Piqua, O.

GEORGE W. HARRIS.
Private; enrolled Aug. 6, 1862. Discharged on Surgeon's certificate at Murfreesboro, Tenn., April 12, 1863. While on the way to Nashville, the train was attacked and captured. It is supposed that he was killed in this attack. Never heard from afterward.

WILLIAM C. HARRIS.
Private; enrolled Aug. 5, 1862. Left sick at Nolensville, Tenn., Dec. 28, 1862. Prisoner of war. Returned to duty Nov. 4, 1863. Wounded in battle at Resaca, Ga., May 14, 1864. Died at Chattanooga, Tenn., June 20, 1864.

ALBERT G. HARNER.
Private; enrolled Aug. 4, 1862. Wounded in action before Kenesaw Mountain, Ga., June 22, 1864. Returned to duty. Mustered out with regiment. Chapmansville, W. Va.

JAMES HETHRINGTON.
Private; enrolled Aug. 2, 1862. Appointed corporal Jan. 20, 1863; Sergeant July 11, 1863; First Sergeant Jan. 24, 1865. Mustered out with regiment. Piqua, O.

WILLIAM HOUSTIN.
Private; enrolled Aug. 1. 1862. Missing on the march near Lexington, Ky., Sept. 1, 1862. Prisoner of war at Camp Chase, O. Exchanged Dec. 10, 1862. Sent to hospital at Murfreesboro, Tenn., May 20, 1863, and to Convalescent Barracks, Louisville, Jan. 21, 1864. Mustered out June 22, 1865.

CLINTON HUBANKS.
Private; enrolled Aug. 4, 1862. Missing on the march near Lexington, Ky., Sept. 1, 1862. Prisoner of war. Exchanged. Returned to duty April, 1863. In hospital June 23, 1863. Discharged on Surgeon's certificate at Louisville, Ky., Aug. 20, 1863. Died.

THOMAS D. HUNTER.
Private; enrolled Aug. 5, 1862. Detailed to regimental wagon April, 1863. Mustered out with regiment. Pleasant Run, Hamilton Co., O.

WILLIAM H. JOHNSTON.
Private; enrolled Aug. 6, 1862. Missing in battle of Stone River, Tenn., Dec. 31, 1862. Prisoner of war at Richmond, Va. Paroled. Sent to Annapolis, Md. Exchanged. Reported for duty June 6, 1863. Sick in hospital at Nashville, Tenn., Nov. 10, 1864. Mustered out at Nashville, Tenn., May 17, 1865. Piqua, O.

FRANK D. JONES.
Private; enrolled Aug. 5, 1862. Missing on the march from Lexington. Ky., Sept. 1, 1862, Discharged on Surgeon's certificate at Columbus, O., Feb. 2, 1863. Lena, O.

DAVID W. LEGG.
Private; enrolled July 28, 1862. Sent to Convalescent Camp at Murfreesboro, Tenn., May 20, 1863. Transferred to Veteran Reserve Corps Oct. 29, 1863. Piqua, O.

LEVI LUNDRY.
Private; enrolled Aug. 4, 1862. Sent to hospital at Danville, Ky., Oct. 19, 1862. Discharged on Surgeon's certificate at Columbus, O., May 2, 1863. Versailles, O.

DAVID N. MANSON.
Private; enrolled Aug. 5, 1862. Missing on the march near Lexington, Ky., Sept. 1, 1862. Prisoner of war. Exchanged Dec. 10, 1862. Detached as Orderly to General M. D. Manson. Returned to duty with company. Mustered out with regiment. Piqua, O.

BENJAMIN F. MATTOX.
Private; enrolled Aug. 5, 1862. Missing on the march near Lexington, Ky., Sept. 1, 1862. Prisoner of war at Camp Chase, O. Exchanged. Returned to duty with regiment Jan. 19, 1863. Wounded in battle of Chickamauga, Ga., Sept. 19, 1863. Returned to duty. Mustered out with regiment. Fletcher, O.

ABRAHAM McCOLLUM.
Private; enrolled Aug. 4, 1862.

JOHN McMASTER.
: Private; enrolled Aug. 4, 1862. Detailed to supply train 1st Division, 14th Army Corps, by order of General Rousseau. Mustered out with regiment. Troy, O.

THOMAS B. MOSIER.
: Private; enrolled Aug. 4, 1862. Mustered out with regiment. Iroquois, D. T.

WILLIAM A. MUNGER.
: Private; enrolled July 28, 1862. Missing in battle of Chickamauga, Ga., Sept. 19, 1863. Prisoner of war at Andersonville, Ga. Died at Danville, Va.; date not known.

HIRAM R. MINOR.
: Private enrolled Aug. 6, 1862. Appointed Corporal at muster-in. Missing on the march near Lexington, Ky., Sept. 1, 1862. Prisoner of war. Returned to duty Jan. 17, 1863. Mustered out with regiment. Solomon City, Kansas.

GRANT C. MINGUS.
: Private; enrolled July 26, 1862. Left sick at Nolensville, Tenn., Dec. 28, 1862. Prisoner of war at Camp Chase, O. Discharged on Surgeon's certificate April 6, 1863.

WILLIAM H. NEEDLES.
: Private; enrolled Aug. 5, 1862. Mustered out with regiment. Died near Lena, O., March 1, 1887.

HENRY NORRIS.
: Private; enrolled Aug. 6, 1862. Missing on the march near Lexington, Ky., Sept. 1, 1862. Prisoner of war at Camp Chase, O. Returned to duty April 4, 1863. Sent to Convalescent Camp near Murfreesboro, Tenn, May 20, 1863. Returned to duty Feb. 1, 1864. Detailed to Ambulance Corps Feb. 5, 1865. Mustered out with regiment. Piqua, Ohio.

GIDEON G. OWEN.
: Musician; enrolled Aug. 2, 1862. Mustered out with regiment. Houston, Shelby Co., Ohio.

ISAAC PECK.
: Private; enrolled Aug. 6, 1862. Transferred to Veteran Reserve Corps by General Order 151, War Department, April 1, 1864. Troy, O.

STEVEN B. PERRY.
: Private; enrolled July 28, 1862. Died in hospital at Nashville, Tenn., April 15, 1863.

BENJAMIN PLACE.
: Private; enrolled Aug. 5, 1862. Appointed Corporal at muster-in. Missing on the march near Lexington, Ky., Sept. 1, 1862. Prisoner of war at Camp Chase, O. Discharged on Surgeon's certificate at Columbus, O., Feb. 26, 1863. Died.

DANIEL W. PLACE.
: Private; enrolled August 5, 1862. Appointed Sergeant at muster-in. Missing on the march near Lexington, Ky., Sept. 1, 1862. Prisoner of war at Camp Chase, O. Discharged on Surgeon's certificate at Columbus, O., Nov. 24. 1862. Sugar Creek P. O., Hancock Co., Ind.

PETER M. PRUGH.
: Private; enrolled July 28, 1862. Detailed as teamster Aug. 24, 1863. Returned to duty with company Jan. 4, 1864. Wounded in action at Resaca, Ga., May 14, 1864. Died in field hospital, near Resaca, Ga., May 18, 1864.

JAMES B. REDMAN.
: Private; enrolled Aug. 12, 1862. Appointed Corporal at muster-in. Missing on the march near Lexington, Ky., Sept. 1, 1862. Prisoner of war at Camp Chase, O. Discharged on Surgeon's certificate at Columbus, O., Feb. 9, 1863. Piqua, O.

WILLIAM H. RHYNARD.
: Private; enrolled Aug. 5. 1862. Missing on the march near Lexington, Ky., Sept. 1, 1862, Prisoner of war at Camp Chase, O. Returned to duty. Mustered out with regiment. St. Paris, O.

CHARLES ROBERTS.
: Private; enrolled Aug. 5, 1862. Wounded in action at Resaca, Ga., May 14, 1864. In hospital at New Albany, Ind., September and October, 1864. Returned to duty. Mustered out with regiment. Springfield, O.

THOMAS ROBERTS.
    Private; enrolled Aug. 5, 1862. Left sick at Nolensville, Tenn., Dec. 28, 1862. Prisoner of war at Camp Chase, O. Reported for duty Nov. 14, 1863. Mustered out with regiment. Conover, Miami Co., O.

JOHN E. ROBERTS.
    Private; enrolled Aug. 5, 1862. Wounded at battle of Stone River, Tenn., Dec. 31, 1862. Mustered out with regiment. Springfield, O.

JOSEPH S. SCHERER.
    Private; enrolled July 28, 1862. Appointed Corporal at muster-in. Discharged on Surgeon's certificate at Columbus, O., Dec. 26, 1862. Richmond, Ind.

CHARLES SHUE.
    Private; enrolled Aug. 4, 1862.

MARTIN H. SMITH.
    Private; enrolled Aug. 1, 1862. Discharged on Surgeon's certificate at Nashville, Tenn., Jan. 30, 1863. Piqua, O.

CHARLES F. SMITH.
    Private; enrolled July 29, 1862.. Missing on the march near Lexington, Ky., Sept. 1, 1862. Prisoner of war. Discharged on Surgeon's certificate, at Nashville, Tenn., April 25, 1863.

MOSES SNYDER.
    Private; enrolled July 24, 1862. Transferred to Veteran Reserve Corps by General Order No. 352, War Department, Oct. 29, 1863. Mustered out at Cairo, Ill., July 13, 1865. Toledo, O.

GEORGE W. SOWERS.
    Private; enrolled Aug. 4, 1862. Discharged on Surgeon's certificate at Louisville, Ky., Oct. 8, 1862, Covington, O.

JACOB STEIGER.
    Private; enrolled Aug. 4, 1862. Missing on the march near Lexington, Ky., Sept. 1, 1862. Prisoner of war at Camp Chase, O. Returned to duty March, 1863. Left sick at Nashville April 7, 1863. Mustered out at Nashville May 18, 1865. Beamsville, Darke County, Ohio.

JAMES M. STEWART.
    Private; enrolled Aug. 5, 1862. Detailed to Pioneer Brigade Dec. 9, 1862. Sick in Nashville, Tenn., January, 1863. Returned to duty with regiment Nov. 4, 1863. Appointed Corporal Jan. 24, 1865. Mustered out with regiment.

ENOCH STOKER.
    Private; enrolled July 24, 1862. Missing on the march near Lexington, Ky., Sept. 1, 1862. Prisoner of war at Camp Chase. Returned to duty. Detached as teamster, February, 1863. Mustered out with regiment. Died Dec. 17, 1879, at Piqua, O.

JOSEPH SYNNOT.
    Private; enrolled July 28, 1862. Mustered out with regiment.

JAMES TAMPLIN.
    Private; enrolled Aug. 5, 1862. Appointed Sergeant at muster-in. Missing on the march near Lexington, Ky., Sept. 1, 1862. Prisoner of war at Camp Chase, O. Returned to duty Jan. 17, 1863. Sick in hospital at Murfreesboro, Tenn. Returned to duty. Mustered out with regiment. Dayton, O.

EZRA P. TAYLOR.
    Private; enrolled Aug. 4, 1862. Mustered out with regiment.

ISRAEL THACKARA.
    Private; enrolled Aug. 5, 1862. Missing on the march near Lexington, Ky., Sept. 1, 1862. Prisoner of war at Camp Chase, O. Discharged on Surgeon's certificate at Columbus, O., April 1, 1863. Corning, Tehama Co., Cal.

AARON TOMIRE.
    Private; enrolled Aug. 5, 1862. Wounded at Chickamauga, Ga., Sept. 19, 1863. In hospital at Nashville Oct. 24, 1863. Transferred to Veteran Reserve Corps by General Order No. 69, War Department, April 2, 1864. Eris, Champaign Co., O.

RECORD OF COMPANY C.

FREDERICK THOMAS.
Private; enrolled Aug. 6, 1862. Transferred to Veteran Reserve Corps by General Order No. 352, War Department, dated Oct. 29, 1863.

JOHN WAY.
Private; enrolled March 13, 1865. Mustered out at Tod Barracks may 13, 1865.

THOMAS WIRT.
Private; enrolled Aug. 5, 1862. Missing on the march near Lexington, Ky., Sept. 1, 1862. Prisoner of war at Camp Chase, O. Rejoined for duty Nov. 9, 1863. Mustered out with regiment. Plattsville, Shelby Co., O.

HENRY F. WHITNEY.
Private; enrolled Aug. 5, 1862. Missing on the march near Lexington, Ky., Sept. 1, 1862. Prisoner of war at Camp Chase, O. Discharged on Surgeon's certificate at Columbus, O., Jan 10, 1863. Lena, O.

KENNETH WHARRY.
Private; enrolled July 31, 1862. Appointed Hospital-Steward, 94th O. V. I. Discharged Oct. 7, 1863.

THOMAS WILGUS.
Private; enrolled Aug. 5, 1862. Mustered out with regiment. Conover, Miami Co., O.

JOHN WOLCOTT.
Private; enrolled Aug. 5, 1862. Discharged on Surgeon's certificate at Columbus, O., March 11, 1863. Lena, O.

MELCHOIR ZUICKEY.
Private; enrolled Aug. 1, 1862. Missing near Lexington, Ky., Sept. 1, 1862. Prisoner of war at Camp Chase, O. Discharged on Surgeon's certificate at Columbus, O., Nov. 15, 1862.

COMPANY D.

CAPTAIN.
JOHN W. FORD.
  Band Leader 10th O. V. I. April to June, 1861. Band Leader 42d O. V. I. September, 1861, to May, 1862. Appointed First Lieutenant 94th O. V. I. Aug. 18, 1862; Captain May 23, 1863. Appointed Assistant Inspector-General 1st Brigade, 1st Division, 14th Corps, Nov. 1, 1863; Acting Assistant Adjutant General, same headquarters, June 29, 1864; Brevet Major U. S. Vols. March 13, 1865. Mustered out with regiment.

FIRST LIEUTENANTS.
ANDREW WIGGIM.
  Appointed Second Lieutenant July 22, 1862. Promoted to First Lieutenant May 23, 1863. Resigned Oct. 29, 1863.

JAMES T. PIERSON.
  Private and Sergeant 11th O. V. I. April to June, 1861. Enrolled as Private in Co. D, 94th O. V. I., Aug. 6, 1862. Appointed Sergeant at muster-in; First Sergeant Dec. 24, 1862. Promoted to Second Lieutenant May 23, 1863; First Lieutenant March 14, 1864; commanding the company since Nov. 1, 1863. Mustered out with regiment. Ouray, Col.

ENLISTED MEN.
DANIEL ANTHONY.
  Private; enrolled Aug. 22, 1862. Died in hospital at Nashville, Tenn., Jan. 8, 1863.

WILLIAM ASHWORTH.
  Enrolled Aug. 13, 1862. Appointed Sergeant at muster-in. Mustered out with regiment. Tippecanoe City, O.

JOHN ATHEY.
  Private; enrolled Sept. 21, 1864. Mustered out with regiment. Tippecanoe City, O.

JOHN BENHAM.
  Private; enrolled Aug. 6, 1862. Discharged on Surgeon's certificate at Murfreesboro, Tenn., April 10, 1863. Tippecanoe City, O.

WILHELM BEARWORTH.
  Private; enrolled Aug. 15, 1862. Detailed to regimental band. Left sick at Nolensville, Tenn., Dec. 28, 1862. Prisoner of war at Camp Chase, O. Discharged on Surgeon's certificate May 25, 1863, at Columbus, O. Tippecanoe City, O.

IRWIN BEARD.
  Private; enrolled Aug. 22, 1862. Detailed to Pioneer Brigade Nov. 22, 1862. Transferred to 1st Regiment U. S. Veteran Volunteer Engineers July 24, 1864.

WILLIAM BLACKBURN.
  Private; enrolled Aug. 15, 1862. Appointed Corporal Aug. 1, 1864. Mustered out with regiment. Potsdam, Miami Co., O.

JESSE BYRKETT.
  Private; enrolled Aug. 15, 1862. Captured near Lexington, Ky., Sept. 1, 1862. Prisoner of war at Camp Chase, O. Re-enlisted in Troop M, 5th U. S. Cavalry, March 30, 1863. Wounded at Appomattox Court-House, Va., April 9, 1865. Discharged on account of wounds. Troy, O.

OTHNEIL BYRKETT.
  Private; enrolled Aug. 22, 1862.

JACOB W. BORTS.
  Private; enrolled Aug. 22, 1862. Mustered out with regiment. Potsdam, Miami Co., O.

DANIEL CHILDERS.
Sergeant; enrolled Aug. 5, 1862. Transferred to Veteran Reserve Corps Aug. 1, 1863.

JOHN CLARK.
Band Musician 10th O. V. I. April to June, 1861. Private; enrolled Aug. 6, 1862, in 94th O. V. I. Detailed to regimental band since muster-in. Mustered out with regiment. Tippecanoe City, O.

SAMUEL J. COBINE.
Private; enrolled July 28, 1862. Captured near Lexington, Ky., Sept. 1, 1862. Prisoner of war at Camp Chase, O. Private 1st U. S. Cavalry Sept. 1, 1863. Mustered out at the close of the war.

SYLVESTER E. COUCH.
11th O. V. I. April to June, 1861. Band Musician 42d O. V. I. 1861. Musician Co. D, 94th O. V. I.; enrolled July 27, 1862. Detailed to the regimental band since muster-in. Mustered out with regiment. Brazil, Ind.

JOSHUA B. COUCH.
Private 11th O. V. I. 1861. Private; enrolled in 94th O. V. I. July 24, 1862. Detailed to regimental band since muster-in. Mustered out with regiment. Dayton, O.

JOHN C. COLLINS.
Enrolled July 23, 1862. Appointed First Sergeant at muster-in. Discharged on Surgeon's certificate at Columbus, O., Dec. 24, 1862. Tippecanoe City, O.

SANFORD L. COLLINS.
Private; enrolled Aug. 6, 1862. Mustered out with regiment. Died at Tippecanoe City, O., July 22, 1885.

STEVEN CONDON.
Private; enrolled Aug. 8, 1862. Captured on the march near Lexington, Ky., Sept. 1, 1862. Discharged on Surgeon's certificate March 30, 1863, at Columbus, O. Died at Covington, O.

PATRICK CLIFFORD.
Private; enrolled August 15, 1862. Discharged at Columbus, O., April 9, 1863, on Surgeon's certificate.

ENOS B. CRUEA.
Private; enrolled Aug. 5, 1862. Discharged March 25, 1863, to re-enlist in marine service. Tippecanoe City, O.

DANIEL B. DAVIS,
Band 10th O. V. I. April to June, 1861. Private; enlisted Nov. 16, 1863, in 94th O. V. I. Detailed to regimental band. Transferred to 74th O. V. V. I. at muster-out of regiment. Tippecanoe City, O.

JOHN DUNCAN.
Private; enrolled Aug. 18, 1862. Discharged on Surgeon's certificate at Lousville, Ky., Nov. 1, 1862. Preston P. O., Hamilton Co., O.

JOHN EDWARDS.
Private; enrolled Aug. 15, 1862. Mustered out with regiment. West Milton, O.

JOHN W. ELLIOTT.
Private; enrolled Aug. 2, 1862. Discharged on Surgeon's certificate at Nashville, Tenn., July 29, 1863.

FRANCIS EVANS.
Private; enlisted Oct. 28, 1864. Transferred to 74th O. V. V. I. at muster-out of regiment, June 5, 1865.

RUFUS C. FENNER.
Private; enrolled Aug. 11, 1862. Discharged on Surgeon's certificate at Nashville, Tenn., Jan. 23, 1863.

ELI H. FENTERS.
Private; enrolled Aug. 11, 1862. Wounded at Stone River, Tenn., Dec. 31, 1862. Discharged at Camp Dennison, O., May 24, 1865.

GEORGE FENTERS.
Private; enrolled Aug. 16, 1862. Left sick at Raleigh, N. C., May 1, 1865. Discharged at New York, May 29, 1865.

JOSIAH FETTERS.
: Private; enrolled Aug. 11, 1862. Died in hospital at Chattanooga, Tenn., June 4, 1864, from a wound received at Resaca, Ga., May 14, 1864.

WILLIAM FILBY.
: Private; enrolled Aug. 14, 1862. Died in hospital at Nashville, Tenn., May 14, 1863.

BENJAMIN FIELDS.
: Private; enrolled Aug. 13, 1862. Transferred to Veteran Reserve Corps Sept. 1, 1863.

SAMUEL FOLKER.
: Private; enrolled Aug. 22, 1862. Discharged at Columbus, O., July 28, 1864, on account of wounds received at Chickamauga, Ga., Sept. 20, 1863. West Milton, O.

JACOB R. FUNK.
: Private; enrolled Aug. 24, 1862. Died in hospital at Bowling Green, Ky., Nov. 18, 1862.

GEORGE W. FRIEND.
: Private; enrolled Aug. 22, 1862. Mustered out with regiment.

JACOB B. FREET.
: Private; enrolled Aug. 11, 1862. Transferred to Veteran Reserve Corps Dec. 15, 1863. Tippecanoe City, O.

WILLIAM GREEN.
: Private; enrolled Aug. 2, 1862. Appointed Corporal May 26, 1863. Mustered out with regiment. Carlisle Station, O.

GEORGE GUCKES.
: Band 10th O. V. I. April to June, 1861. Band Musician 42d O. V. I. 1861. Private; enrolled in 94th O. V. I. Aug. 15, 1862. Detailed to regimental band since muster-in. Mustered out with regiment.

HORACE E. HAMER.
: Private; enrolled Aug. 11, 1862. Died in hospital at Murfreesboro, Tenn., Feb. 15, 1863.

PHILIP HARPER.
: Private; enrolled Aug. 22, 1862. Discharged on Surgeon's certificate at Louisville, Kentucky, March 20, 1863.

WILSON C. HART.
: Band Musician 42d O. V. I. 1861. Private 94th O. V. I.; enrolled Aug. 16, 1862. Detailed to regimental band at muster-in. Died in hospital at Murfreesboro, Tenn., June 20, 1863.

DAVID HART.
: Private; enrolled Aug. 14, 1862. Transferred to Veteran Reserve Corps Sept. 1, 1863. Returned to company by transfer Oct. 27, 1864. Mustered out with regiment.

THOMAS HARTLEY.
: Private; enrolled Aug. 22, 1862. Appointed Sergeant at muster-in. Mustered out with regiment. Tippecanoe City, O.

JAMES HARTLEY.
: Private; enrolled Aug. 11, 1862. Transferred to Veteran Reserve Corps Aug. 11, 1863. Tippecanoe City, O.

ABRAHAM HARSHBARGER.
: Private; enrolled Aug. 11, 1862. Died in hospital at Murfreesboro, Tenn., June 8, 1863.

ROBERT HARDACRE.
: Private; enrolled Aug. 6, 1862. Wounded at Stone River, Tenn., Dec. 31, 1862. Appointed Corporal Feb. 1, 1865. Mustered out with regiment. Sumner, Lawrence County, Illinois.

MATTHIAS HASLER.
: Private; enrolled Aug. 14, 1862. Died at Anderson Station, Tenn., Aug. 18, 1863.

JONATHAN HAWKINS.
: Private; enrolled Aug. 15, 1862. Died at Edgefield Junction, Tenn., Nov. 28, 1862.

ORIN HAYWORTH.
: Private; enrolled Aug. 13, 1862. Slightly wounded at Stone River, Tenn. Mustered out with regiment. Greenville, O.

RECORD OF COMPANY D.   127

JOHN HICKS.
Private; enrolled Aug. 11, 1862. Detached to headquarters 1st Brigade, 1st Division, 14th Corps, as saddler. Left sick at Jeffersonville, Ind., Sept. 3, 1864. Discharged at Louisville, Ky., May 19, 1865.

JOHN W. HICKS.
Private; enrolled Aug. 10, 1862. Mustered out with regiment. West Milton, O.

WILLIAM HOECKEY.
Private; enrolled Aug. 15, 1862. Mustered out with regiment.

JOSEPH E. HICKERSON.
Corporal; enrolled Aug. 11, 1862. Appointed Sergeant May 26, 1863. Died in hospital at Nashville, Tenn., Nov. 6, 1863.

SYLVESTER H. HOUCK.
Corporal; enrolled Aug. 6, 1862. Transferred to Veteran Reserve Corps Jan. 15, 1864.

SAMUEL HOWE.
Private; enrolled Aug. 11, 1862. Detached to Pioneer Brigade Nov. 22, 1863. Transferred to 1st Regiment U. S. Veteran Volunteer Engineers July 24, 1864.

HARVEY HUGHES.
Private; enrolled Aug. 11, 1862. Wounded at Stone River, Tenn., Dec. 31, 1862. Transferred to Veteran Reserve Corps Nov. 1, 1863.

TANZY HUTCHINS.
Private; enrolled Aug. 7, 1862. Died in hospital at Nashville, Tenn., March 2, 1863.

BENJAMIN F. HUTCHINS.
Private; enrolled Aug. 21, 1862. Died in Hospital at Murfreesboro, Tenn., April 17, 1863.

WILLIAM HUTCHINS.
Private; enrolled Aug. 11, 1862. Discharged on Surgeon's certificate at Columbus, O., May 2, 1863. Died.

SAMUEL HUTCHINS.
Private; enrolled Sept. 23, 1864. Mustered out with regiment.

JAMES JAY.
Private; enrolled Oct. 5, 1863. Transferred to 74th O. V. V. I. at muster-out of regiment June 5, 1865.

FRANKLIN KAUFFMAN.
Private; enrolled Sept. 21, 1864. Mustered out with regiment. Tippecanoe City, O.

WILLIAM H. KESSLER.
Private; enrolled July 28, 1862. Appointed Corporal Aug. 1, 1863. Wounded at Missionary Ridge Nov. 25, 1863. Promoted Sergeant Jan. 1, 1864; First Sergeant Feb. 1, 1865. Mustered out with regiment. West Milton, O.

MARTIN KESSLER.
Enrolled Aug. 16, 1862. Appointed Corporal at muster-in. Wounded at Tate's Ferry, Kentucky River, Aug. 31, 1862. Died at Nashville, Tenn., Aug. 24, 1863.

JOHN O. KESSLER.
Private; enrolled Oct. 10, 1863. Wounded in front of Atlanta August, 1864. Transferred to 74th O. V. I. at muster-out of regiment. Troy, O.

FRANKLIN KING.
Band 10th O. V. I. April to June, 1861. Private; enrolled 94th O. V. I. July 28, 1862. Detailed to regimental band at muster-in. Discharged Nov. 16, 1862, at Columbus, O. Re-enlisted Oct. 17, 1864. Detached as Band Leader, Post Band, Columbus, O. Discharged at Tod Barracks May 15, 1865. New York.

PHILIP KNARRE.
Private; enrolled Aug. 22, 1862. Appointed Corporal May 26, 1863; Sergeant July 1, 1863. Detached to Columbus, O., on recruiting service, by Special Field Order No. 39, 1865. Discharged at Columbus June 10, 1865. Died at Tippecanoe City, O., 1884.

JOSEPH KENDIG.
Private; enrolled Aug. 14, 1862. Transferred to Veteran Reserve Corps Jan. 15, 1864. Dayton, O.

JOB LEAVELL.
: Corporal; enrolled Aug. 2, 1862. Discharged on Surgeon's certificate at Columbus, O., Jan. 19, 1863.

BENJAMIN LINE.
: Corporal; enrolled Aug. 11, 1862. Transferred to Veteran Reserve Corps Jan. 15, 1864. Died.

GEORGE LOVELOCK.
: Private; enrolled Sept. 20, 1864. Mustered out with regiment.

JOHN MAHAFFEY.
: Musician; enrolled Aug. 5, 1862. Died in hospital at Annapolis, Md., April 7, 1864.

OLIVER MILLIGAN.
: Private; enrolled Aug. 8, 1862. Discharged on Surgeon's certificate at Camp Benton, Mo., Feb. 11, 1863. Died.

MARTIN MILLER.
: Private; enrolled Aug. 13, 1862. Mustered out with regiment. New Bremen, O.

SAMUEL MOORE.
: Private; enrolled Aug. 11, 1862. Discharged on Surgeon's certificate at Columbus, O., Feb. 11, 1863.

HENRY T. MORRISON.
: Band 10th O. V. I. April to June, 1861. Band musician 42d O. V. I. 1861. Private 94th O. V. I.; enrolled Aug. 9, 1862. Detailed to regimental band since muster-in. Mustered out with regiment. Died at Tippecanoe City, O.

ISRAEL S. NACE.
: Band 10th O. V. I. April to June, 1861. Private, Co. D, Aug. 15, 1862. Detailed to regimental band since muster-in. Mustered out with regiment. Brownville, Neb.

ENOCH PATTY.
: Enrolled Aug. 15, 1862; appointed Corporal. Discharged on Surgeon's certificate at Lebanon, Ky., April 13, 1863. Died in 1881.

REINHOLD PETER.
: Private; enrolled Aug. 15, 1862. Discharged on Surgeon's certificate at Cincinnati, O., Nov. 24, 1862. Logansville, Logan Co., O.

THOMAS ROCKEY.
: Private; enrolled Aug. 5, 1862. Detailed to supply train, 1st Division, 14th Corps. Mustered out with regiment.

RICHARD E. SAUNDERS.
: Private; enrolled Aug. 11, 1864. Mustered out with regiment. Atlanta, Ill.

MARSHALL SMITH.
: Private; enrolled Aug. 2, 1862. Discharged on Surgeon's certificate at Columbus, O., Jan. 6, 1863.

JAMES D. TREADWAY.
: Private; enrolled Aug. 11, 1862. Missing on the march near Lexington, S. C. Prisoner of war Feb. 15, 1865. Discharged at Camp Chase, O., June 13, 1865. Brandt, O.

CHARLES TRUPP.
: Band 10th O. V. I. April to June, 1861. Private; enrolled Aug. 15, 1862, 94th O. V. I. Detailed to regimental band since muster-in. Mustered out with regiment. Tippecanoe City, O.

ISAIAH VANDEVER.
: Corporal; enrolled Aug. 8, 1862. Appointed Sergeant May 1, 1864. Mustered out with regiment. Webster, Darke Co., O.

HAZEL WELDAY.
: Wagoner; enrolled Aug. 22, 1862. Discharged on Surgeon's certificate at Columbus, May 2, 1863. West Charleston, O.

NATHAN WELDAY.
: Private; enrolled Aug. 2, 1862. Died in hospital at Nashville, Tenn., Jan. 23, 1863.

ADAM J. WESLER.
: Private; enrolled Aug. 6, 1862. Killed in action at Kenesaw Mountain, Ga., July 1, 1864.

RECORD OF COMPANY D. 129

JOHN J. WESLER.
   Band 10th O. V. I. April to June, 1861. Private; enrolled Aug. 15, 1862, 94th O. V. I. Detailed to regimental band since muster-in. Sent to hospital at Raleigh, N. C., April 25, 1865. Discharged at Mower General Hospital, Philadelphia, Pa., June 20, 1865. Tippecanoe City, O.

JOSEPH P. WESLER.
   Private; enrolled Aug. 6, 1862. Detailed to regimental band Aug. 10, 1864. Mustered out with regiment. Beatrice, Neb.

IRVIN WIGLEY.
   Private; enrolled Oct. 4, 1864. Died in hospital at Ward's Island, New York Harbor, March 4, 1865.

TILLMAN WILSON.
   Private; enrolled Aug. 14, 1862. Killed in action at Perryville, Ky., Oct. 8, 1862.

GEORGE WOLF.
   Private; enrolled Aug. 19, 1862. Died in hospital at Nashville, Tenn., July 17, 1863.

JOHN WORLEY.
   Private; enrolled Aug. 6, 1862. Mustered out with regiment. Tippecanoe City, O.

DAVID WORT.
   Private; enrolled Aug. 1, 1862. Mustered out with regiment. Tippecanoe City, O.

AMOS WORTS.
   Private; enrolled Aug. 2, 1862. Transferred to 2d U. S. Artillery Sept. 22, 1862, by order of Secretary of War. West Milton, O.

DAVID YOUNGS.
   Private; enrolled Aug. 7, 1862. Mustered out with regiment. Carmi, Ill.

MARTIN YOUNG.
   Private; enrolled Aug. 17, 1862. Discharged on Surgeon's certificate at Columbus, O., Aug. 13, 1863.

COMPANY E.

CAPTAINS.
DAVID STEELE.
  Sergeant Co. G, 2d Iowa Infantry, May, 1861, to April, 1862. Appointed Captain 94th O. V. I. July 23, 1862. Wounded at battle of Stone River, Tenn., Dec. 31, 1862. Died at Murfreesboro, Tenn., Jan. 13, 1863.

SAMUEL H. SHERLOCK.
  Enrolled as private, Co. C, Aug. 6, 1862. Appointed Sergeant-Major Jan. 28, 1863; Adjutant March 31, 1863. Promoted to Captain March 3, 1864; assigned to Co. E. Detached to headquarters 1st Regiment, 1st Division, 14th Army Corps, as Assistant Inspector-General. Brevet Major United States Volunteers March 13, 1865. Mustered out with regiment. Fort Smith, Ark.

FIRST LIEUTENANTS.
JOHN A. BEALE.
  Appointed July 23, 1862. Died at Nashville, Tenn., Jan. 2, 1863.

JOHN KINGERY.
  Enrolled as private Aug. 7, 1862. Appointed Sergeant at muster-in. Promoted to First Sergeant Dec. 1, 1862; 2d Lieutenant March 14, 1863; 1st Lieutenant April 7, 1863. Resigned July 19, 1863.

JAMES MITCHELL.
  Enrolled as private Aug. 7, 1862. Appointed Sergeant at muster-in. Promoted to First Sergeant March 21, 1863; 2d Lieutenant April 7, 1863; 1st Lieutenant March 1, 1864. Wounded at battle of Resaca, Ga., May 14, 1864. Returned to duty. Resigned Sept. 7, 1864. Crescent City, Fla.

EDWARD CONNER.
  Enrolled as private, Co. F, July 23. 1862. Appointed First Sergeant at muster-in. Promoted to 1st Lieutenant Oct. 10, 1864. Assigned to Co. E; in command of company from that date. Mustered out with regiment.

SECOND LIEUTENANT.
SAMUEL WALTON.
  Appointed July 23, 1862. Absent without leave. Dismissed Jan. 22, 1863, by order of General Rosecrans.

ENLISTED MEN.
SIMON P. ALEY.
  Private; enrolled Aug. 11, 1862. Transferred to Veteran Reserve Corps, by order of War Department, Jan. 14, 1864. Dayton, O.

HENRY ALEY.
  Private; enrolled Aug. 10, 1862. Died in hospital at Louisville, Ky., Nov. 17, 1862.

GEORGE H. ANDREW.
  Enrolled Aug. 8, 1862. Appointed Corporal at muster-in. Died in hospital at Murfreesboro, Tenn., March 19, 1863.

JOSEPH W. BECK.
  Private; enrolled July 31, 1862. Sent to hospital at Chattanooga, Tenn., Feb. 24, 1864. Provision for discharge made by General Order No. 77, series 1865, War Department.

GILBERT BROWDER.
  Private; enrolled Aug. 7, 1862. Died in hospital at Nashville, Tenn., Feb. 1, 1863.

CHARLES BELL.
  Private; enrolled July 23, 1862. Mustered out with regiment. Spring Valley, Greene County, Ohio.

RECORD OF COMPANY E.

SAMUEL A. BOWERMASTER.
Private; enrolled Aug. 7, 1862. Discharged on Surgeon's certificate at Columbus, O., March 22, 1863. Died at Bowersville, Greene Co., O.

WILLIAM BRANNON.
Private; enrolled Aug. 7, 1862. Transferred to Veteran Reserve Corps Nov. 6, 1863.

CYRUS BROWN.
Private; enrolled Aug. 11, 1862. Appointed Corporal April 7, 1863; Sergeant Jan. 8, 1865. Mustered out with regiment. New Jasper, Greene Co., O.

JERRY BUTLER.
Private; enrolled Oct. 5, 1863. Absent, sick at Jeffersonville, Ind., Nov. 1, 1864. Returned to duty. Detailed to Ambulance Corps. Transferred to 74th O. V. V. I. at muster-out of regiment.

DAVID W. CARPENTER.
Private; enrolled Aug. 9, 1862. Appointed Corporal Oct. 20, 1863. Wounded at Kenesaw Mountain June 22, 1864. In hospital at Nashville, Tenn. Provision for discharge made by General Order No. 77, War Department, 1865. Milledgeville, Fayette Co., O.

OSCAR CHRISTIE.
Private; enrolled Aug. 6, 1862. Killed in battle of Resaca, Ga., May 14, 1864.

LORINZO CLARK.
Private; enrolled Aug. 13, 1862. Transferred to 74th O. V. I. at muster-out of regiment. Harshmanville, Montgomery Co., O.

MICHAEL CLOHESSEY.
Private; enrolled Aug. 11, 1862.

DANIEL CLOHESSEY.
Private; enrolled July 23, 1862.

HIRAM R. CONN.
Private; enrolled Aug. 13, 1862. Discharged on Surgeon's certificate at Cincinnati, O., Feb. 26, 1863. Van Wert, O.

ADAM G. CORNWELL.
Private; enrolled Aug. 7, 1862. Wounded at battle of Perryville, Ky., Oct. 8, 1862. Absent in hospital at Cleveland, O., until discharge, May 30, 1865. Byron, Greene County, Ohio.

WILLIAM CORNWELL.
Private; enrolled Aug. 7, 1862. Discharged on Surgeon's certificate at Nashville, Tenn., May 18, 1863. Byron, Greene Co., O.

LOUIS C. COTTRELL.
Private; enrolled Aug. 11, 1862. Wounded at battle of Stone River, Tenn., Dec. 31, 1862. In hospital at New Albany, Ind., February, 1863. Transferred to Veteran Reserve Corps Jan. 10, 1864.

JOHN M. COTTRELL.
Private; enrolled Aug. 13, 1862. Absent, sick at New Albany, Ind., since Oct. 2, 1862. Transferred to Veteran Reserve Corps Jan. 10, 1864.

CHRISTOPHER C. COY.
Private; enrolled Aug. 10, 1862. Appointed Corporal Jan. 8, 1865. Mustered out with regiment. Trebine's Station, O.

ABRAHAM COY.
Private; enrolled Aug. 2, 1862. Killed in battle of Perryville, Ky., Oct. 8, 1862.

JOSEPHUS COVER.
Enrolled Aug. 8, 1862. Appointed Corporal at muster-in. Died in hospital at Danville, Ky., Oct. 26, 1862.

ISAAC COVER.
Private; enrolled Aug. 2, 1862.

JOHN DAVIS.
Private; enrolled Aug. 6, 1862. Transferred to Veteran Reserve Corps, 1865, by general order of War Department. Apha, Greene Co., O.

EDWARD H. DE WITT.
Wagoner; enrolled Aug. 11, 1862.

GEORGE DICKERSON.
Private; enrolled Aug. 11, 1862. Discharged on Surgeon's certificate at Louisville, Ky., Nov. 29, 1862.

SOLOMON DODGE.
Private; enrolled Aug 10, 1862. Transferred to 18th U. S. I. Dec. 6, 1862.

THOMAS C. DUNN.
Private; enrolled Aug. 11, 1862.

TISEN EVAN.
Private; enrolled Aug. 1, 1862. Died in hospital at Nashville, Tenn., Dec. 22, 1862.

JOHN F. ECHERT.
Private; enrolled Aug. 13, 1862. Detailed as teamster. Mustered out with regiment.

WILLIAM H. H. FAUBER.
Enrolled Aug. 7, 1862. Appointed Corporal at muster-in. Died in hospital at Louisville, Ky., Oct. 2, 1862.

WILLIAM FINDLAY.
Private; enrolled Aug. 12, 1862. Wounded in battle of Resaca, Ga., May 14, 1864. Discharged at Camp Chase, O., Nov. 29, 1864, by order of General Joe Hooker. Spring Valley, Greene Co., O.

JAMES M. FLANNIGAN.
Private; enrolled Aug. 9, 1862.

WILLIAM FOGWELL.
Private; enrolled Aug. 7, 1862. Absent, sick at Camp Dennison, O., since Feb. 28, 1865. Discharged under provisions of General Order No. 77, War Department, 1865. Died.

ALONZO FUGATE.
Private; enrolled Feb. 22, 1865. Transferred to 74th O. V. I. at muster-out of regiment. Bowersville, Greene Co., O.

HARRISON FUGATE.
Private; enrolled Aug. 7, 1862. Appointed Corporal April 7, 1863. Wounded in battle of Resaca, Ga., May 14, 1864. Returned to duty. Appointed Sergeant Jan. 8, 1865. Mustered out with regiment. Bowersville, Greene Co., O.

THOMAS J. GALLION.
Private; enrolled Aug. 11, 1862. Died at Louisville, Ky., Dec. 17, 1862.

JOHN A. GOE.
Private; enrolled Aug. 14, 1862.

PHILIP H. HARSHMAN.
Private; enrolled Aug. 13, 1862. Absent, sick at Savannah, Ga., since Jan. 20, 1865. Discharged under General Order 77, War Department, series 1865. Zimmermanville, Greene Co., O.

ABEL D. HAUGHEY.
Private; enrolled Aug. 8, 1862. Appointed Sergeant April 7, 1863. Wounded in action at Kenesaw Mountain June 22, 1864. Transferred to Veteran Reserve Corps Oct. 23, 1864. Boxley, Hamilton Co., Ind.

FRANK HAVERSTICK.
Private; enrolled Aug. 6, 1862. Appointed Corporal Jan. 8, 1865. Mustered out with regiment. Zimmermanville, Greene Co., O.

JAMES M. HAWES.
Private; enrolled Aug. 9, 1862. Absent, sick at Nashville, Tenn., Dec. 6, 1864. Discharged by order of General Hooker Feb. 2, 1865, Columbus, O. Bowersville, Greene County, Ohio.

HENRY HELMER.
Private; enrolled Aug. 6, 1862. Detailed to Ambulance Corps. Mustered out with regiment. Alpha, Greene Co., O.

CHARLES HUFFMAN.
Enrolled Aug. 8, 1862. Appointed Corporal at muster-in; Sergeant March 14, 1863; First Sergeant April 7, 1863. Mustered out with regiment. Died at St. Joseph, Mo., February, 1884.

RECORD OF COMPANY E.

THOMAS S. HUSTON.
Private; enrolled Aug. 12, 1862. Appointed Corporal April 7, 1863; Sergeant July 15, 1864. Mustered out with regiment. Spring Valley, Greene Co., O.

GEORGE W. HUSTON.
Private; enrolled Aug. 12, 1862. Killed in battle of Resaca, Ga., May 14, 1864.

JOHN HUSSY.
Private; enrolled Aug. 11, 1862. Appointed Corporal Jan. 8, 1865. Mustered out with regiment. Bowersville, Greene Co., O.

ADDISON M. JONES.
Private; enrolled Aug. 13, 1862. Absent, sick at Columbus, O., Jan. 1, 1865. Mustered out at Cleveland, O., May 30, 1865. Bowersville, O.

EMMET JOBE.
Private; enrolled Aug. 9, 1862. Discharged on Surgeon's certificate at Nashville, Tenn., Feb. 11, 1863. Re-enlisted in 8th O. V. C. Captured at Cedar Creek, Va., Oct. 19, 1864. Prisoner of war at Salisbury, N. C. Died while in prison.

DANIEL A. JONES.
Private; enrolled Aug. 12, 1862. Transferred to Veteran Reserve Corps Oct. 29, 1863.

DAVID KELLY.
Private; enrolled Aug. 5, 1862. Mustered out with regiment. Xenia, O.

FRED. H. KEMPT.
Enrolled Aug. 8, 1862. Appointed Corporal at muster-in. Absent, sick in hospital at New Albany, Ind., from July 1, 1863. Transferred to Veteran Reserve Corps Jan. 22, 1864.

JACOB KNEE.
Private; enrolled Aug. 5, 1862. Detached on special duty at Columbus, O., March 1, 1863. Returned to duty with company. Mustered out with regiment.

ADAM KERSHNER.
Private; enrolled Aug. 11, 1862. Wounded at battle of Chickamauga, Ga., Sept. 19, 1863. Absent in hospital at Jeffersonville, Ind. Provision for discharge made by General Order 77, War Department, 1865.

JOHN H. KOOGLER.
Private; enrolled Aug. 11, 1862. Mustered out with regiment. Zimmermanville, Greene Co., O.

OLIVER H. P. KRISE.
Enrolled Aug. 11, 1862. Appointed Corporal at muster-in. Transferred to Veteran Reserve Corps by War Department order June 6, 1863. Alpha, Greene Co., O.

FRED. B. LEDBETTER.
Private; enrolled Aug. 8, 1862. Wounded in action before Atlanta, Ga., July 22, 1864. Mustered out at Nashville, Tenn., May 25, 1865. Xenia, O.

ELIJAH H. LEWIS.
Private; enrolled Aug. 8, 1862. Transferred to Veteran Reserve Corps, Oct. 29, 1863.

ALLEN LUCAS.
Enrolled Aug. 9, 1862. Died at Murfreesboro, Tenn., March 17, 1863.

SOLOMON LUCAS.
Private; enrolled Aug. 7, 1862. Detailed to Pioneers Dec. 11, 1862. Transferred to 1st Regiment U. S. Veteran Volunteer Engineers, S. F. O. 77, Department of the Cumberland. Xenia, O.

JAMES W. LUCAS.
Enrolled Aug. 9, 1862. Appointed Sergeant at muster-in. Detailed to Pioneers. Transferred to 1st Regiment U. S. Veteran Volunteer Engineers July 22, 1864, by S. F. O. 77, Department of the Cumberland. Battle Creek, Mich.

HENRY J. LUTZ.
Private; enrolled Aug. 8, 1862. Mustered out with regiment. Arcadia, Hamilton Co., Indiana.

WILLIAM H. MARTIN.
Private; enrolled Aug. 10, 1862. Mustered out with regiment. Dayton, O.

THE NINETY-FOURTH OHIO.

JACOB MILLER.
 Enrolled Aug. 11, 1862. Appointed Corporal at muster-in; Sergeant April 7, 1863, Drowned October, 1863, at Chattanooga, Tenn.

JOSEPH MILLER.
 Private; enrolled Aug. 7, 1862. Killed in battle of Perryville, Ky., Oct. 8, 1862.

THOMAS McGAUHEY.
 Private; enrolled Oct. 5, 1863. Transferred to 74th O. V. I. at muster-out of regiment. Xenia. O.

SAMUEL NEAL.
 Private; enrolled Aug. 11, 1862. Sent to hospital at Louisville, Ky., Oct. 1, 1862. Mustered out at Louisville, Ky., May 19, 1865.

WILLIAM NOLAN.
 Enrolled Aug. 11, 1862. Appointed Corporal at muster-in. Deserted from Lexington, Ky., Sept. 1, 1862.

EDWARD S. PALMER.
 Private; enrolled Aug. 14, 1862. Absent, sick at Cincinnati, O., from Jan. 6, 1864, to March 1, 1864. Returned to duty. Mustered out with regiment, Fairfield, Green Co., Ohio.

JOHN S. PERKINS.
 Private; enrolled Aug, 13, 1862. Sick in hospital at Nashville, Tenn., from Dec. 18, 1862, to February, 1864. Returned to duty. Mustered out with regiment. Bowersville, Greene Co., O.

SAMUEL H. PIERCE.
 Enrolled Aug. 10, 1862. Appointed First Sergeant at muster-in. Discharged on Surgeon's certificate at Columbus, Dec. 1, 1862. Died.

ROBERT PRATT.
 Private; enrolled Aug. 7, 1862. Mustered out with regiment. Died.

MILO A. RICHESON.
 Private; enrolled Aug. 6, 1862. Mustered out with regiment. Webster, Kosciusko Co., Indiana.

WILLIAM B. RICHESON.
 Private; enrolled Aug. 6, 1862. Mustered out with regiment. Died.

JOHN RIDENOUR.
 Private; enrolled Aug. 12, 1862. Mustered out with regiment.

MARTIN SESLAR.
 Private; enrolled Aug. 13, 1862. Appointed Corporal April 7, 1863; Sergeant Jan. 8, 1865. Mustered out with regiment. Jamestown, O.

ADAM SITES.
 Private; enrolled Aug. 13, 1862. Died at Murfreesboro, Tenn., March 1, 1863.

LOSSING H. SHADLEY.
 Private; enrolled Aug. 13, 1862.

WILLIAM SHANE.
 Private; enrolled Aug. 6, 1862. Mustered out with regiment. Xenia, O.

JOHN N. SHANK.
 Private; enrolled Aug. 6. 1862. Died near Bridgeport, Ala., Jan. 7, 1864.

WILLIAM SMITH.
 Private; enrolled Aug. 11, 1862. Transferred to Veteran Reserve Corps July 27, 1863. Van Wert, O.

GEORGE M. SMITH.
 Private; enrolled Aug. 9, 1862. Died at Lebanon. Ky., Nov. 11, 1862.

WILLIAM F. SNEDIKER.
 Musician; enrolled Aug. 12, 1862. Mustered out with regiment. Fairfield, Greene County, Ohio.

MADISON SPAHR.
 Private; enrolled Aug. 11, 1862. Died at Bowling Green, Ky., Nov. 29, 1863.

RECORD OF COMPANY E.

ARCHIBALD STEEN.
    Private; enrolled Aug. 7, 1862. Absent, sick at Louisville, Ky., from Oct. 29, 1862, to February, 1864. Discharged at Camp Dennison, O., Feb. 13, 1864. New Jasper, O.

JOHN A. STEELE.
    Private; enrolled Aug. 11, 1862. Discharged by order of General Rosecrans May 8, 1863, at Nashville, Tenn. Xenia, O.

JOHN W. STEELE.
    Private; enrolled Aug. 6, 1862. Appointed Corporal April 7, 1863; Sergeant Oct. 20, 1863. Killed in action at Buzzard's Roost, Ga., May 10, 1864.

HENRY STORY.
    Private; enrolled Aug. 12, 1862. Absent, sick since June 23, 1864., at Murfreesboro, Tenn. Mustered out at Columbus, O., June 28, 1865. Bowersville, O.

JAMES R. STEWART.
    Private; enrolled Aug. 6, 1862. Died at Danville, Ky., Dec. 2, 1862.

JOHN C. STEWART.
    Private; enrolled Aug. 6. 1862. Transferred to Veteran Reserve Corps Oct. 22, 1864, by order of War Department.

DAVID W. SWIGART.
    Enrolled Aug. 4, 1862. Appointed Sergeant at muster-in. Transferred to D. P. N. W. Dec. 3, 1863, by order of War Department. Fairfield, O.

WILLIAM TINGLEY.
    Private; enrolled Aug. 12, 1862. Discharged on Surgeon's certificate at Camp Chase, O., Nov. 28, 1864.

MICHAEL TOBIAS.
    Private; enrolled Aug. 11, 1862. Missing on the march to Bowling Green, Ky., Oct. 27, 1862. Prisoner of war. Returned to duty March 31, 1863. Mustered out with regiment. Piqua, O.

JOHN TOBIAS.
    Private; enrolled Aug. 12, 1862. Missing on the March to Bowling Green, Ky., Oct. 27, 1862. Prisoner of war. Returned to duty March 31, 1863. Mustered out with regiment. Alpha, Green Co., O.

HENRY W. TOBIAS.
    Private; enrolled Aug. 11, 1862. Missing on the march from Bowling Green, Ky., Oct. 27, 1862. Prisoner of war. Returned to duty March 31, 1863. Absent, sick at Murfreesboro, Tenn., June 23, 1863. Returned to duty March 1, 1864. Mustered out with regiment. Piqua, O.

JAMES M. TOWNSEND.
    Private; enrolled Aug. 1, 1862. Mustered out with regiment. Latrobe, Athens Co., O.

HARRISON TRUBY.
    Private; enrolled Aug, 11, 1862.

JOHN M. VAN CLEAF.
    Private; enrolled Aug. 11, 1862. Appointed Corporal Oct. 20, 18863. Wounded in action at Kenesaw Mountain, Ga., June 22, 1864. Mustered out with regiment. Dayton, O.

JAMES R. WEAVER.
    Private; enrolled Aug. 5, 1862. Discharged on Surgeon's certificate at Alpha, O., March 24, 1863. Alpha, Greene Co., O.

JOHN W. WIKEL.
    Private; enrolled Aug, 13, 1862. Died at Annapolis, Md., Feb. 9, 1863.

JOSHUA WINGET.
    Private; enrolled Aug. 12. 1862. Absent, sick since June 3, 1864. Mustered out at Columbus, O., July 3, 1865.

DOREMUS WILLISON.
    Private; enrolled Aug. 7, 1862. Died at Byron, O., Feb. 24, 1863.

COMPANY F.

CAPTAIN.

THOMAS H. WORKMAN.
Appointed July 26, 1862. Captured at Lexington, Ky., Sept. 1, 1862. Resigned Nov. 14, 1862. Richmond, Ind.

FIRST LIEUTENANTS.

HENRY A. TOMLINSON.
Appointed Second Lieutenant July 22, 1862. Promoted to First Lieutenant Jan. 25, 1863. Resigned June 21, 1863. Re-enlisted in Co. F Feb. 26, 1865. Detached to Post Band, Columbus, O. Mustered out May 15, 1865. Died at Greenville, O.

WILLIAM D. PUTNAM.
Enrolled July 23, 1862. Appointed Sergeant at muster-in. Promoted to Second Lieutenant Jan. 25, 1863; First Lieutenant Jan. 19, 1864. In command of Company C since July 21, 1864. Mustered out with regiment. Died at Harmer, O., 1884.

ENLISTED MEN.

JOHN ARENS.
Wagoner; enrolled Aug. 2, 1862. Sick at Louisville, Ky., 1862. Discharged on Surgeon's certificate. Ft. Recovery, O.

AMOS A. AKES.
Private; enrolled July 26, 1862. Captured at Chickamauga, Ga., Sept. 19, 1863. Prisoner of war. Died at Andersonville, Ga., June 10, 1864.

LUKE ARNOLD.
Private; enrolled July 25, 1862. Mustered out with regiment. Ansonia, Darke Co., O.

JOHN J. BAUGHMAN
Private; enrolled July 23, 1862. Died at Murfreesboro, Tenn., June 28, 1863.

HENRY BECK.
Enrolled July 25, 1862. Appointed Corporal at muster-in. Detailed to colors. Appointed Sergeant Dec. 1, 1864. Mustered out with regiment. Greenville, O.

DAVID BEERS.
Private; enrolled Aug. 7, 1862. Detached to office of Assistant Topographical Engineers 14th Army Corps Sept. 6, 1862. Mustered out with regiment. Greenville, O.

THERON BELL.
Musician; enrolled Aug. 2, 1862. Discharged on Surgeon's certificate at Columbus, O., Dec. 27, 1862.

ALBERT H. BERRY.
Private; enrolled July 24, 1862. Mustered out with regiment.

WILLIAM H. BIRELY.
Enrolled July 23, 1862. Appointed Corporal at muster-in. Wounded at Kentucky River, Aug. 31, 1862. Discharged Oct. 23, 1862. Arcanum, O.

ABRAHAM BLACK.
Private; enrolled July 28, 1862. Discharged on Surgeon's certificate at Columbus, O., Oct. 6, 1863. Greenville, O.

JACOB BLACKFORD.
Private; enrolled Aug. 2, 1862. Mustered out with regiment. Mt. Heron, Darke Co., O.

GEORGE BRENNER.
Private; enrolled July 25. 1862. Captured near Lexington, Ky., Sept. 1, 1862. Discharged on Surgeon's certificate at Columbus, O., Feb. 20, 1863.

RECORD OF COMPANY F.

FRANK F. BOOKWALTER.
Private; enrolled Aug. 2, 1862. Discharged on Surgeon's certificate at Nashville, Tenn., March 18, 1863. Died.

HEZEKIAH V. BROWN.
Private; enrolled Feb. 23, 1864. Transferred to 74th O. V. V. I. at muster-out of regiment. Portland, Ind.

AZARIAH BRUSS.
Private; enrolled Aug. 1, 1862. Captured near Black River, N. C., March 16, 1865. Prisoner of war at Annapolis, Md., April 1, 1865. Discharged at Camp Chase, O., June 13, 1865. Arcanum, O.

DAVID BYRAM.
Private; enrolled July 20, 1862. Transferred to 1st Regiment U. S. Veteran Volunteer Engineers by Special Field Order No. 77, Department of the Cumberland, July 0, 1864. Discharged at Nashville, Tenn., Sept. 26, 1865. Springfield, O.

ANDREW BRYANT.
Private; enrolled Aug. 7, 1862. Transferred to Veteran Reserve Corps Aug. 1, 1863. New Carlisle, St. Joseph Co., Ind.

GEORGE BRYANT.
Private; enrolled Aug. 1, 1862. Left sick in hospital at Goldsboro, N. C., April 10, 1865. Discharged at Albany, N. Y., May 30, 1865. Galien, Berrien Co., Mich.

EDMOND S. COLE.
Private; enrolled July 31, 1862. Mustered out with regiment. Union City, Ind.

ANDREW CROWELL.
Enrolled July 28, 1862. Appointed Corporal at muster-in. Sick in hospital at muster-out of regiment. Discharged under provisions of General Order No. 77, War Department.

WILLIAM H. CROWELL.
Private; enrolled July 28, 1862. Wounded at battle of Resaca, Ga., May 14, 1864. Died in field hospital near the battle-field May 20, 1864.

ADELBERT CRANDALL.
Private; enrolled Aug. 2, 1862. Captured near Lexington, Ky., Sept. 1, 1862. Discharged on Surgeon's certificate at Columbus, O., April 18, 1863.

ALEXANDER C. DAVIS.
Private; enrolled July 24, 1862. Discharged on Surgeon's certificate at Columbus, O., Oct. 13, 1862.

OBEDIAH DENISE.
Private; enrolled Aug. 3, 1862. Discharged on Surgeon's certificate at Columbus, O., Jan. 1, 1863. Greenville, O.

SAMUEL DeRUSH.
Private; enrolled Aug. 2, 1862. Captured at Chickamauga, Ga., Sept. 19, 1863. Prisoner of war at Andersonville, Ga. Died June 5, 1864.

ROBERT DEVOR.
Private; enrolled July 26, 1862. Died at Louisville, Ky., Dec. 20, 1862.

OLNEY DEVOR.
Private; enrolled Aug. 2, 1862. Sent to Convalescent Camp near Murfreesboro, Tenn., June 23, 1863. Returned to duty. Mustered out with regiment. Died.

JOHN DOUGHERTY.
Private; enrolled Aug. 1, 1862. Left sick at Nolensville, Tenn., Dec. 28, 1862. Captured Dec. 30, 1862. Discharged on Surgeon's certificate March 18, 1863. Hector, Ind.

HUGH DOUGHERTY.
Private; enrolled July 24, 1862. Left sick at Nolensville, Tenn., Dec. 28, 1862. Captured Dec. 30, 1862. Discharged on Surgeon's certificate at Columbus, O., May 14, 1863. Bluffton, Indiana.

ABRAHAM DOUGHERTY.
Private; enrolled July 23, 1862. Discharged on Surgeon's certificate at Bowling Green, Ky., Jan 23, 1863. Died.

SMITH DYE.
Enrolled as private. Appointed Commissary Sergeant July 29, 1863, by Special Order No. 49, headquarters 94th O. V. I. Mustered out with regiment. Greenville, O.

ISAAC DYE.
Private; enrolled Aug. 2, 1862. Discharged on Surgeon's certificate at Columbus, O., March 19, 1865.

JAMES EUBANKS.
Private; enrolled July 28, 1862. Discharged at Louisville, Ky., April 6, 1863, on Surgeon's certificate of disability. New Madison, O.

HENRY V. EUBANKS.
Enrolled July 29, 1862. Appointed Corporal at muster-in. Died in camp near Murfreesboro, Tenn., Feb. 2, 1863.

ALLEN W. FUNK.
Private; enrolled July 26, 1862. Transferred to Veteran Reserve Corps Aug. 1, 1863. Died 1886.

SAMUEL M. GUY.
Private; enrolled July 24, 1862. Discharged on Surgeon's certificate at Columbus, O., Nov. 3, 1863. Greenville, O.

WESLEY GREENWAULT.
Private; enrolled July 24, 1862. Left sick at Nolensville, Tenn., Dec. 28, 1862. Captured Dec. 30, 1862. Returned to duty. Appointed Corporal Nov. 1, 1864. Mustered out with regiment. Tippecanoe City, O.

CHARLES HAAS.
Private; enrolled Aug. 12, 1862. Discharged on Surgeon's certificate at Columbus, O., Oct. 24, 1862.

THOMAS J. HAFNAGLE.
Private; enrolled Aug. 2, 1862. Mustered out with regiment. Union City, Ind.

FRANK HAMILTON.
Private; enrolled Aug. 1, 1862. Discharged on Surgeon's certificate at Columbus, O., March 5, 1863. Winchester, Ind.

CHARLES H. HECKER.
Private; enrolled Aug. 26, 1862. Discharged on Surgeon's certificate at Louisville, Ky., Oct. 24, 1862. Louisburgh, O.

WILLOUGHBY J. HECKER.
Private; enrolled July 25, 1862. Left sick at Nolensville, Tenn., Dec. 28, 1862. Captured Dec. 30, 1862. Prisoner of war at Camp Chase, O. Returned to duty. Mustered out with regiment. Weaver's Station, Darke Co., O.

WILLIAM J. HIMES.
Private; enrolled July 23, 1862. Detailed to Pioneers. Sent to his home in Ohio on account of sickness.

GEORGE V. HIPPLE.
Private, Co. K, 11th O. V. I., "Three Months." Enrolled July 29, 1862. Appointed Corporal at muster-in; Sergeant Nov. 1, 1864. Mustered out with regiment. Killed in Missouri by a railway train March 12, 1883.

CHARLES M. HOOD.
Private; enrolled July 24, 1862.

ISAAC A. JAY.
Private; enrolled Aug. 7, 1862. Captured near Blackwater, N. C., March 16. 1865. Prisoner of war at Annapolis, Md., April 1, 1865. Discharged at Camp Chase, O., June 13, 1865. Jaysville, Darke Co., O.

JOHN H. JUDAY.
Private; enrolled Aug. 1, 1862. Mustered out with regiment. El Dorado, O.

EMANUEL JUDAY.
Private; enrolled Aug. 1, 1862. Discharged on Surgeon's certificate at Louisville, Ky., July 20, 1863. El Dorado, O.

RECORD OF COMPANY F. 139

HENRY KRICKENBERGER.
 Private; enrolled Aug. 1, 1862. Discharged on Surgeon's certificate at Nashville, Tenn., Feb. 13, 1863.

OSCAR B. LAMOTTE.
 Enrolled July 24, 1862. Appointed Corporal at muster-in. Left sick at Nolensville, Tenn., Dec. 28, 1862. Captured December 30, 1862. Prisoner of war at Camp Chase, O. Returned to duty. Promoted Sergeant January 1, 1865. Mustered out with regiment. Bloomington, Ill.

JOHN T. LAWRENCE.
 Private; enrolled Aug. 3, 1862. Transferred to 1st Regiment U. S. Veteran Volunteer Engineers July 20, 1864, by S. F. O. No. 77, headquarters Department of the Cumberland. New Madison, O.

ISAAC N. LOCKET.
 Private; enrolled July 27, 1862. Appointed Hospital Steward Oct. 20, 1863, by Special Order No. 39, headquarters 94th O. V. I. Mustered out with regiment. New Madison, Ohio.

WILLIAM H. MARTIN.
 Private; enrolled July 30, 1862. Died in Hospital at Nashville, Tenn., April 25, 1863.

DAVID MARQUITH.
 Private; enrolled Aug. 2, 1862. Left sick at Bridgeport, Ala., Sept. 4, 1863. Discharged at Camp Dennison, O., May 24, 1865. Greenville, O.

JOHN S. McCLURE.
 Enrolled July 30, 1862. Appointed Corporal at muster-in. Captured at Chickamauga, Ga., Sept. 20, 1863. Escaped from Danville, Va. Returned to duty May 10, 1864. Mustered out with regiment. Union City, Ind.

HIRAM McCLURE.
 Private; enrolled July 31, 1862. Wounded in action at Stone River, Tenn., Dec. 31, 1862. Mustered out with regiment. Union City, Ind.

HENRY McCLURE.
 Enrolled July 29, 1862. Appointed Sergeant at muster-in. Transferred to Veteran Reserve Corps Aug. 1, 1863.

JAMES McCAMPBELL.
 Private; enrolled July 28, 1862. Detached as teamster, headquarters Department of the Cumberland, since Dec. 22, 1863. Provision for discharge made by General Order No. 77, War Department, 1865. Died.

WILLIAM H. McCONNELL.
 Private; enrolled July 29, 1862. Detailed for duty at headquarters 94th O. V. I., 1862. Mustered out with regiment. Greenville, O.

JOHN McCONNELL.
 Private; enrolled Aug. 1, 1862. Discharged on Surgeon's certificate at Cincinnati, O., March 18, 1863.

DAVID H. MILLER.
 Private; enrolled July 25, 1862. Appointed Corporal Nov. 1, 1864. Mustered out with regiment. De Lisle P. O., Darke Co., O.

ARTHUR F. MILLER.
 Private; enrolled July 31, 1862. Absent, sick in hospital, since Dec. 28, 1863. Mustered out under General Order No. 77, War Department, 1865.

JOHN MILLER.
 Private; enrolled Aug. 2, 1862. Killed in action at Atlanta, Ga., Aug. 21, 1864.

ELIAS MUMAH.
 Private; enrolled July 30, 1862. Mustered out with regiment. Hill Grove, Darke Co., Ohio.

REUBEN OHLER.
 Private; enrolled July 31, 1862. Mustered out with regiment. Union City, Ind.

GEORGE W. PAULUS.
 Private; enrolled July 25, 1862. Captured at Chickamauga, Ga., Sept. 19, 1863. Prisoner of war. Died at Andersonville, Ga., Aug. 22, 1864.

THE NINETY-FOURTH OHIO.

GEORGE W. PERRY.
Enrolled Aug. 1, 1862. Appointed Sergeant at muster-in. Promoted to First Sergeant Jan. 1, 1865. Mustered out with regiment. Greenville, O.

HENRY PIPPINGER.
Private; enrolled Aug. 12, 1862. Died in hospital at Nashville, Tenn., Dec. 20, 1862.

JOSEPH RAY.
Private; enrolled July 30, 1862. Transferred to Veteran Reserve Corps May 1, 1865. Mustered out at Cincinnati, O., June 28, 1865. New Madison, O.

DAVID A. RIES.
Private; enrolled July 27, 1862. Discharged on Surgeon's certificate at Louisville, Ky., Sept. 23, 1862. Died.

JOHN H. RIES.
Private; enrolled July 29, 1862. Wounded at Stone River, Tenn., Dec. 31, 1862. Discharged on Surgeon's certificate at Louisville, Ky., May 16, 1863. Greenville, O.

CORNELIUS ROGERS.
Private; enrolled July 28, 1862. Discharged on Surgeon's certificate at Louisville, Ky., Dec. 19, 1862. Tracy, Iowa.

ANDREW C. RUPLE.
Private; enrolled July 29, 1862. Left sick at Kingston, Ga., Nov. 12, 1864. Discharged at St. Louis, Mo., Aug. 17, 1865. Greenville, O.

JOHN RYAN.
Private; enrolled July 30, 1862. Captured at Chickamauga, Ga., Sept. 20, 1863. Prisoner of war. Died at Andersonville, Ga.

DANIEL H. RYAN.
Private; enrolled Aug. 24, 1862. Mustered out with regiment. Greenville, O.

THOMAS B. SHADE.
Private; enrolled Aug. 1, 1862. Discharged on Surgeon's certificate at Louisville, Ky., Nov. 23, 1862.

GEORGE W. SHARP.
Private; enrolled July 29, 1862. Mustered out with regiment. Celina, O.

JOHN SINNARD.
Private; enrolled Aug. 1, 1862. Transferred to Veteran Reserve Corps Aug. 1, 1863. German P. O., Darke Co., O.

WILLIAM E. SMITH.
Private; enrolled July 24, 1862. Left sick at Nolensville, Tenn., Dec. 28, 1862. Captured Dec. 30, 1862. Prisoner of war at Camp Chase, O. Returned to duty. Appointed Corporal Aug. 25, 1863. Wounded at Chickamauga, Ga., Sept. 19, 1863. Returned to duty. Mustered out with regiment. Monticello, Ill.

SAMUEL F. SPROWL.
Private; enrolled July 30, 1862. Mustered out with regiment.

ABRAHAM STUDALAKER.
Private; enrolled July 27, 1862. Discharged on Surgeon's certificate at Goldsboro, N. C., March 27, 1865.

ESTEP STEVENSON.
Private; enrolled July 27, 1862. Left sick at Nolensville, Tenn., Dec. 28, 1862. Captured Dec. 30, 1862. Prisoner of war at Camp Chase, O. Returned to duty. Mustered out with regiment. Greenville, O.

SQUIRE W. STUBBS.
Private; enrolled July 26, 1862. Appointed Corporal at muster-in. Transferred to Veteran Reserve Corps Aug. 1, 1863. Greenville, O.

WILSON W. SWATHWOOD.
Private; enrolled July 25, 1862. Missing on the march to Goldsboro, N. C., March 16, 1865. Paroled prisoner at Annapolis, Md., April 1, 1865. Discharged at Camp Chase, O., June 16, 1865.

MALYN SWARTZ.
Private; enrolled Aug. 1, 1862. Discharged on Surgeon's certificate at Columbus, O., Nov. 6, 1862. Greenville, O.

RECORD OF COMPANY F.

ANDERSON TILMAN.
  Private; enrolled July 24, 1862, Mustered out with regiment. De Lisle, O.
WALTER J. TODD.
  Private; enrolled Aug. 2, 1862. Discharged on Surgeon's certificate at Columbus, O., May 20, 1863. Greenville, O.
ISAAC TUCKER.
  Private; enrolled Aug. 2, 1862. Died in hospital at Murfreesboro, Tenn., June 19, 1863.
ELI UNDERWOOD.
  Private; enrolled Aug. 1, 1862. Transferred to Veteran Reserve Corps Aug. 1, 1863.
JOHN VANTILBURGH.
  Enrolled July 28, 1862. Appointed Sergeant at muster-in. Wounded at Kenesaw Mountain June 22, 1864. Mustered out at Camp Dennison, O., May 24, 1865. Indianapolis, Ind.
WILLIAM H. VANTILBURGH.
  Private; enrolled July 26, 1862. Died at Bowling Green, Ky., Nov. 23, 1862.
GEORGE E. VANDYKE.
  Private; enrolled July 25, 1862. Left sick at Nolensville, Tenn., Dec. 28, 1862. Captured Dec. 30, 1862. Discharged on Surgeon's certificate at Columbus, O., May 14, 1863. Ansonia, Darke Co., O.
ELI WAGAMAN.
  Private; enrolled July 31, 1862. Died in hospital at Nashville, Tenn., Dec. 24, 1862.
PERRY F. WIKLE.
  Private; enrolled Aug. 2, 1862. Killed at Kentucky River (Tates Creek pike) Aug. 31, 1862.
MILO J. WILSON.
  Private; enrolled July 26, 1862. Mustered out with regiment. Scranton, Pa.
MANLIUS WILCOX.
  Private; enrolled July 30, 1862. Died in hospital at Nashville, Tenn., Feb. 21, 1863.
DAVID R. WILLIAMS.
  Private; enrolled Aug. 7, 1862. Left sick at Louisville, Ky., Oct. 1, 1862. Provision for discharge made by General Order No. 77, War Department, series 1865.
NATHAN W. WILCOX.
  Private; enrolled July 30, 1862.
EPHRAIM YOST.
  Private; enrolled Aug. 1, 1862. Transferred to Veteran Reserve Corps Jan. 16, 1864. Greenville, O.

COMPANY G.

CAPTAIN.

NATHAN M. McCONKEY.
　　Appointed First Lieutenant Aug. 8, 1862. Promoted to Captain Jan. 20, 1864. Mustered out with regiment. Died near Springfield, O., July 9, 1882

FIRST LIEUTENANTS.

GEORGE W. WILSON.
　　Appointed Second Lieutenant Aug. 8, 1862. Promoted to First Lieutenant Jan. 20, 1864. Mustered out Aug. 24, 1864, to accept promotion to Captain 1st Regiment U. S. Veteran Volunteer Engineers. Mustered out at the close of the war. London, O.

MORRISON M. MARQUITH.
　　Enrolled as private Co. F Aug. 11, 1862. Appointed Sergeant-Major April 17, 1863, Special Order No. 27, headquarters 94th O. V. I. Promoted to First Lieutenant Sept. 22, 1864. Assigned to Co. G. In command of Co. F since Dec. 1, 1864. Mustered out with regiment. West Liberty, O.

ENLISTED MEN.

JOHN W. BALL.
　　Private; enrolled Aug. 8, 1862. Appointed Corporal April 5, 1864. Mustered out with regiment.

BENJAMIN BARRINGER.
　　Private; enrolled Aug. 9, 1862. Discharged on Surgeon's certificate at Louisville, Ky., April 6, 1863.

ISAAC L. BAUMGARDNER.
　　Private; enrolled Aug. 2, 1862. Discharged on Surgeon's certificate at Chattanooga, Tenn., Dec. 22, 1863.

GEORGE W. BAUMGARDNER.
　　Private; enrolled Aug. 2, 1862. Missing near Black Stock, S. C., Feb. 23, 1865. Prisoner of war. Mustered out under General Order No. 77, War Department, 1865.

JAMES BEASON.
　　Private; enrolled Aug. 9, 1862. Died at Murfreesboro, Tenn., Jan. 25, 1863.

GEORGE W. BEASON.
　　Private; enrolled Aug. 11, 1862. Died at Nashville, Tenn., Jan. 9, 1863.

WALES A. BELL.
　　Private; enrolled Oct. 10, 1863. Killed in battle of Resaca, Ga., May 14, 1864.

HENRY C. BIRELY.
　　Private; enrolled Oct. 11, 1863. Transferred to 74th O. V. I. at muster-out of regiment. La Rue, O.

WILLIAM H. BRIGHAM.
　　Enrolled Aug. 6, 1862. Appointed Corporal at muster-in.

GEORGE W. BYMASTER.
　　Private; enrolled Aug. 8, 1862. Wounded at battle of Resaca, Ga., May 14, 1864. Mustered out at Louisville, Ky., May 19, 1865. Springfield, O.

WILLIAM H. CLAYTON.
　　Private; enrolled Aug. 8, 1862. Discharged on Surgeon's certificate at Louisville, Ky., Oct. 15, 1862.

DAVID COVER.
　　Private; enrolled Aug. 11, 1862.

RECORD OF COMPANY G. 143

MALYN COX.
Private; enrolled Aug. 6, 1862. Died at Murfreesboro, Tenn., March 3, 1863.

JAMES B. CROSS.
Enrolled July 25, 1862. Appointed First Sergeant at muster-in. Promoted to First Lieutenant March 3, 1864. Awaiting muster. Killed in battle of Resaca, Ga., May 14, 1864.

SAMUEL G. CREAMER.
Private; enrolled July 31, 1862. Mustered out with regiment.

ANDREW CREAMER.
Private; enrolled Aug. 5, 1862, Died at Louisville, Ky., Nov. 15, 1862.

CORNELIUS CHRIST.
Private; enrolled Aug. 8, 1862.

ARCHIBALD DAVIS.
Private; enrolled Ang. 4, 1862. Died at Louisville, Ky., Dec. 5, 1862.

JACOB M. DEMORY.
Private; enrolled Oct. 10, 1863. Died at Chattanooga, Tenn., Aug. 3, 1864.

JOHN W. DULANEY.
Private; enrolled Aug. 5, 1862. Captured at Chickamauga, Ga. Died at Andersonville, Ga., July 16, 1864.

JOHN DUTRO.
Private; enrolled Aug. 11, 1862, Killed in action at Bentonville, N. C., March 19, 1865.

JACOB M. ELLSWORTH.
Enrolled Aug. 2, 1862. Appointed Corporal at muster-in. Charged with desertion from Louisville, Ky., Oct. 20, 1862. The following copy is made from detachment rolls in the Adjutant-General's office, Columbus, O.: "Mustered out to date from Oct. 20, 1862, in compliance with indorsement on papers in the case. The charge of desertion is removed by special order, headquarters Department of the Lakes, Detroit, Mich., Nov. 7, 1867, Brevet Major-General Robinson commanding."—GEORGE D. RUGGLES, A. A. G.

JESSE M. EVANS.
Private; enrolled Aug. 2, 1862. Discharged at Bowling Green, Ky., Feb. 12, 1863.

WILLIAM EVANS.
Private; enrolled Aug. 11, 1862. Sick in hospital at Chattanooga, Tenn., May 2, 1864. Mustered out at Cincinnati, O., May 27, 1865. Huntsville, Logan Co., O.

WILLIAM C. EVERHART.
Private; enrolled July 31, 1862. Transferred to Veteran Reserve Corps by General Order No. 352, War Department, series of 1864. Mustered out at the close of the war. Horrs P. O., Clarke Co., O.

WILLIAM F. FAUBER.
Enrolled Aug. 8, 1862. Appointed Sergeant at muster-in.

THOMAS B. FINNEY.
Musician; enrolled Aug. 6, 1862. Mustered out with regiment. Died.

JOSEPH H. FISHER.
Private; enrolled Sept. 2, 1863. Discharged on Surgeon's certificate at Camp Dennison, O., Sept. 27, 1864. National Military Home, Dayton, O.

ENOS N. FERGUSON.
Private; enrolled Aug. 7, 1862. Discharged on Surgeon's certificate at Louisville, Ky., July 31, 1863.

ABSALOM J. FULLER.
Private; enrolled Aug. 6, 1862. Detached to Pioneer Corps 1863. Mustered out at Louisville, Ky., May 13, 1865.

BENJAMIN GOLDEN.
Enrolled Aug. 7, 1862. Appointed Sergeant as muster-in. Transferred to Veteran Reserve Corps by General Order No. 271, War Department, 1863. Catawba, Clarke Co., O.

JACOB HAMMOND.
Private; enrolled Aug. 6, 1862. Discharged on Surgeon's certificate at Nashville, Tenn., Jan. 10, 1863.

DAVID B. HALE.
  Enrolled Aug. 7, 1862. Appointed Corporal at muster-in; Sergeant March 17, 1864. Wounded at Resaca, Ga., May 14, 1864. Returned to duty June 14, 1864. Slightly wounded at Bentonville, N. C., March 19, 1865. Mustered out with regiment. West Liberty, Ohio.

GEORGE W. HARRIS.
  Enrolled Aug. 5, 1862. Appointed Corporal at muster-in. Died at Murfreesboro, Tenn., Jan. 21, 1863.

WILLIAM J. HARRIS.
  Private; enrolled Aug. 5, 1862. Discharged on Surgeon's certificate at Louisville, Ky., Sept. 17, 1863. Somerford, Medina Co., O.

SAMUEL HARTLEY.
  Private; enrolled Aug. 7, 1862. Mustered out with regiment. Catawba, Clarke Co., O.

THOMAS HARDIN.
  Private; enrolled Aug. 5, 1862. Wounded in battle of Resaca, Ga., May 14, 1864. Died May 20, 1864, at Chattanooga, Tenn.

JACOB HARNISH.
  Private; enrolled Aug. 11, 1862. Missing in action at Stone River, Tenn., Dec. 31, 1862. risoner of war. Mustered out at Camp Chase, O., June 28, 1865.

MARFLITT HAWKINS.
  Enrolled Aug. 7, 1862. Appointed Corporal at muster-in; Sergeant April 5, 1864. Mus- ered out with regiment. Linwood, Hamilton Co., O.

WILLIAM HILL.
  Private; enrolled Aug. 9, 1862. Appointed Corporal March 14, 1864. Wounded in action at Bentonville, N. C., March 19, 1865. Died at Newbern, N. C., April 5, 1865.

JOHN HOOVER.
  Private; enrolled July 31, 1862. Discharged on Surgeon's certificate at Chattanooga, Tenn., Nov. 8, 1863. Died at the National Military Home, Dayton, O., April 30, 1878.

JOHN W. JOHNSON.
  Private; enrolled Aug. 8, 1862. Died at Murfreesboro, Tenn., Jan. 31, 1863.

SANDESKY JONES.
  Private; enrolled Aug. 7, 1862. Mustered out with regiment. North Topeka, Kas.

WILLIAM JONES.
  Private; enrolled Aug. 9, 1862. Appointed Corporal April 15, 1864. Mustered out with regiment. Metcalf P. O., Edgar Co., Ills.

SYLVESTER JONES.
  Private; enrolled Aug. 5, 1862. Died Nov. 28, 1862, from the effects of a wound received at Perryville Oct. 8, 1862.

JESSE JUDY.
  Private; enrolled Aug. 9, 1862. Sent to hospital at Marietta, Ga., July 15, 1864. Pro- vision made for discharge by General Order No. 77, War Department, series 1865.

HENRY O. LAYBOURN.
  Private; enrolled Aug. 9, 1862. Died at Nashville, Tenn., Oct. 23, 1863.

JAMES LANG.
  Private; enrolled Aug. 8. 1862. Transferred to Veteran Reserve Corps by General Order No. 352, War Department, series 1864. Mustered out June 13, 1865, at Cairo. Ills.

JULIUS LINTNER.
  Private; enrolled Aug. 2, 1862. Mustered out with regiment. Mechanicsburg, O.

JAMES LOCKHART.
  Private; enrolled Aug. 2, 1862. Killed in battle at Stone River, Tenn., Dec. 31, 1862.

JOHN LOCKHART.
  Private; enrolled Aug. 2, 1862. Mustered out with regiment. Catawba.

JOHN H. LOCKHART.
  Private; enrolled Aug. 7, 1862. Left sick in hospital at Bowling Green, Ky., 1862. Discharged from hospital.

RECORD OF COMPANY G.

MICHAEL MACKLIN.
 Private; enrolled Aug. 10, 1862. Mustered out with regiment. Died at Soldiers' Home, Dayton, O., May 24, 1881.

HIRAM L. McCONKEY.
 Enrolled Aug. 7, 1862. Appointed Sergeant at Muster-in. Appointed First Sergeant May 14, 1864. Mustered out with regiment. Catawba, O.

GEORGE W. McCORKLE.
 Private; enrolled Aug. 9, 1862. Mustered out with regiment. Somerford, Medina Co. Ohio.

LEVI McLINTOC.
 Wagoner; enrolled Aug. 14, 1862. Died at Murfreesboro, Tenn., Feb. 5, 1863.

JAMES MELONA.
 Private; enrolled Aug. 9, 1862. Discharged at Chattanooga, Tenn., Jan. 27, 1864.

CHRISTIAN MUMA.
 Private; enrolled Aug. 2, 1862. Died at Lebanon, Ky., Oct. 30, 1862.

WILLIAM H. NEAR.
 Private; enrolled Aug. 6, 1862. Wounded in action at Resaca, Ga., May 14, 1864. Mustered out at Columbus, O., July 3, 1865. Catawba, O.

JAMES NEAR.
 Private; enrolled Aug. 2, 1862. Transferred to Veteran Reserve Corps by General Order No. 352, War Department, series 1864. Catawba, O.

ISAAC D. PRICE.
 Private; enrolled Aug. 5, 1862. Discharged on Surgeon's certificate at Cleveland, O., Sept. 23, 1864. Brookfield, Trumbull Co., O.

JOCKLIN H. PHILLIPS.
 Enrolled Aug. 2, 1862. Appointed Sergeant at muster-in. Missing on the march near Black River, N. C., March 16, 1865.

FRANCIS M. PALMER.
 Private; enrolled Aug. 7, 1862. Died at Bowling Green, Ky., Nov. 18, 1862.

GEORGE L. PEARSON.
 Private; enrolled Aug. 7, 1862. Mustered out with regiment. Catawba, O.

JOHN S. RICHIE.
 Private; enrolled Aug. 7, 1862. Captured at White Pond, S. C., Feb. 12, 1865. Provision for discharge made by General Order No. 77, War Department, series 1865.

ISAAC M. ROBERTS.
 Private; enrolled Aug. 7, 1862. Mustered out with regiment. New Moorefield, Clarke County, Ohio.

DANIEL M. ROBERTS.
 Private; enrolled Aug. 7, 1862. Transferred to Veteran Reserve Corps by General Order No. 352, War Department, series 1864. Mexico, Mo.

ELI ROPP.
 Private; enrolled Aug. 2, 1862. Appointed Corporal Jan. 16, 1865. Mustered out with regiment.

JOHN W. ROPP.
 Private; enrolled Aug. 2, 1862. Mustered out with regiment. Catawba, O.

ER. ROHR.
 Private; enrolled Aug. 11, 1862. Died at Nashville, Tenn., March 2, 1863.

WILLIAM B. SHANKS.
 Private; enrolled Oct. 24, 1863. Transferred to 74th O. V. I. at muster-out of regiment. Dunkirk, Hardin Co., O.

WILLIAM SMALLWOOD.
 Private; enrolled July 14, 1862. Transferred to Veteran Reserve Corps by General Order No. 352, 1864, War Department. Mustered out Feb. 7, 1865, on Surgeon's certificate.

GEORGE SLUSSER.
 Private; enrolled Aug. 19, 1862. Discharged on Surgeon's certificate at Nashville, Tenn., Aug. 5, 1863. National Military Home, Dayton, O.

JOEL STEVENSON.
Private; enrolled Aug. 7, 1862. Died at Nashville, Tenn., Feb. 26, 1863.

ALEXANDER STEVENSON.
Private; enrolled Aug. 7, 1862. Died at Nashville, Tenn., Dec. 13, 1862.

JESSE TARBUTTON.
Enrolled Aug. 2, 1862. Detailed as musician 1863. Mustered out with regiment. Catawba, O.

STEVEN D. TAYLOR.
Private; enrolled Aug. 9, 1862. Killed in battle of Stone River, Tenn., Dec. 31, 1862.

FLAVIUS TAVENDER.
Private; enrolled Aug. 2, 1862. Transferred to Veteran Reserve Corps by General Order No. 352, 1864, War Department.

AARON S. TURNER.
Enrolled Aug. 5, 1862. Appointed Corporal at muster-in. Mustered out with regiment. Marysville, O.

FRANKLIN B. TURNER.
Enrolled Aug. 5, 1862. Appointed Corporal at muster-in. Transferred to 1st Regiment Veteran Volunteer Engineers by Special Field Order No. 77, headquarters Department of the Cumberland, July 20, 1864. Belvidere, Neb.

WILLIAM WALLACE.
Private; enrolled Aug. 8, 1862. Discharged on Surgeon's certificate at Louisville, Ky., Feb. 17, 1863.

HENRY WILSON.
Private; enrolled Aug. 21, 1862. Mustered out with regiment.

JOHNSON WILSON.
Private; enrolled Aug. 5, 1862. Mustered out with regiment. Vienna Cross Roads, O.

JOHN WILSON.
Private; enrolled Aug. 5, 1862. Transferred to Veteran Reserve Corps by General Order No. 276, War Department, series 1863. London, O.

HARRISON WILSON.
Enrolled Aug. 5, 1862. Appointed Corporal at muster-in. Discharged on Surgeon's certificate at Murfreesboro, Tenn., April 22, 1863. London, O.

EDMOND B. WILTISON.
Private; enrolled Aug. 7, 1862. Mustered out with regiment. Catawba, O

JOSEPH WALTMAN.
Private; enrolled Aug. 9, 1862. Missing near Black Stock, S. C., Feb. 23, 1865. Prisoner of war. Mustered out at Camp Chase, O., June 13, 1865. Catawba, O.

FELIX WINGFIELD.
Private; enrolled Aug. 7, 1862. Discharged at Louisville, Ky., March 12, 1863, on account of wounds received at battle of Perryville, Ky., Oct. 8, 1862.

ISAIAH WOOD.
Private; enrolled Aug. 6, 1862. Appointed Corporal March 14, 1864. Discharged at Camp Dennison, O., Dec. 2, 1864, on account of wounds received at battle of Resaca, Ga. Catawba, O.

WILLIAM YOUNG.
Private; enrolled Aug. 7, 1862. Died at Murfreesboro, Tenn., April 15, 1863.

COMPANY H.

CAPTAINS.

JAMES KYLE.
Appointed Captain Aug. 8, 1862. Resigned Feb. 20, 1863. Died at Xenia Oct. 9, 1887.

DAVID T. DAVIDSON.
Appointed Second Lieutenant July 23, 1862. Left sick at Nolensville, Tenn., Dec. 28, 1862. Prisoner of war. Returned to duty. Promoted to Captain March 10, 1863. Resigned Nov. 5, 1863. Xenia, O.

ANDREW GOWAN.
Enrolled as private Aug. 7, 1862. Appointed Sergeant at muster-in. Promoted to Second Lieutenant April 7, 1863; First Lieutenant April 16, 1864; Captain Jan. 20, 1865. Mustered out with regiment.

FIRST LIEUTENANTS.

ALFRED L. TRADER.
Appointed July 23, 1862. Missing on the march near Lexington Sept. 1, 1862. Prisoner of war. Returned to duty February, 1863. Resigned March 25, 1863. Died at Xenia, O., March 21, 1870.

HARVEY N. ARNOLD.
Private Co. K, 11th O. V. I., April to June, 1861. Enrolled as private Co. I, 94th O. V. I., Aug. 11, 1862. Appointed First Sergeant at muster-in. Promoted to First Lieutenant Jan 6, 1865. Assigned to Company H. Mustered out with regiment. Greenville, O.

ENLISTED MEN.

JAMES H. ARCHIBALD.
Private; enrolled Oct. 20, 1863. Transferred to 74th O. V. I. at muster-out of regiment. Died at National Military Home, Dayton, O., May 12, 1869.

WILLIAM BAIR.
Enrolled Aug. 7, 1862. Appointed First Sergeant at muster-in. Discharged at Columbus, O., Dec. 30, 1862, by general order of War Department. Died Dec. 12, 1886, at Baltimore, Md.

ANDREW H. BLACK.
Private; enrolled Aug. 13, 1862. Discharged on Surgeon's certificate at Camp Dennison, O., Sept. 30, 1863. Xenia, O.

JACOB BROCIES.
Private; enrolled Aug. 11, 1862. Detailed to headquarters' train, Department of the Cumberland, Dec. 27, 1863. Mustered out at Chattanooga, Tenn., June 8, 1865. Crawfordsville, Ind.

JOHN G. BULL.
Private; enrolled Aug. 11, 1862. Appointed Corporal March 1, 1863. Discharged on Surgeon's certificate at Camp Dennison, O., Oct. 25, 1864.

JOHN H. BULL.
Private; enrolled Aug. 8, 1862. Detailed as provost guard, headquarters 1st Brigade, 1st Division, 14th Army Corps, Colonel Scribner, December, 1862. Returned to duty with company. Wounded at battle of Resaca, Ga., May 14, 1864. Died from wounds June 23, 1864.

JAMES E. BULL.
Private; enrolled Aug. 12, 1862. Mustered out with regiment.

DANIEL BUCKLEY.
Private; enrolled Aug. 9, 1862. Discharged on Surgeon's certificate at Nashville, Tenn., Feb. 27, 1863. Eris, Champaign Co., O.

DAVID D. CHANEY.
Private; enrolled Aug. 11, 1862. Discharged on Surgeon's certificate at Louisville, Ky., Aug. 8, 1863.

JOHN A. CHRISTY.
Private; enrolled Aug. 8, 1862. Died in hospital at Danville, Ky., Nov. 6, 1862.

JAMES CLARK.
Private; enrolled Aug. 13, 1862. Died in hospital at Murfreesboro, Tenn., May 25, 1863.

WILLIAM CLIFTON.
Private; enrolled July 27, 1862. Transferred to Veteran Reserve Corps by general order of War Department 1863.

ROBERT T. COOPER.
Private; enrolled Aug. 12, 1862. Mustered out with regiment. Washington, Dubois Co., Ind.

HUGH M. COOPER.
Private; enrolled Aug. 8, 1862. Sent to hospital at Cincinnati, O., March 20, 1863. Provision for discharge made by General Order No. 77, War Department, 1865. Died at Monmouth, Ill., Feb. 18, 1871.

DANIEL CONNARD.
Private; enrolled Aug. 2, 1862. Missing on the march from Kentucky River, Sept. 1, 1862. Prisoner of war at Camp Chase, O. Returned to duty Jan. 17, 1863. Appointed Corporal Nov. 1, 1864. Mustered out with regiment. Addison, Champaign Co., O.

WILLIAM H. CRAWFORD.
Private; enrolled Aug. 13, 1862. Discharged on Surgeon's certificate at Columbus, O., April 18, 1863. Wapakoneta, O.

LEWIS H. DEAN.
Private; enrolled Aug. 12, 1862. Mustered out with regiment. Pawnee City, Neb.

GIBBERT DEHART.
Private; enrolled Aug. 13, 1862. Wounded at Perryville, Ky. Killed in battle of Resaca, Ga., May 14, 1864.

JAMES DOOLE.
Private; enrolled Aug. 11, 1862. Killed in a skirmish near Kentucky River, Sept. 1, 1862.

LEWIS DUKE.
Private; enrolled Aug. 9, 1862. Mustered out with regiment.

HENRY H. EAVEY.
Private; enrolled Aug. 12, 1862. Missing on the march near Lexington, Ky., Sept. 1, 1862. Prisoner of war at Camp Chase, O. Discharged on Surgeon's certificate at Columbus, O., Oct 21, 1862. Xenia, O.

GRANVILLE P. EDSALL.
Private; enrolled Aug. 13, 1862. Missing on the march near Lexington, Ky., Sept. 1, 1862. Prisoner of war at Camp Chase, O. Transferred to Veteran Reserve Corps April 10, 1864, by general order of War Department. Eaton, O.

HENRY EICHMAN.
Enrolled July 29, 1862. Borne on the rolls as Henry Oakman. Detailed to regimental hospital. Mustered out with regiment. Xenia, O.

JOHN EYLER.
Private; enrolled Aug. 11, 1862. Missing on the march near Lexington, Ky., Sept. 1, 1862. Prisoner of war at Camp Chase, O. Returned to duty Jan. 17, 1863. Mustered out with regiment. Xenia, O.

RECORD OF COMPANY H.

WILLIAM H. FOREMAN.
Wagoner; enrolled Aug. 9, 1862. Discharged on Surgeon's certificate at Louisville, Ky., April 8, 1863. Died at Xenia, O.

SAMUEL FURGESON.
Private; enrolled June 23, 1862. Missing at battle of Chickamauga, Ga., Sept. 19, 1863. Prisoner of war at Andersonville, Ga. Provision for discharge made by General Order No. 77, War Department, series 1865. Died.

GEORGE R. GILLETT.
Musician; enrolled Aug. 9, 1862. Left sick at Nolensville, Tenn., Dec. 28, 1862. Prisoner of war at Camp Chase, O. Returned to duty. Appointed Chief Musician 94th O. V. I. Nov. 9, 1864. Mustered out with regiment. Minden, Neb.

WILLIAM N. GILLETT.
Private; enrolled Aug. 9, 1862. Detailed to Ambulance Corps, headquarters 1st Divison, 14th Army Corps Feb. 6, 1864. Mustered out with regiment. Died.

LEWIS GILBERT.
Private; enrolled July 28, 1862. Missing on the march near Lexington, Ky., Sept. 1, 1862. Prisoner of war at Camp Chase, O. Returned to duty. Mustered out with regiment. Cedarville, O.

SAMUEL GOWDY.
Private; enrolled Aug. 12, 1862. Mustered out with regiment. Died.

JAMES A. GOWDY.
Private; enrolled Aug. 11, 1862. Discharged on Surgeon's certificate at Louisville, Ky., Nov. 10, 1862. Died.

GEORGE V. GOODE.
Private; enrolled Aug. 8, 1862. Captured near Lexington, Ky., Sept. 1, 1862. Prisoner of war at Camp Chase, O. Discharged on Surgeon's certificate at Columbus, O., Nov. 11, 1862. Re-enlisted in gunboat service.

WILLIAM H. H. GOE.
Private; enrolled Aug. 11, 1862. Appointed Sergeant June 10, 1863. Mustered out with regiment.

JASPER N. GREEN.
Private; enrolled July 29, 1862. Captured at Lexington, Ky., Sept. 1, 1862. Prisoner of war. Returned to duty. Died June 26, 1864, from wounds received at battle of Resaca, Ga., May 14, 1864.

JAMES A. HARPER.
Private; enrolled Aug. 11, 1862. Discharged on Surgeon's certificate at Nashville, Tenn., Feb. 27, 1863. Xenia, O.

SAMUEL HEATHCOCK.
Private; enrolled Aug. 9, 1862. Mustered out with regiment. Cedarville, O.

WILLIAM P. HOLTZOPLE.
Private; enrolled Aug. 12, 1862. Mustered out with regiment. Xenia, O.

FINLEY HOPKINS.
Private; enrolled Aug. 8, 1862. Missing on the march near Lexington, Ky., Sept. 1, 1862. Prisoner of war at Camp Chase, O. Discharged on Surgeon's certificate at Columbus, O., Oct. 24, 1862. Xenia, O.

JACOB P. HORNER.
Private; enrolled Aug. 8, 1862. Discharged on Surgeon's certificate at Cincinnati, O., March 12, 1863. Died at Cedarville, O., July 21, 1882.

WESLEY HUDSON.
Private; enrolled Aug. 11, 1862. Wounded before Atlanta, Ga., Aug. 7, 1864. In hospital at Camp Dennison, O., April 28, 1865. Discharged under General Order No. 77, War Department, 1865. Xenia, O.

JOHN R. JACOBY.
Private; enrolled Aug. 12, 1862. Killed in battle at Perryville Oct. 8, 1862.

THE NINETY-FOURTH OHIO.

ANDREW JACKSON.
Private; enrolled Aug. 8, 1862. Wounded in battle at Perryville, Ky., Oct. 8, 1862. Detailed to headquarters 1st Brigade, 1st Division, 14th Army Corps, by Special Order No. 9, dated March 20, 1863. Detached to Ordinance Office, Nashville, Tenn., Nov. 16, 1864. Mustered out at Nashville, Tenn., June 3, 1865. Cedarville, O.

WILLIAM JONES.
Private; enrolled Aug. 11, 1862. Discharged on Surgeon's certificate at Nashville, Tenn., Jan. 13, 1863. Died.

ALERED JONES.
Private; enrolled Aug. 11, 1862. Killed in battle at Resaca, Ga., May 14, 1864.

PATTERSON JONES.
Private; enrolled Aug. 11. 1862. Borne on the rolls as "Patrick Jones." Mustered out with regiment. Died at Covington, O., September, 1887.

ISAAC P. KELLY.
Private; enrolled Aug, 6, 1862. Detailed in Louisville, Ky. Mustered out. Died at Louisville, Ky., September, 1887.

JAMES H. KYLE.
Private; enrolled Aug. 13, 1862. Appointed Corporal June 10, 1863. Wounded at Bentonville, N. C., March 19, 1865. Lost right arm. Discharged at New York Sept. 28, 1865. Xenia, O.

ISAAC R. LANE.
Enrolled Aug. 5, 1862. Appointed Corporal at muster-in; Sergeant, Aug. 16, 1863. Detailed to office of Assistant Adjutant-General, headquarters 14th Army Corps, Dec. 30, 1863. Mustered out with regiment. Barnesville, O.

THOMAS LEARY.
Private; enrolled July 31, 1862.

ABNER L. LEACH.
Private; enrolled Aug. 14, 1862. Detailed as teamster. Mustered out with regiment.

JAMES LIDDELL.
Private; enrolled Aug. 8, 1862. Mustered out with regiment. Xenia, O.

ROBERT LITTLE.
Private; enrolled Aug. 12, 1862. Discharged on Surgeon's certificate at Cowan Station, Tenn., Aug. 11, 1863. Paxton, Ills.

JOHN C. LOVETT.
Private; enrolled July 28, 1862. Missing on the march near Lexington, Ky., Sept. 1, 1862. Prisoner of war at Camp Chase. Returned to duty. Mustered out with regiment. Xenia, O.

ISAAC MARTIN.
Private; enrolled Aug. 9, 1862. Appointed Sergeant March 1, 1863. Discharged on Surgeon's certificate Aug. 8, 1863. Xenia, O.

EVAN B. McCORD.
Private; enrolled Aug. 15, 1862.

PHILIP L. McDOWELL.
Enrolled Aug. 8, 1862. Appointed Corporal at muster-in. Discharged on Surgeon's certificate at Nashville, Tenn., Feb. 5, 1863. Kenton, O.

HUGH McQUISTON.
Private; enrolled Aug. 12, 1862. Left sick at Nolensville, Tenn., Dec. 28, 1862. Prisoner of war at Camp Chase, O. Discharged on Surgeon's certificate at Columbus, O., March 25, 1863. Xenia, O.

JAMES P. McFARLAND.
Private; enrolled Aug. 8, 1862. Appointed Corporal March 1, 1863; Sergeant, Nov. 1, 1864. Mustered out with regiment. South Charleston, O.

RECORD OF COMPANY H.

JOHN G. McPHERSON.
Enrolled Aug. 8, 1862. Appointed Corporal at muster-in; Sergeant, April 7, 1863; First Sergeant, May 15, 1864. Mustered out with regiment. Xenia, O.

JOHN A. MILLER.
Private; enrolled Aug. 11, 1862. Discharged on Surgeon's certificate at Louisville, Ky., April 8, 1863. Died 1886.

CHARLES H. MILLER.
Enrolled Aug. 12, 1862. Appointed Corporal at muster-in. Missing on the march to Lexington, Ky., Sept. 1, 1862. Prisoner of war. Discharged on Surgeon's certificate at Cincinnati, O., Nov. 19, 1862. Cincinnati, O.

CLINTON C. NICHOLS.
Enrolled Aug. 7, 1862. Appointed Sergeant at muster-in. Discharged on Surgeon's certificate at Louisville, Ky., Nov. 10, 1863. Wilmington, O.

SIMEON OLDHAM.
Private; enrolled Aug. 12, 1862. Discharged on Surgeon's certificate at Columbus, O., Oct. 29, 1862. Xenia, O.

ABNER W. OLDHAM.
Private: enrolled Aug. 13, 1862. Discharged on Surgeon's certificate at Camp Dennison, O., December, 1863. Xenia, O.

DAVID A. PATTERSON.
Private; enrolled Aug. 11, 1862. Mustered out with regiment. Cincinnati, O.

JOHN A. PHILLIPS.
Private; enrolled July 29, 1862. Mustered out with regiment. Cedarville, O.

VESPASIAN POTTLE.
Musician; enrolled Aug. 13, 1862. Mustered out with regiment. Dayton, O.

GEORGE W. POTTLE.
Enrolled Aug. 13, 1862. Appointed Corporal at muster-in. Discharged on Surgeon's certificate at Nashville, Tenn., April 25, 1863. Spring Valley, Greene Co., O.

HARRISON K. PUTNAM.
Private; enrolled Aug. 11, 1862. Transferred to Mississippi Marine Brigade, at St. Louis, April 2, 1863, by general order of War Department.

ALBERT RADER.
Private; enrolled Aug. 8, 1862. Missing on the march from Kentucky River Sept. 1, 1862. Prisoner of war at Camp Chase, O. Discharged on Surgeon's certificate at Columbus, O., Oct. 24, 1862. Xenia, O.

LEVI RADER.
Enrolled Aug. 11, 1862. Appointed Corporal at muster-in. Discharged on Surgeon's certificate at Madison, Ind., Dec. 5. 1863. Jamestown. O.

JOHN F. SHEARER.
Enrolled Aug. 8, 1862. Appointed Corporal March 1, 1863; Sergeant Jan. 7, 1863; First Sergeant June 10, 1863. Killed in battle of Resaca, Ga., May 14, 1864.

JOHN M. SELLERS.
Private; enrolled Aug. 8, 1862. Discharged on Surgeon's certificate at Louisville, Ky., Nov. 1, 1862. Xenia, O.

GEORGE SHARP.
Private; enrolled Aug. 6, 1862. Discharged; date and place not known.

JAMES A. SMEIGH.
Private; enrolled Aug. 12, 1862. Discharged on Surgeon's certificate at Columbus, O., April 6, 1863.

JAMES STALEY.
Private; enrolled Aug. 9, 1862. Missing near Perryville, Ky., Oct. 9, 1862. Prisoner of war. Returned to duty, Discharged on Surgeon's certificate at Nashville, Tenn., July 30, 1863. Xenia, O.

SAMUEL H. STRICKLE.
Private; enrolled Aug. 10, 1862. Discharged on Surgeon's certificate at Camp Dennison, O., June 12, 1863. Wilmington, O.

WILLIAM STRAWBERG.
Private; enrolled Oct. 27, 1863. Died in hospital at Nashville, Tenn., July 19, 1864.

CORNELIUS STOUP.
Private; enrolled Aug. 12, 1862. Wounded at battle of Resaca, Ga., May 14, 1864. Died June 27, 1864.

FRED. P. STEWART.
Private; enrolled July 3, 1862. Discharged by special order of War Department April 11, 1864. Died 1886.

NATHANIEL STUDEVANT.
Private; enrolled Aug. 2, 1862. Wounded in a skirmish near Kentucky River Sept. 1, 1862. Died Sept. 10, 1862.

WILLIAM STUDEVANT.
Private; enrolled Aug. 2, 1862. Transferred to Veteran Reserve Corps September, 1863, by General Order No. 201, War Department. Died.

SAMUEL SUTTLES.
Private; enrolled Aug. 2, 1862.

OBEDIAH SYLVESTER.
Private; enrolled Aug. 8, 1862. Transferred to Veteran Reserve Corps January, 1864, by general order of War Department. Celina, O.

JAMES M. THIRKIELD.
Enrolled July 29, 1862. Appointed Corporal at muster-in. Missing on the march near Lexington, Ky., Sept. 1, 1862. Prisoner of war at Camp Chase, O. Discharged on Surgeon's certificate at Columbus, O., Oct. 29, 1862. Ogden, Utah.

CHARLES H. THOMAS.
Enrolled Aug. 7, 1862. Appointed Sergeant at muster-in. Captured on the march near Lexington, Ky., Sept. 1, 1862. Prisoner of war at Camp Chase, O. Returned to duty Jan. 17, 1863. Detailed to headquarters 1st Division, 14th Army Corps, May 11, 1863, by Special Order No. 73, General Rousseau. Returned to duty with company. Mustered out with regiment. Williamsburg, O.

WILLIAM C. THOMPSON.
Private; enrolled Aug. 11, 1862. Died in hospital at Nashville, Tenn., Jan. 2, 1863.

CHRISTIAN VANHORN.
Private; enrolled July 29, 1862. Killed in battle of Bentonville, N. C., March 19, 1865.

DAVID VULTZ.
Private; enrolled Aug. 12, 1862. Missing at battle of Chickamauga, Ga., Sept. 19, 1863. Prisoner of war at Andersonville, Ga. Mustered out at Camp Chase, O., June 13, 1865.

ROBERT P. WALKER.
Private; enrolled Aug. 11, 1862. Discharged on Surgeon's certificate at Louisville, Ky., Nov. 5, 1862. Xenia, O.

GEORGE C. WINTER.
Private; enrolled Aug. 12, 1862. Transferred to Veteran Reserve Corps April 10, 1864, by General Order No. 150, War Department. Died.

DAVID M. WINTER.
Private; enrolled Aug. 12, 1862. Appointed Corporal June 10, 1863; Sergeant Nov. 1, 1864. Mustered out with regiment. Duncansville, Crawford Co., Ill.

HUGH M. WEIR.
Private; enrolled Aug. 12, 1862. Discharged on Surgeon's certificate at Louisville, Ky., Dec. 10, 1862. Died 1874.

DAVID W. WILLIAMSON.
Enrolled Aug. 12, 1862. Appointed corporal at muster-in. Discharged on Surgeon's certificate at Columbus, O., April 9, 1863. Xenia, O.

JOHN W. WHITEMAN.
Private; enrolled Aug. 12, 1862. Detailed to train, headquarters 1st Division, 14th Army Corps, Nov. 10, 1863. Returned to duty with company. Mustered out with regiment.

JESSE WRIGHT.
Private; enrolled Aug. 8, 1862. Discharged on Surgeon's certificate Dec. 6, 1863, at Louisville, Ky. Xenia O.

GEORGE M. WRIGHT.
Private; enrolled Aug. 11, 1862. Missing near Bentonville, N. C., March 19, 1865. Prisoner of war. Mustered out at Camp Chase, O. June 16, 1865. Greenville, O.

COMPANY I.

CAPTAINS.

WESLEY GORSUCH.
  Second Lieutenant 11th O. V. I. April to June, 1861; Captain 94th O. V. I. Aug. 6, 1862. Resigned Feb. 24, 1863. Greenville, O.

CHARLES R. MAUS.
  Appointed Second Lieutenant Aug. 23, 1862. Promoted to Captain Feb. 26, 1863. Resigned Jan. 6; 1865. Gettysburgh, O.

SAMUEL JUDY.
  Sergeant Co. K, 11th O. V. I., April to June, 1861; Second Lieutenant, 44th O. V. I., September, 1861, to March, 1862. Enrolled as private Co. I, 94th O. V. I., Aug. 11, 1862. Appointed Sergeant at muster-in. Promoted to Second Lieutenant April 8, 1863; First Lieutenant Jan. 19, 1864. Captain March 27, 1865. Mustered out with regiment. Greenville, O.

FIRST LIEUTENANT.

GEORGE D. FARRER.
  Appointed Aug. 6, 1862. Dismissed June 6, 1863, by General Order No. 131, headquarters Department of the Cumberland, General Rosecrans, commanding.

ENLISTED MEN.

GILBERT ADAMS.
  Private; enrolled Aug. 11, 1862. Re-enlisted in 8th O. V. C. February, 1864 Mustered out at close of the war.

NATHAN L. ALLEN.
  Private; enrolled Aug. 11, 1862. Discharged on Surgeon's certificate Dec. 4, 1862, at Bowling Green, Ky. Died.

DANIEL ALSPAUGH.
  Private; enrolled Aug. 8, 1862. Appointed Corporal Aug. 27, 1863; Sergeant Jan. 25, 1865. Mustered out with regiment. Died.

AARON W. ARNOLD.
  Private, Co. K., 11th O. V. I., April to June, 1861. Enrolled Aug. 11, 1862, 94th O. V. I. Appointed Corporal at muster-in. Captured at Bardstown, Ky., October, 1862. Discharged on Surgeon's certificate May 1, 1863. at Columbus, O. Re-enlisted in 8th Ohio Independent Battery. Greenville, O.

JACOB ARN.
  Private; enrolled Aug. 8, 1862. Died of wounds received at battle of Stone River, Tenn., Jan. 1, 1863.

WILLIAM BIDDLE.
  Private; enrolled Aug. 9, 1862. Appointed Corporal at muster-in. Promoted to First Corporal June 30, 1863. Mustered out with regiment. New Madison, O.

JOHN BIDDLE.
  Private; enrolled Aug. 7, 1862. Appointed Corporal Jan. 1, 1865. Mustered out with regiment. Weaver's Station, Darke Co., O.

JAMES BITEMAN.
  Private; enrolled Aug. 3, 1862. Transferred to 1st Regiment U. S. Veteran Volunteer Engineers, by Special Field Order No. 77, headquarters Department of the Cumberland, July 24, 1864.

RECORD OF COMPANY I.

AMOS BOOMERSHINE.
Private; enrolled Aug. 8, 1862. Died in hospital at Nashville, Tenn., Dec. 7, 1862.

JAMES L. BRADY.
Private; enrolled Aug. 7, 1862. Discharged on Surgeon's certificate at Louisville, Ky., Nov. 26, 1862. Vineland, Douglas Co., Kansas.

JOHN BROOKS.
Private; enrolled Aug. 11, 1862. Mustered out with regiment. Greenville, O.

SAMUEL K. BROWN.
Private; enrolled Aug. 8, 1862. Discharged on Surgeon's certificate at Louisville, Ky., Nov. 26, 1862. Died.

JESSE T. BRUSH.
Private; enrolled Aug. 5, 1862. Appointed Corporal at muster-in. Wounded in front of Atlanta, Ga. Mustered out with regiment. Lancaster, Pa.

ABRAHAM BRUMBAUGH.
Private; enrolled Aug. 11, 1862. Mustered out with regiment. Gettysburgh, O.

JACOB BIRCH.
Private; enrolled Aug. 12, 1862. Died near Greenville, Ohio, Dec. 26, 1862.

JOHN CANNON.
Private; enrolled Aug. 17, 1862. Died in hospital at Graysville, Ga. April 1, 1864.

JOHN C. CECIL.
Private; enrolled Aug. 11, 1862. Sent to Raleigh, N. C., sick, April, 1865. Mustered out from Lovell General Hospital, Portsmouth Grove, R. I., July 6, 1865. Pleasant Hill, O.

AHIJAH COATE.
Private; enrolled Aug. 5, 1862. Died in hospital at Murfreesboro, Tenn., Jan. 25, 1862.

DENMAN R. COOPER.
Private; enrolled Aug. 5, 1862. Appointed Corporal Sept. 26, 1864. Mustered out with regiment. Arkansas City, Kansas.

RICHARD COPPERSMITH.
Private; enrolled Aug. 8, 1862.

JOHN B. M. COTTRELL.
Private; enrolled Aug. 25, 1862. Discharged on Surgeon's certificate at Camp Dennison, O.; date not found on roll.

GEORGE W. CRANE.
Private; enrolled Aug. 11, 1862. Appointed Corporal at muster-in; Sergeant Aug. 27, 1863. Mustered out with regiment. Indianapolis, Ind.

PHINEAS R. CROMER.
Private; enrolled Aug. 5, 1862. Sick in hospital at Nashville, Tenn., March 25, 1863. Returned to duty. Mustered out with regiment. Gettysburgh, O.

JAMES DEAN.
Private; enrolled Aug. 11, 1862. Left sick in hospital March 6, 1864. Returned to duty. Mustered out with regiment.

JOHN DERSHAM.
Private; enrolled Aug. 8, 1862. Mustered out with regiment. Died at Gettysburgh, O., 1873.

HENRY F. DORSEY.
Private; enrolled Aug. 5, 1862. Died in hospital at Nashville, Tenn., Dec. 5, 1862.

GEORGE W. DUTRO.
Private; enrolled Aug. 11, 1862. Appointed Chief Musician Nov. 9, 1864. Mustered out with regiment. Portland, Ind.

HENRY DYE.
Private; enrolled Aug. 11, 1862. Appointed Sergeant at muster-in. Discharged on Surgeon's certificate at Columbus, O., March 26, 1863. Died near Troy, O.

JACOB ETTER.
Private; enrolled Aug. 6, 1862. Wounded in battle at Perryville, Ky., Oct. 8, 1862. Died in hospital at Murfreesboro, Tenn,, May 5, 1863.

JOHN ESTABROOK.
Private; enrolled Aug. 9, 1862. Discharged on Surgeon's certificate at Columbus, O., April 24, 1863. Plattsville, Shelby Co., O.

JAMES FAILEY.
Private; enrolled Aug. 6, 1862. Mustered out with regiment. Died.

MICHAEL FEESER.
Private: enrolled Aug. 12, 1862. Discharged on Surgeon's certificate at Nashville, Tenn., Oct. 9, 1863. Died at Greenville, O., March 14, 1886.

WILLIAM FOLIN.
Private; enrolled Aug. 18, 1862. Mustered out with regiment. Skeel's Cross Roads, Mercer Co., O.

JOHN L. FRANK.
Private; enrolled Aug. 11, 1862. Appointed Sergeant at muster-in; Second Sergeant, April 7, 1863; First Sergeant, Jan. 25, 1865. Mustered out with regiment. Union City, Indiana.

LEVI FRYBARGER.
Private; enrolled Aug. 6, 1862. Detached as Wagon Master, Headquarters 1st Brigade, 1st Division, 14th Corps, July 1, 1863. Mustered out with regiment. Eureka, Kas.

JOHN C. GATES.
Private Co. B, 44th O. V. I., 1861; enrolled as private Co. I, 94th O. V. I., Aug. 5, 1862. Appointed Corporal at muster-in; Sergeant, April 7, 1863. Detailed to colors (regimental color). Wounded in action at Resaca, Ga., May 14, 1864. Returned to duty. Mustered out with regiment. Clear Lake, Wis.

JOSEPH GILBERT.
Private; enrolled Aug. 5, 1862. Died in hospital at Nashville, Tenn., Dec. 23, 1862.

WILLIAM B. GRISSOM.
Private; enrolled Aug. 26, 1862. Died in hospital at Bowling Green, Ky., Nov. 29, 1862. Buried in National Cemetery at Nashville, Tenn. Grave, 544.

JOHN D. GRISSOM.
Private; enrolled Aug. 26, 1862. Died in hospital at Louisville, Ky., Sept. 8, 1863.

SAMUEL GILBERT.
Private; enrolled Aug. 8, 1862. Transferred to Mississippi Marine Brigade, by War Department order, May 3, 1863.

SAMUEL GROW.
Private; enrolled Aug. 15, 1862. Died in hospital at Lebanon, Ky., Jan. 1, 1863.

EMANUEL HARDMAN.
Private; enrolled Aug. 11, 1862. Died at Nashville, Tenn., Feb. 15, 1863.

DAVID HARDMAN.
Private; enrolled Aug. 1, 1862. Died in hospital at Nashville, Tenn., Jan. 31, 1863.

JOHN D. HARTZELL.
Private; enrolled Aug. 9, 1862. Discharged on Surgeon's certificate at Columbus, O., Sept. 25, 1862.

JOHN C. HAYS.
Private; enrolled Aug. 8, 1862. Appointed Corporal at muster-in. Transferred to 1st Regiment U. S. Vet. Vol. Engineers, Special Field Order No. 77. Department of the Cumberland, July 24, 1864. Greenville, O.

JACOB HEB.
Private; enrolled Aug. 5, 1862. Mustered out with regiment. Otwell Mills P. O., Darke County, Ohio.

RECORD OF COMPANY I.

JAMES B. HILLER.
Private; enrolled Aug. 10, 1862, Appointed Sergeant at muster-in; Third Sergeant April 7, 1863. Mustered out with regiment. Greenville, O.

JOSIAH HILL.
Private; enrolled Aug. 6, 1862. Mustered out with regiment. Panther Creek P. O., Darke Co., O.

HENRY J. HOBBS.
Private; enrolled Aug. 6, 1862. Died from wounds received in front of Atlanta, Ga., Aug. 24, 1864.

ISAAC HOLLEPETER.
Private; enrolled Aug. 8, 1862. Killed in skirmish at Kentucky River Aug. 31, 1862.

JACOB HOLLINGER.
Private; enrolled Aug. 5, 1862. Mustered out with regiment. Webster, Darke Co., O.

DAVID C. JUDY.
Private; enrolled Aug. 7, 1862. Discharged on Surgeon's certificate at Nashville, Tenn., Jan. 15, 1863. Died.

JOHN F. JUDY.
Private; enrolled Aug. 11, 1862. Discharged on Surgeon's certificate at Louisville, Ky., Feb, 12, 1863. Union City, Ind.

BENJAMIN F. LEVENSBERGER.
Private; enrolled Aug. 25, 1862.

WASHINGTON LINDAMOOD.
Private; enrolled Aug. 9, 1862. Mustered out with regiment.

EPHRIAM LONGNECKER.
Private; enrolled Aug. 5, 1862. Transferred to Veteran Reserve Corps, by General Order No. 271, War Department, 1863. Pleasant Hill, O.

WILLIAM H. H. MARTIN.
Private; enrolled Aug. 8, 1862. Mustered out with regiment. Greenville, O.

JEREMIAH M. MARTIN.
Private; enrolled Aug. 3, 1862. Mustered out with regiment. Greenville, O.

WILLIAM McDONALD.
Private; enrolled Aug. 7, 1862. Prisoner of war at Nolensville, Tenn., Dec. 28, 1862. Discharged on Surgeon's certificate at Columbus, O., April 1, 1863. Re-enlisted in 8th Ohio Independent Battery. Arcanum, O.

THOMAS McKEE.
Private; enrolled Aug. 11, 1862. Appointed Corporal Aug. 27, 1863. Missing at battle of Chickamauga, Ga. Prisoner of war at Andersonville, Ga. Returned to duty. Mustered out with regiment. Ansonia, O.

JACOB MICHAEL.
Private; enrolled Aug. 12, 1862. Died in hospital at Murfreesboro, Tenn., Aug. 17, 1863.

SAMUEL MORELOCK.
Private; enrolled Aug. 5, 1862.

WILLIAM F. MORROW.
Private; enrolled Aug. 7, 1862. Mustered out with regiment. Ansonia, O.

DANIEL NEICE.
Private; enrolled Aug. 7, 1862. Discharged on Surgeon's certificate at Camp Dennison, O., Aug. 4, 1863. Gettysburgh, O.

JAMES O. SULLIVAN.
Private; enrolled Aug. 11, 1862. Died in hospital at Murfreesboro, Tenn. Feb. 15, 1863.

JOSEPH PARKS.
Private; enrolled July 23, 1862. Discharged on Surgeon's certificate at Nashville, Tenn., Feb. 1, 1863. Died.

THE NINETY-FOURTH OHIO.

JOHN PATTERSON.
Private; enrolled Aug. 7, 1862. Died at Murfreesboro, Tenn., March 23, 1863.

JAMES G. PAXTON.
Private; enrolled Aug. 8, 1862. Died at Graysville, Ga., April 7, 1864.

SILAS RECK.
Private; enrolled Aug. 6, 1862. Appointed Corporal Sept. 26, 1864. Mustered out with regiment.

SAMUEL RECK.
Private; enrolled Aug. 7, 1862. Died at Stevenson, Ala., Nov. 1, 1863.

JOSIAH REED.
Private; enrolled Aug. 24, 1862. Wounded at battle of Stone River, Tenn., Dec. 31, 1862. Sick in hospital at Nashville, Tenn., September, 1864. Mustered out at Nashville May 15, 1865. Died at Troy, O.

MARTIN RISSER.
Private; enrolled Aug. 11, 1862. Died in hospital at Nashville, Tenn., Jan. 19, 1863.

WILLIAM ROHR.
Private; enrolled Aug. 23, 1862. Appointed Corporal Aug. 27, 1863. Wounded at battle of Bentonville, N. C., March 19, 1865. Mustered out at Camp Dennison, O., May 24, 1865. Rose Hill, Darke Co., O.

LEMUEL RUSH.
Private; enrolled Aug. 11, 1862. Appointed Corporal at muster-in. Died at Nashville, Tenn., Feb. 27, 1863.

JAMES SEBRING.
Private; enrolled Aug. 7, 1862. Appointed Corporal Jan. 1, 1865. Mustered out with regiment. Died in Illinois.

ISAAC W. SEBRING.
Private; enrolled Aug. 7, 1862. Appointed Corporal at muster-in. Left sick in hospital at Nashville, Tenn., Nov. 1, 1864. Mustered out June 10, 1865, at Nashville, Tenn. Gordon, Darke Co., O.

JOHN J. H. SOTHERN.
Wagoner; enrolled Aug. 11, 1862. Died in hospital at New Albany, Ind., Nov. 26, 1862.

REUBEN SPAYD.
Private; enrolled Aug. 11, 1862. Discharged on Surgeon's certificate at Columbus, O., April 25, 1863. Died at Greenville, O., Jan. 20, 1886.

JACOB STAHL.
Private; enrolled Aug. 5, 1862. Mustered out with regiment. Arcanum, O.

MOSES TEAGUE.
Private; enrolled Aug. 11, 1862. Transferred to Veteran Reserve Corps by General Order No. 21, War Department, Jan. 14, 1864. Gettysburgh, O.

WILLIAM H. TENNENT.
Private; enrolled Aug. 8, 1862. Slightly wounded at Kentucky River Aug. 31, 1862. Mustered out with regiment. Gettysburgh, O.

JOSEPH TRUMP.
Private; enrolled Aug. 6, 1862. Mustered out with regiment. Poplar Ridge, Darke Co., O.

JOSEPH VOEKLE.
Private; enrolled Aug. 8, 1862. Transferrred to Veteran Reserve Corps by General Order No. 358, War Department, Nov. 6, 1863. Died at Gettysburgh, O., Sept. 3, 1882.

ISAAC W. WEAVER.
Private; enrolled Aug. 25, 1862. Mustered out with regiment. Versailles, O.

JACOB WIKLE.
Private; enrolled Aug. 5, 1862. Mustered out with regiment.

RECORD OF COMPANY I.

CHRISTOPHER WISE.
Private; enrolled Aug. 12, 1862. Mustered out with regiment. Lincoln, Ill.

JOHN WISENER.
Private; enrolled Aug. 7, 1862. Mustered out with regiment. Darke P. O., Darke Co., O.

GEORGE W. WISSINGER.
Private; enrolled Aug. 8, 1862. Wounded at Resaca, Ga., May 14, 1864. Mustered out with regiment. Webster, Darke Co., O.

HENRY WITTERS.
Private; enrolled Aug. 6, 1862. Transferred to 74th O. V. I. at muster-out of regiment.

JACOB L. WOLF.
Private; enrolled Aug. 11, 1862. Died of wounds received near Atlanta, Ga., Aug. 15, 1864.

JOHN WOLF.
Private; enrolled Aug. 12, 1862. Mustered out with regiment. Skeel's Cross Roads, Mercer Co., O.

AARON YODER.
Private; enrolled Aug. 6, 1862. Died in hospital at Nashville, Tenn., Feb. 15, 1863.

COMPANY K.

CAPTAINS.
CHAUNCEY RIFFLE.
Corporal Co. K, 11th O. V. I., April to June, 1861; Sergeant 4th O. V. C., 1861. Mustered out. Appointed Captain 94th O. V. I. Aug. 11, 1862. Resigned Dec. 18, 1864. Surgeon's certificate forwarded. Richmond, Ind.

FRANK A. HARDY.
Private Co. I, 3d Ohio Volunteers, June 11, 1846. to June 24, 1847. Appointed Second Lieutenant Co. C, 94th O. V. I., July 22, 1862. Captured near Lexington, Ky., Sept. 1, 1862. Assigned to duty at Camp Chase, O., Nov. 22, 1862. Promoted to First Lieutenant July 15, 1863. Rejoined the regiment Oct. 7, 1863. Wounded at Kenesaw Mountain June 22, 1864. In hospital at Nashville. Assigned to command in Veteran Reserve Corps. Rejoined. Promoted to Captain. Assigned to Co. K May 20, 1865. Mustered out with regiment. Piqua, O.

FIRST LIEUTENANTS.
SAMUEL F. ARMOLD.
Appointed July 25, 1862. Resigned Dec. 25, 1862. Surgeon's certificate forwarded. Hill Grove, Darke Co., O.

DANIEL D. HUNTER.
Enrolled Aug. 10, 1862. Appointed First Sergeant at muster-in. Promoted to First Lieutenant Dec. 28, 1862. Resigned Oct. 12, 1863. Surgeon's certificate forwarded. Greenville, O.

JOHN A. HIVLING.
Enrolled as private Co. H July 29, 1862. Captured near Lexington, Ky., Sept. 1, 1862. Prisoner of war at Camp Chase, O. Returned to duty. Appointed Second Lieutenant April 16, 1863; First Lieutenant March 1, 1864. Assigned to Co. K. Captured near Goldsboro, N. C., March 26, 1865. Mustered out May 26, 1865. Xenia, O.

SECOND LIEUTENANTS.
GEORGE H. MADDOX.
Appointed July 23, 1862. Discharged Feb. 17, 1863.

JOHN P. PATTERSON.
Enrolled as Private Co. H Aug. 13, 1862. Appointed Sergeant at muster-in. Promoted to Second Lieutenant April 7, 1863. Assigned to Co. K. Resigned Nov. 14, 1863. Cincinnati, O.

ENLISTED MEN.
MARK ANTHONY.
Private; enrolled July 26, 1862. Sent to hospital at Chattanooga, Tenn., Nov. 24, 1863. Transferred to Veteran Reserve Corps. North Star, Darke Co., O.

S. M. ANKENY.
Private; enrolled Aug. 9, 1862. Died at Bowling Green, Ky., Nov. 18, 1862.

ISAAC ARNOLD.
Private; enrolled July 25, 1862. Sent to hospital from Chattanooga, Tenn. Discharged at Camp Dennison, O., Jan. 20, 1864, by order of General Hooker. Died.

CHARLES H. BAYMAN.
Private; enrolled Aug. 18, 1862. Wounded in action at Resaca, Ga., May 14, 1864. Returned to duty. Mustered out with regiment. Covington, O.

RECORD OF COMPANY K.

URIAH M. BROWDER.
Musician; enrolled July 26, 1862. Mustered out with regiment. Litchfield, Ill.

LEWIS S. BOWSER.
Private; enrolled Aug. 13, 1862. Transferred to 1st Regiment U. S. Vet. Vol. Engineers July 24, 1864, Special Field Orders No. 77, Department of the Cumberland. Winchester, Ind.

MARTIN BEDINGER.
Musician; enrolled Aug. 10, 1862. Prisoner of war at Andersonville, Ga. Died May 3, 1864.

ABRAHAM J. BYARD.
Private; enrolled Aug. 5, 1862. Died at Nashville, Tenn., Jan. 29, 1863.

BURTON BINKLEY.
Private Co. K. 11th O. V. I., April to June, 1861. Private Co. K. 94th O. V. I.; enrolled Aug. 9, 1862. Detailed to Pioneers Dec. 9, 1862. Sick in hospital June, 1865. Mustered out. Greenville, O.

WILLIAM H. BAILEY.
Private; enrolled Aug. 13, 1862. Died at Nashville, Tenn., Dec. 22, 1863.

WESLEY J. BICKLE.
Private; enrolled Aug. 22, 1862.

CHARLES BINKLEY.
Private; enrolled Aug. 1, 1862. Discharged on Surgeon's certificate at Columbus, O., Nov. 26, 1862. Re-enlisted in Indiana Volunteers.

WILLIAM C. BERRY.
Private; enrolled Aug. 6, 1862. Appointed Corporal March 30, 1864. Mustered out with regiment. Versailles, Darke Co., O.

WILLIAM CARTER.
Private; enrolled Aug. 15, 1862. Appointed Corporal Aug. 16, 1863. Mustered out with regiment. Rose Hill, Darke Co., O.

ELIJAH CURTIS.
Private; enrolled Aug. 18, 1862. Wounded in battle at Missionary Ridge Nov. 25, 1863. Returned to duty. Mustered out with regiment. Yorkshire, Darke Co., O.

JESSE CURTIS.
Private; enrolled July 26, 1862. Sent to hospital at Chattanooga, Tenn. Returned to duty. Died in an ambulance while on the way to Jonesboro, Ga., Aug. 30, 1864.

WILLIAM S. COTTRELL.
Enrolled Aug. 10, 1862. Appointed Sergeant at muster-in. Died at Bowling Green, Ky., Nov. 25, 1862.

CONSTANT COLE.
Private; enrolled Aug. 13, 1862. Died at Bowling Green, Ky., Nov. 15, 1862.

TITUS W. DOVE.
Private; enrolled July 26, 1862. Sick in hospital at Nashville at muster-out of regiment. Mustered out June 15, 1865. Osgood, Darke Co., O.

OREN DEEDS.
Private; enrolled Aug. 13, 1862. Discharged on Surgeon's certificate at Nashville, Tenn., March 7, 1863.

WILLIAM DETH.
Private; enrolled Aug. 9, 1862. Discharged on Surgeon's certificate at Bowling Green, Ky., Dec. 1, 1862.

JOHN EDINGTON.
Private; enrolled Aug. 10, 1862.

GEORGE W. EDINGTON.
Private; enrolled Aug. 3, 1862.

RESIN FOREMAN.
Private; enrolled July 28, 1862. Missing on the march near Lexington, Ky., Sept 1, 1862. Prisoner of war at Camp Chase, O. Returned to duty. Mustered out with regiment.

GRANVILLE W. FIFER.
Private; enrolled Aug. 6, 1862. Left in hospital at Murfreesboro, Tenn., March 21, 1863. Transferred to Veteran Reserve Corps April 1, 1865. Hageman, Darke Co., O.

JOSEPH FIFER.
Enrolled Aug. 11, 1862. Appointed Corporal at muster-in. Discharged on Surgeon's certificate at Louisville, Ky., Feb. 5, 1863. Greenville, O.

ENOS FISHER.
Private; enrolled Aug. 8, 1862. Transferred to 74th O. V. I. at muster-out of regiment. Columbus, Kas.

JAMES FINFROCK.
Private; enrolled Dec. 23, 1863. Sent to hospital at Chattanooga, Tenn., Feb. 9, 1864. Mustered out at Camp Dennison, O., May 24, 1865.

THOMAS GOODALL.
Private; enrolled Aug. 17, 1862. Appointed Corporal Jan. 1, 1863; Sergeant, March 30, 1864. Mustered out with regiment.

JONATHAN GIBSON.
Private; enrolled Aug. 10, 1862. Mustered out with regiment. North Star, Darke County, Ohio.

AUGUSTUS GOUBEAU.
Private; enrolled Aug. 13, 1862. Wounded in action at Bentonville, N. C., March 19, 1865. Mustered out at Camp Dennison, O., May 24, 1865. Osgood, Darke Co., O.

JOHN W. GANGER.
Private; enrolled Aug. 11, 1862. Mustered out with regiment. North Star, Darke Co., Ohio.

ISAIAH GILBERT.
Private; enrolled July 28, 1862. Discharged on Surgeon's certificate at Nashville, Tenn,, March 15, 1863.

BENJ. F. GILBERT.
Private; enrolled Aug. 15. 1862. Transferred to 74th O. V. I. at muster-out of regiment.

JOHN C. GILBERT.
Private; enrolled Aug. 13, 1862. Transferred to Veteran Reserve Corps Nov. 15, 1863.

THOMAS C. GILBERT.
Private; enrolled Aug. 13, 1862. Died at Nashville, Tenn., Dec. 16, 1862. Buried at Covington, O.

JAMES GOSLEY.
Private; enrolled Aug. 13, 1862. Sent to Convalescent Camp, near Murfreesboro, Tenn., June 23, 1863. Transferred to Veteran Reserve Corps Aug. 1, 1863. North Star, Darke County, Ohio.

JOHN A. HARBISON.
Private; enrolled Aug. 5, 1862. Detached to hospital at Nashville Oct. 9, 1863, by general order headquarters Army of the Cumberland. Returned to duty with company. Mustered out with regiment. Ansonia, Darke Co., O.

ABEL A. HARNESS.
Enrolled Aug. 10, 1862. Appointed Sergeant at muster-in. Left sick in hospital at Bridgeport, Ala, Sept. 6, 1863. Mustered out at Nashville, Tenn., June 10, 1865. Troy, O.

RICHARD D. HOLE.
Private; enrolled Aug. 9, 1862. Sick at Camp Dennison, O., since March 1, 1865. Mustered out May 24, 1865. Independence, Montgomery Co., Kas.

NATHAN W. HOLE.
Enrolled Aug. 5, 1862. Appointed Corporal at muster-in. Transferred to Veteran Reserve Corps Nov. 1, 1863. Independence, Montgomery Co., Kas.

JOHN HILLER.
Private; enrolled Aug. 9, 1862. Discharged on Surgeon's certificate at Columbus, O., April 7, 1863, St. Paris, O.

ISAAC G. HILLER.
Enrolled Aug. 9, 1862. Appointed Corporal at muster-in. Transferred to Veteran Reserve Corps Dec. 15, 1863, by order of War Department. Greenville, O.

SAMUEL HOOVER.
Private; enrolled Aug. 11, 1862. Discharged on Surgeon's certificate at Louisville, Ky., Dec. 16, 1862.

JONATHAN HAPNER.
Private; enrolled July 30, 1862.

JOSEPH B. HECK.
Private; enrolled Aug. 9, 1862.

LORENZO D. HECK.
Private; enrolled Aug. 9, 1862.

WILLIAM H. H. JEFFRIES.
Private; enrolled Aug. 10, 1862. Died at Nashville, Tenn., Feb. 23, 1863.

HENRY KERNS.
Private; enrolled Aug. 2, 1862. Mustered out with regiment. North Star, Darke Co., O.

MICHAEL W. KERNS.
Private; enrolled Aug. 1, 1862. Transferred to Veteran Reserve Corps April 6, 1864.

JOHN KLEM.
Private; enrolled Aug. 8, 1862. Mustered out with regiment. Philadelphia, Ind.

LEWIS KEISTER.
Private; enrolled Aug. 8, 1862. Died at Murfreesboro, Tenn., May 10, 1863.

JACOB LYON.
Private; enrolled Aug. 10, 1862. Mustered out with regiment.

JAMES G. MARTIN.
Wagoner; enrolled Aug. 13, 1862. Discharged on Surgeon's certificate Nov. 10, 1862, at Louisville, Ky. Woodington, O.

JEFFERSON R. MARTIN.
Enrolled Aug. 10, 1862. Appointed Sergeant at muster-in. Wounded in action at Stone River, Tenn., Dec. 31, 1862. Appointed First Sergeant March 30, 1864. Mustered out with regiment. Farmland, Ind.

WILLIAM I. MARTIN.
Enrolled Aug. 5, 1862. Appointed Corporal at muster-in. Left sick at Nolensville, Tenn., Dec. 28, 1862. Prisoner of war at Camp Chase, O. Returned to duty. Appointed Sergeant Nov. 1, 1864. Mustered out with regiment. Greenville, O.

WILLIAM G. MARSHALL.
Private; enrolled Aug. 8, 1862. Appointed Corporal Aug. 16, 1863. Mustered out with regiment. Royal Centre, Cass Co., Ind.

JOHN J. MARSHALL.
Private; enrolled Aug. 11, 1862. Wounded at battle of Resaca, Ga., May 14, 1864. Returned to duty. Mustered out with regiment. Houston, Shelby Co., O.

ANDREW J. MACK.
Private; enrolled Aug. 8, 1862. Mustered out with regiment.

PHILLIP MAGNESS.
Private; enrolled Aug. 2, 1862. Died at Murfreesboro, Tenn., May 15, 1863.

JAMES S. M. McCLANAN.
Private; enrolled Aug. 22, 1862. Died at Nashville, Tenn., Jan. 17, 1863.

JOSIAH McCOUGHEY.
Private; enrolled Aug. 6, 1862.

JOHN McCOLISTER.
Private; enrolled July 25, 1862. Discharged on Surgeon's certificate at Cincinnati, O., Feb. 16, 1863. Udall, Cowley Co., Kansas.

MATTISON McCOLISTER.
Private; enrolled July 25, 1862. Discharged on Surgeon's certificate at Louisville, Ky., Aug. 27, 1863.

DANIEL McNEAL.
Private; enrolled Aug. 9, 1862. Transferred to 4th U. S. Cavalry at Nashville, Tenn., Dec. 7, 1862.

JOSEPH MORGAN.
Enrolled Aug. 10, 1862. Appointed Corporal at muster-in. Died at Chattanooga, Tenn., Nov. 28, 1863.

JOHN S. NORRIS.
Enrolled Aug. 9, 1862. Appointed Sergeant at muster-in. Discharged on Surgeon's certificate at Louisville, Ky., March 19, 1863.

JOHN POTTER.
Private; enrolled Aug. 9, 1862. Killed in battle of Resaca, Ga., May 14, 1864.

SILAS P. RIFFLE.
Private; enrolled Aug. 6, 1862. Sent to Convalescent Camp, near Murfreesboro, Tenn., May 21, 1863. Provision for discharge made by General Order No. 77, War Department, series 1865. Ansonia, O.

JACOB ROLAND.
Private; enrolled Aug. 9, 1862. Transferred to 4th U. S. Cavalry at Nashville, Tenn., Dec. 7, 1862.

JOSEPH RORBINS.
Private; enrolled Aug. 5, 1862. Mustered out with regiment.

ISAAC N. W. REED.
Private; enrolled Aug. 3, 1862. Missing at battle of Chickamauga, Ga., Sept. 20, 1863. Prisoner of war. Discharged at Camp Chase, O., June 16, 1885. Ansonia, O.

THOMAS D. REED.
Enrolled Aug. 7, 1862. Killed in battle of Resaca, Ga., May 14, 1864.

WILLIAM REED.
Private; enrolled Aug. 3, 1862. Sent to Convalescent Camp, near Murfreesboro, Tenn., Nov. 21, 1863. Mustered out under General Order No. 77, War Department, series 1865.

CYRUS ROYER.
Private, Co. K. 11th O. V. I., April to June, 1861. Enrolled Aug. 8, 1862, in 94th O. V. I. Appointed Corporal at muster-in. Died at Nashville, Tenn., Dec. 5, 1862.

JOHN H. SANDERS.
Private; enrolled Aug. 10, 1862. Mustered out with regiment. Celina, O.

MOSES SANDERS.
Private; enrolled Aug. 9, 1864. Mustered out with regiment. Ansonia, O.

ISAAC N. T. SUPINGER.
Private; enrolled Aug. 10, 1862. Mustered out with regiment.

ABEL M. SHOOK.
Private; enrolled Aug. 10, 1862. Mustered out with regiment. North Star, Darke Co., Ohio.

JOHN L. STARR.
Private; enrolled July 25, 1862. Mustered out with regiment. North Star, Darke Co., O.

RECORD OF COMPANY K.

JAMES R. STEVENSON.
Private; enrolled Aug. 15, 1862. Left sick at Nashville, Tenn., Dec. 8, 1862. Mustered out under General Order No. 77, War Department, 1865. Cedar Rapids, Ia.

OZRO M. SEARL.
Private; enrolled Aug. 8, 1862. Discharged on Surgeon's certificate at Louisville, Ky., Dec. 18, 1862. Ansonia, O.

JOHN STOLTZ.
Private; enrolled July 25, 1862. Discharged on Surgeon's certificate at Columbus, O., Oct. 1, 1862. Logansport, Ind.

HARROL SYMMS.
Private; enrolled Aug. 4, 1862. Discharged on Surgeon's certificate at Camp Dennison, O., May 9, 1864.

NELSON SNYDER.
Private; Enrolled Aug. 2, 1862. Transferred to 1st Regiment U. S. Veteran Volunteer Engineers July 24, 1864, by Special Field Order, Department of the Cumberland.

SAMUEL SHOOK.
Private; enrolled Aug. 13, 1862. Appointed Corporal Nov. 1, 1864. Mustered out with regiment. Marion, Ind.

HENRY STRAIGHT.
Private; enrolled Aug. 13, 1862. Died in hospital at Bowling Green, Ky., Nov. 11, 1862.

WILLIAM SILVER.
Private; enrolled July 25, 1862. Transferred to Veteran Reserve Corps Nov. 1, 1863.

GEORGE T. SILVER.
Private; enrolled Aug. 11, 1862.

WILLIAM THOMAS.
Private; enrolled Aug. 5, 1862.

WILLIAM M. TURPEN.
Private; enrolled July 28, 1862. Left sick at Nolensville, Tenn., Dec. 28, 1862. Prisoner of war at Camp Chase, O. Returned to duty. Wounded in action at Mission Ridge, Tenn., Nov. 25, 1863. Appointed Corporal Feb. 1, 1865. Mustered out with regiment. Died at Versailles, O., July 1877.

EDWARD L. TEEL.
Private; enrolled Aug. 5, 1862. Mustered out with regiment.

DAVID TRISSEL.
Private; enrolled July 29, 1862. Transferred to Veteran Reserve Corps Nov. 1, 1863. Mustered out at Cairo, Ill., July 13, 1865. Ansonia, Darke Co., O.

JAMES TEEGARDEN.
Private; enrolled Aug. 13, 1862. Died in hospital at Nashville, Tenn., Dec. 3, 1862.

JOHN M. TULLIS
Private; enrolled Aug. 10, 1862. Transferred to Veteran Reserve Corps Aug. 11, 1863. Richmond, Ind.

OSMAN VAN SKOIK.
Private; enrolled Aug. 8, 1862. Mustered out with regiment. Ansonia, Darke Co., O.

ABRAHAM WINGER.
Private; enrolled Aug. 13, 1862. Mustered out with regiment. Celina, O.

ALEXANDER WHITE.
Private; enrolled Aug. 11, 1862. Killed in action at Lookout Mountain Nov. 24, 1863.

THOMAS B. WHITE.
Private; enrolled Aug. 6, 1862. Wounded in battle at Stone River, Tenn., Dec. 31, 1862. Discharged on account of wounds April 28, 1863. Ansonia, O.

WILLIAM WHITMAN.
Private; enrolled Aug. 9, 1862.

NOAH J. WORTS.
  Enrolled Aug. 5, 1862. Appointed Corporal at muster-in. Died at Camp Dennison, O., April 5, 1863.
ANDREW WESTFALL.
  Private; enrolled Aug. 1, 1862. Missing near Bentonville, N. C., March 20, 1865. Prisoner of war. Mustered out at Camp Chase, O., June 16, 1865.
JAMES H. WARD.
  Private; enrolled Aug. 7, 1862.
ELIJAH C. WARD.
  Private; enrolled Nov. 2, 1863. Transferred to 74th O. V. I., at muster-out of regiment.
DANIEL H. WARD.
  Private; enrolled Aug. 13, 1862. Transferred to Veteran Reserve Corps Nov. 1, 1863.
WILLIAM H. H. WARD.
  Private; enrolled Aug. 11, 1862. Appointed Corporal Jan. 1, 1863; Sergeant March 30, 1864. Mustered out with regiment. Versailles, Darke Co., O.
MOSES WORTH.
  Private; enrolled Aug. 5, 1862. Appointed Corporal March 30, 1864; Sergeant Feb. 1, 1865. Mustered out with regiment. Union City, Ind.
VALENTINE WOLF.
  Private; enrolled Oct. 23, 1863. Wounded at battle of Resaca, Ga., May 14, 1864. Transferred to 74th O. V. 1. at muster-out. Versailles, O.
JOHN WADE.
  Private; enrolled Aug. 6, 1862. Discharged on Surgeon's certificate at Louisville, Ky., May 8, 1863.

www.ingramcontent.com/pod-product-compliance
Lightning Source LLC
Chambersburg PA
CBHW030329100526
44592CB00010B/630